1/94

3000 800026 29665
St. Louis Community College

D0055954

WITHDRAWN

 St. Louis Community College

Forest Park
Florissant Valley
Meramec

Instructional Resources
St. Louis, Missouri

WITHDRAWN

St. Louis Community College
at Meramec
Library

LOUIE LOUIE

LOUIE LOUIE

The History and Mythology of the World's Most Famous Rock'n'Roll Song; Including the Full Details of Its Torture and Persecution at the Hands of the Kingsmen, J. Edgar Hoover's F.B.I., and a Cast of Millions; and Introducing, for the First Time Anywhere, the Actual Dirty Lyrics

DAVE MARSH

NEW YORK

The author gives grateful acknowledgment to the following for permission to quote from copyrighted material: "Love You So," written by Ron Holden, copyright Golden Unlimited Music (admin. Super Songs), copyright renewed, international copyright secured, all rights reserved; "Do You Love Me," Berry Gordy, Jobete Music Co., Inc., © June 1962; "Dirty Water" © 1965 Equinox Music, c/o AVI Music Publishing Group, Inc.; "Wild Thing" by Chip Taylor © 1965 EMI Blackwood Music Inc. All rights reserved. International copyright secured. Used by permission; "Spanish Castle Magic" (© 1968) and "Castles Made of Sand" (© 1968) written by Jimi Hendrix/copyright Bella Godiva Music Inc. All rights reserved. Used by permission; "Brother Louie," words and music by E. Brown and T. Wilson, copyright © 1973 by Finchley Music Corp., rights administered in the U. S. and Canada by All Nations Music, rights for the World excluding the U. S. Canada administered by RAK Music Publishing Ltd., international copyright secured, all rights reserved; Specified selection from "A Supermarket in California" from *Collected Poems* by Allen Ginsberg. Copyright 1955 by Allen Ginsberg. Reprinted by permission of HarperCollins Publishers, Inc.

Copyright © 1993 Dave Marsh

All rights reserved. No part of this book may be used or reproduced in any manner whatsoever without written permission of the Publisher. Printed in the United States of America. For information address Hyperion, 114 Fifth Avenue, New York, New York 10011.

Library of Congress Cataloging-in-Publication Data

Marsh, Dave.
    Louie Louie : the history and mythology of the world's most famous
rock 'n' roll song . . . / Dave Marsh. — 1st ed.
        p.   cm.
    ISBN 1-56282-865-7
    1. Rock music—United States—History and criticism.   2. Berry,
Richard, 1935–   Louie Louie.   I. Title.
ML3534.M39   1993
782.42166—dc20   93-24725
                                                              CIP
                                                              MN

Designed by Sandra Choron

Produced by March Tenth, Inc.

FIRST EDITION

10   9   8   7   6   5   4   3   2   1

*For Richard Berry,
who gave birth to this unruly child,
and Rockin' Robin Roberts,
who first raised it to glory*

Contents

Acknowledgments   ix

1 "Let's Give It to 'Em, Right Now!"   1

2 A Tale of 300 Ditties   3

3 Birth of the "Lou"s   12

4 "Louie" in Limbo   41

5 "Louie" Unleashed   47

6 Spanish Castle Magic   73

7 "Louie" Come Home   81

8 Every Termite a King   102

9 "Louie" Who?   106

10 Combating Merchants of Filth:
The Role of "Louie Louie"   114

11 The "Louie" Generation   139

12 In Search of the Ultimate "Louie"   156

13 "Louie" Marches On   172

14 The Return of "Louie Louie"   191

15 "Louie" Reaches Nirvana   200

Maximum "Louie Louie":
A Discography   208

Index   239

Acknowledgments

Bob Miller stuck by the story of "Louie Louie" through two publishing houses, five years, and several long, dark nights. I'm deeply grateful for his unyielding support, without which this book would not exist. Equal gratitude must go to my agent, Sandra Choron, who never gives up, and to my editor, Tom Miller, who persevered through a process that must have seemed at turns both incomprehensible and never-ending.

Greil Marcus shares my obsession with the song and encouraged me both early and late. So does Doc Pelzell, whose research assistance and insights were as valuable as the discographical material he and Jeffrey "Stretch" Riedle supplied. Eric Predoehl's opening up of the FBI's "Louie" file is certainly the most clever and creative use ever made of the Freedom of Information Act in the service of rock'n'roll. His commitment to "Louie Louie," best expressed in his forthcoming documentary film, extended to providing much of the graphic material contained here. Invaluable research assistance was also provided by Keith Abbott, Pat Baird at BMI, Harold Bronson, Art Chantry, Paul de Baros, Scott Isler, Cub Koda, Steve Propes, Bob Rolontz, and Joel Selvin. Bruce Springsteen very kindly made me feel like an idiot for not spotting Boston's use of the "Louie" code sooner. Thanks also to Karen Hall, for reading and advising me on the early chapters. And if it weren't for Carol Green, I'd just stay home.

If most of the principals in the "Louie" saga had not made themselves available to me, there would be no book. My biggest debts are owed to Richard Berry, Buck Ormsby, and Jack Ely, each of whom gave me a great deal of himself in the course of our interviews. I hope that the tremendous character each of these men possesses comes through here. Thanks also to Rich

Dangel, Mr. and Mrs. Max Feirtag, Richard Foos, Arnie Ginsburg, Ron Holden, Chuck Rubin, Marv Schlachter, and Governor Matt Welch.

It is customary to thank one's family for bearing up through the horribly selfish processes involved in writing a book. Barbara Carr, my wife, always handles this well. My elder daughter, Sasha, escaped all the nastiness this time by going off to college, then moving to Mexico. But on this project, my main supporter at home proved to be my younger daughter, Kristen Ann Carr, who unfailingly asked each day, "Did you get any work done?" It troubles my heart to know that she will never read these pages, but yes, sweetheart, and I'm finally finished with this one.

1

"Let's Give It to 'Em, Right Now!"

*L*et's get straight to the point. You've journeyed here in hopes of an answer to a single, simple question—the basic question from which flows the whole sordid story. To wit:

What *are* the real lyrics, anyway?

A most excellent question, pilgrim, the very one that renders you worthy of a quest such as this. Profound in its very stupidity. So elementary that my original intention had been to answer it straightaway, if only to show that the mystery of "Louie Louie" does not subsist within it.

But lo! It came to pass in the fullness of time that composer Richard Berry—hallowed be his mighty name—licensed the rights to his masterpiece and, as happens every time anybody makes a business deal in this yarn, the situation got all fouled up. Berry sold his license to a company wondrously titled Windswept Pacific, which sounds about right. Windswept Pacific sublicensed the print rights to a firm known as Warner/Chappell, a division of the multi-tentacled megalith called Time Warner.

So, thirty years after it first hit the charts, "Louie Louie" had slipped at last into the mighty corporate maw. No big deal, it happens to (practically) everybody. However, Warner/Chappell seems to have been infiltrated by a master of the occult rites of rock'n'roll lore, and this gremlin apparently decided that it would be a major error to allow the authentic "Louie Louie" lyrics, as composed by Richard Berry in 1956 and initially published by Limax Music, to appear in a volume devoted to explicating these sacred mysteries. Either that or they just didn't have anybody handy who could or would cope with the prospect of reading *an entire book* about one of their revenue-generators. One way or the other, three months after Warner/Chappell received the manuscript of *Louie Louie*, they still hadn't been able to figure out whether the lyrics might safely appear here.

And that's OK. Perhaps the whimsical guardians of rock'n'roll spirit have, on this occasion, proved more helpful than they intended. Maybe it's *better* for a book about a song with what surely must be the most notorious set of lyrics in creation, let alone rock'n'roll, to contain not a single, solitary scrap of them. If only to show that *the point ain't just the lyrics.*

Nevertheless, you now have some choices to make. On the one hand, you can hie yourself down to the local music store and see if they happen to stock a sample of the sheet music. Just glance it over; you certainly don't need to buy one on *my* account. On the other hand, you could decide that, given such a cosmic property as "Louie Louie," the likes of Warner/Chappell couldn't understand or appreciate it anyway and, therefore, the "official" version of the lyrics would be highly suspect, and keep on thinking that you're hearing the things that you've *always* heard.

As for myself, I've read the original lyrics and I believe what they say. But you're under no obligation to share my faith. Millions now living do not and never will. From time to time, I've wondered myself. But you gotta trust somebody. Don't you?

2

A Tale of 300 Ditties

I t is the best of songs, it is the worst of songs. A rock'n'roll song, a calypso song, a sea chanty, a filthy, dirty, obscene song, the story of rock'n'roll in a nutshell, the most ridiculous piece of junk in the history of damnation. A stupid song, a brilliant song, an R&B oldie, a punk rock classic, a wine cooler commercial, an urban legend, a sacred text, a song with roots, a glimpse of the future, the song that defines our purpose, the very voice of barbarism. A song that casts a spell, a song that ought to have been forgotten and many times has been—and for all that, a song that roots into the brain until there's no erasing it. Barely a song at all—three chords and a cloud of dust; the song that really does remain the same—no matter the reinterpretations it suffers. An old story, an untold story.

This is "Louie Louie." Love it or leave it. But if you choose to leave, don't look over your shoulder, for what you'll see—a garden of delights, a profanation of the very idea of "music" (music *properly understood*, that is), the true and total history of what once we were and have become—will not turn you into anything so benign as a pillar of salt. It'll make you over as a complete rockin' maniac.

If you tell it right, "Louie" 's story in all its weirdness offers answers to a whole host of questions, ranging from the high ap-

peal of low art all the way up to central existential quandaries—
questions of life and death, if not for you and me, at least for our
culture.

That's undoubtedly a preposterous and impossible statement. Ignore every word of it. No rock'n'roll song lovingly recalled for the incompetence and incoherence of its most famous
version could bear such portents. Ask Wynton Marsalis. Ask Allan Bloom. Ask Albert Goldman. Ask Tipper Gore. Ask Harry
Connick, Jr., and Sr. But don't ask me to tell you that, because
I'm not that big a sucker. Things mean what they mean. You can
deny "Louie Louie" all significance, write it off as just a damnable adolescent fixation, insist that it's symbolic of the end of
civilization at the end of the century. But it goes right on meaning more than what that kind of snobbery will allow.

Don't take my word for it. Frank Zappa, that exemplar of
what happens if you study L.A. doo-wop too deeply, gets to the
prime meat of the musical matter in his 1989 opus, *The Real
Frank Zappa Book*, when he speaks of his compositions using
"stock modules" to create aural textures, among them sounds
derived from "Twilight Zone," "Mister Rogers," cornball bandleader Lester Lanin, "and things that sound either **exactly like**
or **very similar** to 'Louie Louie.' " These textures, Zappa contends, "are **archetypal American musical icons**, and their
presence in an arrangement puts a spin on any lyric in their vicinity. When present, these modules 'suggest' that you interpret
those lyrics within parentheses." Zappa also notices that
"Louie" is built around one of the two basic 1950s rock'n'roll
chord patterns (I-IV-V).

Besides being a song, though, "Louie Louie" is a bunch of
other things, not all of them apparent to the untutored eye and
ear. For that matter, what *is* a song these days: A chord pattern?
A bunch of lyrics sung or recited with so tangled a tongue that
not even FBI scientists could decipher them? A bundle of rights
to be sold, acquired, poached, and permutated? Or just *Duh duh
duh. duh duh*?

"Louie Louie" raises all those questions but it's also an answer,
and answers are a big deal, because they're the rarest thing
around. "Louie Louie" is a Yes to the No that rock'n'roll in all

its diversity has always pronounced to the commonplace culture around it. Once you get it, you have to realize that that No was only worthwhile as a pathway to a Yes that affirms the human heart and soul. It's an affirmation of the glory of absolute nonsense.

What "Louie Louie" affirms is everyday, unchic, unbohemian, unhip radiance. Its primitive chords, its half-baked melody, trace the path to the apogee of spirit from the perigee of nonsense and finds them one. "Louie" is a genuinely transcendent object, a song to which we can dance out the concept expressed so simply by Henry David Thoreau: "Heaven is under our feet." So long as we never forget that the floor of heaven itself is not devoid of banana peels.

We live in a world of trash, of dispensable icons, of Ten-Day Wonders and This Year's Models. This season's Boy George gives way in short order to Andrew Dice Clay; and they are not so much polar opposites as brothers under the skin, their brotherhood confirmed in the rapidity of their fading away. Andy Warhol may not have accurately measured the half-life of fame. It surely persists longer than fifteen minutes, which accounts for the proportionate rise in boredom as a determining factor in everyday life. But Warhol got it exactly right about the general ambition of life in a mediacracy. Trash is no longer a dispensable piece of fun but an indispensable appliance of contemporary existence. So teach our postmodern pedagogues, Paglia be thy name.

A sentiment we could all salute, if only the postmodernists had the ability to discern degrees of quality in trash, between the Elephant Trash (Ronald Reagan, Sylvester Stallone) that tramples everything in its hegemonic path, because it denies that anything outside itself is real, and the Termite Trash (Madonna, Jesse Jackson) that somehow maintains a breath of life, because it hints that everything is real and thus empowers even its antagonists. Rock'n'roll started out as termite trash, an insidious burrowing thing that always contained more than was possible given its surface dimensions, but it changed as it went from "Sh-Boom" to "Wooly Bully" to adaptations of Moussorgsky and expropriations by Philip Glass. So rock is now inhabited by two species of trash, one termite and one elephant. At this point, sorting one from the other could be a full-time job.

From this perspective, "Louie Louie" is rock'n'roll's grand story—or at least, as grand as any story rock'n'roll has to tell. It has made the full journey from the days of total termite status to the ambiguities of today. From the less-than-a-footnote it started out to be, "Louie Louie"—like rock'n'roll—has become a story about splits and bifurcations, about unity and unifications. It is, necessarily, something of a joke, because so many people had so much trouble—and so much fun—accepting the obvious about its nature and origins.

"Louie Louie" has fascinated me since 1964, when some-body slipped me a copy of the "true" lyrics as I was stepping off a school bus. I stumbled back into the story while I was trying to tell another yarn—my book about the 1,001 greatest records ever made. "Louie Louie," from what I could see, sort of boiled all those stories down into one.

This time I determined to get to the bottom of it. But "Louie" 's story turned out to be bottomless. Every firm answer was contingent on something that threw off more perplexing questions. And yet, the answers could not be denied.

I'm not claiming "Louie Louie" is a mystery without a solu-tion. On the contrary, the solution stares us all in the face every time we hear the song. The mystery is *not* what this song—be-yond the basic *duh duh duh. duh duh*—has to tell you or me or the next guy. How could that kind of secret be concealed within what is after all nothing more than a black vinyl 45 rpm record?

The answer to that mystery is so simple that I willingly give anyone who has arrived in these pages for no other purpose than to learn what "Louie Louie" really says the entire solution right now. What "Louie Louie" has to tell you and me and the next guy is this:

It all depends.

Your next question (presuming it isn't some whiny-assed var-iation of "But are they really singing dirty words?") is obvious: Depends on *what?* Ah, there's the true mystery. To solve that one, you'll have to stick around for a while. But again, knowing that these days nobody converses, even on paper, because nobody has the attention span; knowing that we just sit there and soak up TV, radio, or maybe the stereo *if* anybody has the energy to get up and change tapes; aware as I am that we inhabit a world without patience—in that light I shall immediately offer an outline of what it depends upon.

In 1989, Joe Roth directed a movie called *Coupe de Ville*. Considering that, only a few weeks after it was released (to good critical and poor commercial reception), Roth gave up directing to become president of 20th Century-Fox, perhaps it's fair to imagine that *Coupe de Ville* represents his final verdict on the role of artistry and creativity in our time. Perhaps not, too, but at the heart of Roth's movie lies an effort to figure out family, home, parents, brotherhood, community, human understanding, and the general futility of it all—and the crowning metaphor of his film is "Louie Louie."

What happens is plain enough: In the summer of 1963, a father (transplanted from Detroit to Florida, on early retirement) assigns his three sons to drive from Michigan to Tampa with a present for their mother: a mint condition, powder blue 1952 convertible Cadillac Coupe de Ville.

The brothers take their journey together badly, as they are accustomed to taking everything involving one another badly. The oldest, Marvin, just released from the military, is a starched, tight-ass martinet, a bully in temperament and demeanor. Buddy, the middle son, is a University of Michigan nerd, the kind of slide-rule guy regularly demeaned by the irredeemable radical snobs of *The Big Chill* on their way across the quad. And Bobby, youngest of the three, is a teenage hoodlum, filterless chain-smoker, baiter of teachers, bane of parents, the only brother with a sense of cool, the only one without any sense of responsibility or even tolerance.

Midway through the film, the brothers are cruising a two-lane blacktop somewhere in the South, Marvin at the wheel. The Caddy is no longer pristine; its left front headlight's shot, a hole has been burnt in the backseat, the fenders are now dented and muddy. Enraged, Marvin grabs the knob of the radio, which is blaring the Temptations' masterpiece "Since I Lost My Baby" (which wouldn't actually be recorded for another two years, but never mind) and switches the station hard to the right. The radio erupts: "*duh duh duh. duh duh.*" Bobby, riding shotgun with a cigarette in his mouth, smiles broadly at the first hint of the Kingsmen and leans forward, turns the volume knob all the way up. Then he leans back, puts his T-shirt-clad arms behind his head, and clamps down on that smoke—FDR in a DA. In the backseat, Buddy squints up his eyes and sings along: "Louie Louie, let's dance real slow."

Bobby moves his jaws to the same beat, but what emerges is "Oh, baby, got you way down low." Buddy leans forward: "Way down low?"

"*Those are the words*," Bobby explains impatiently. "It's a hump song."

"What's a 'hump song'?"

"When you hump. It's about humping."

"Oh, get off!"

"Listen," Bobby says with total certainty. On the radio, the record is in the middle of a brief instrumental break. Then the vocal comes back in. Bobby again sings along:

"I take her fuckin' all alone / She's never a girl I'd lay at home."

"Those are not the words," says Buddy, doubt rankling.

"Have it your way," says Bobby, arrogance unperturbed.

"No," Buddy says, still wavering; maybe his dweeb friends back in Ann Arbor got *this* wrong, too. He tries to be convincing, but he's trying to convince himself. "It's about dancing. The song is a dance. 'Louie Louie' is a dance. 'Do the Lou-ee Lou-ay.'"

"Are you the only guy in the world who has never heard these lyrics?" Bobby explodes in frustration. Addressing his older brother as a moron, he says slowly, "It's a hump song. It's about humping."

"It's about being in love and dancing," Buddy says haplessly. He's beaten. Just then they pull into a gas station. Marvin, wanting a fill-up, leans on the horn for the attendant, who ignores the three kids in the jalopy.

Bobby sings along again: " 'Each night at ten, I lay her again.' Didja hear that?"

"Did he say 'lay?' " asks Buddy, amazed (and relieved, no doubt, to find an outlet for agreement). "He said 'lay,' didn't he? Oh, my God, it's dirty. It's a dirty song! Oh, my God . . ."

"You gonna throw up?" asks Bobby, poor winner that he is. But Buddy doesn't notice. He's still incredulous at the revelation of the connection, undreamt of in all his philosophy classes, that there's a connection between "Louie" and humping.

By now, Marvin has had enough—of his brothers and of the gas station attendant's recalcitrance. He clambers out from under the steering wheel and goes to the back of the car, searching for the gas tank. He speaks through clenched teeth, as if dealing with orphaned idiots and with the authority of someone who has done his service time and therefore knows the world: "It's not a hump song, and it's not a dance song. It's a *sea chanty.*" Bobby looks at him, dumbfounded. "He's talking about going to sea and leaving his girl . . ." Marvin begins.

Bobby cuts him off: "A sea chanty? You mean like 'Yody-hody, shiver me timbers?' "

This sends Marvin over the edge again. "I mean, like you don't know what you're talkin' about!" he screams. "He's not sayin', 'Each night at ten, I lay her again.' He's sayin', 'Three nights and days, I sailed the sea.' "

"You are so fulla shit," says Bobby derisively and Buddy chimes in: "No, no, no. I'm sure I heard him say 'lay.' "

"He *did* say 'lay,' " says Bobby.

"He *didn't* say 'lay,' " contends Marvin. "*Bobby* said 'lay.' "

"So why is it called 'Lou-ee Lou-ay?' " asks Buddy, master of the non sequitur.

"It's a code word for 'the Land of Enchantment,' " says Bobby. Nothing disturbs this kid's confidence.

"No, see, in the third verse he says, 'Let's cut a rug, babe, we're so in love,' " says Buddy, sure that if his new facts are wrong, the old ones must have had their integrity restored.

"No," Bobby says, derisive as ever. "In the third verse he says, 'She's got a wang on, I move it above.' "

"*He is talking about Jamaica!*" shouts Marvin at the peak of his pique because Bobby, without dropping a beat, has just flipped up the tail fin, exposing the gas cap big brother has been seeking.

"What's a 'wang-on?' " asks Buddy.

On the radio, the record has reached its crucial third verse. As the singer comes back in, each brother picks up the lyrics— his own set. The result is cacophony perfected.

"See, what does that tell ya?" asks Bobby.

"It tells me, for one thing, that you've never been laid," says Marvin, with terrible certainty.

"How do you know?" asks Bobby. At last, his confidence shows a hint of cracking.

"Because anybody who's been laid knows that women don't get a wang-on," says Marvin, ending the conversation decisively. They fill up and drive on.

Marvin gets in the last word at the movie's end, when, after updating us on family developments since that summer, he asserts, "By the way, 'Louie Louie'? It's a sea chanty."

But Marvin (and maybe this goes for Joe Roth, too) isn't interested in solving the mystery of "Louie Louie." He is interested in having his own way. This marks him (or them) as novices in the "Louie" mysteries. It is the task of the true "Louie" adept to avoid doing any such thing—in fact, to avoid showing why any interpretation of the song is right or wrong. To the contrary, the deeply committed initiate's obligation is to prove, once and for all, that they *all* are true. And false. In this way, and this way only, can the true measure of "Louie Louie" and all that it represents ever be comprehended.

And that doesn't mean that Richard Berry ever wrote a dirty word or that the Kingsmen ever sang one. Well, maybe *one*.

Rock lovers and rock haters both assume that great rock'n'roll songs are, or ought to be, dreamed up on the spot. Rock fans think this proves the music's tremendous spontaneity and dedication to amateurism or, at least, the proposition that doing it mostly boils down to putting your heart in the right place. Rock bashers promulgate rock-on-the-spot because it reinforces their sense of it as throwaway garbage made solely to generate big bucks and/or gonadal excitement, with an underlying purpose either cynical or Satanic.

Problem is, neither rock lovers nor rock haters generally know shit about how rock is made. Great rock songs aren't born,

they're sweated out, and fables like the one about how Keith
Richard dreamed the riff to "Satisfaction," even if they're true,
mainly just distract you from the reality of the thousands of fin-
gertip blisters Keith developed learning the catalog of Chuck
Berry riffs down to the cellular level. You think you get to dream
in guitar riffs for free?

"Louie Louie" entered the annals of rock'n'roll mythology ac-
cidentally in the summer of 1963, when a quintet of Portland
teenagers assayed a demo studio version that stumbled into public display by a weird series of chance developments. But
"Louie," the song, and its place in those teenagers' repertoire,
was anything but a product of happenstance.

In 1963 "Louie Louie" was already seven years old. It had
been a regional hit not once but twice. The Kingsmen may not
even have been the first group to record the song *that week*.

Furthermore, "Louie" certainly wasn't born in Portland, nor
even in Seattle among the white garage rockers of the Pacific
Northwest. The mystery of "Louie Louie" came to life in the
imagination of Richard Berry, a twenty-one-year-old black man,
already a recording studio and songmill veteran, who happened
to be sitting in the dressing room of the Harmony Park Ballroom
in Anaheim, California, on a Sunday night in 1956, when a
group called Ricky Rillera and the Rhythm Rockers went into a
cha-cha whose opening riff cried out *duh duh duh. duh duh.*

3

Birth of the "Lou"s

Harmony Park Ballroom, Anaheim, California, Summer 1956

Richard Berry sat in the cramped, muggy dressing room of the barn-like dance hall. The 1,200 capacity ballroom was packed with local low-riders for the regular Sunday night gig of the Rhythm Rockers, a ten-piece band led by Bobby and Barry Rillera, Filipino-American brothers from Orange County. As the group's featured singer, Richard sat out the first part of the set while the band got the energy going with instrumentals.

Berry had sung with the Rillera brothers for more than a year, appearing on a few of their Friday and Saturday dates around East L.A. and always on Sundays at Harmony Park, 40 miles south of Los Angeles. The Harmony Park dates were promoted by Orange County promoter Ralph Perez for members of local car clubs, those legendary low-riders who slung the frames of their slow-running hot rods so close to the ground that they gave off sparks as they rolled. Low-riders loved doo-wop; even thirty years later, those silken R&B harmonies remained the preferred pop sound of their barrio. "They would feature me doing the rock'n'roll, rhythm and blues songs—my songs, a couple of other people's stuff," Richard recalled. "I did two shows a night and bam! I'd be gone."

12

All that came through the dressing room door was a steady rhythmic thump. Yet early in this night's set a beat pulsing through the walls made Richard sit up, hot-wired. *Duh duh duh. duh duh,* it said. Berry heard it and he *knew.* Humming that riff, while the song resolved into a standard cha-cha, he applied a pencil to the only paper at hand, a bag crumpled up on the floor and scribbed a few lines, the outline of a lyric.

Although he was only 21 years old, Richard Berry had already became a street-smart L.A. record hustler, the studio rat who seemed born to stay up all night, singing into a mike for pleasure and profit. Berry possessed the studio hustler's arsenal of skills, including singing, piano playing, arranging, bandleading, and—potentially most profitably—songwriting. He was moderately good looking and knew something about style, wearing his hair waved with the front swept into a pompadour.

Onstage Berry asked the Rilleras to name that tune, "the one with that great bass and piano intro." The Rilleras rattled off titles. "You know," Richard finally said, "the one that goes *duh duh duh. duh duh.*"

"Oh, *that,*" the Rilleras immediately told him. "That was 'El Loco Cha Cha.' Great, huh?"

"Yeah. Who's it by?"

"Rene Touzet."

Richard Berry awoke late the next morning in the house where he'd grown up, on West 54th Street in the black ghetto of Los Angeles. *Duh duh duh. duh duh* ran through his mind as he dressed and went out to a record shop to buy Rene Touzet's new record on the GNP label. He couldn't remember the title exactly and he wasn't even sure he had the artist right. Rene Touzet seemed such an unlikely name—wasn't it French? Even thirty-five years later, Berry would remember the anxiety of waiting for the needle to drop into the groove of "El Loco Cha Cha." "But when I played it, I said, '*That's* the song.' " It wasn't hard to tell: *duh duh duh. duh duh,* claves, bass, and piano said by way of introduction. *Duh duh duh. duh duh* they said at the close.

Beyond that, "El Loco Cha Cha" is a conventional cha-cha, although, as Barry Rillera notes, "Touzet had a real way of getting the cha-cha beat smooth, but *real solid.*" And that smooth-but-solid *duh duh duh. duh duh* put Richard Berry on the trail of the most unforgettable tune of his life.

Also, Richard possessed personality. People flat-out liked him, from the Rillera brothers to the fabled arranger/producer Maxwell Davis, who picked Berry up every day and drove him to the Modern Records studio, where Davis was musical director. Davis told Berry how the music world worked, let him sit at the studio piano and toy with songwriting, gave him the chance to prepare vocal arrangements—a fabulous education in a world where *doing* was the fundamental mode of instruction. Davis did this for the same reason that the Rillera brothers selected Richard as their part-time front man: Of all the guys who could do the job, he was the best to be around.

Berry's voice was strong, pure, and—most important—adaptable. He could sing lead frantically like Little Richard, or in a deeper Muddy Waters–style blues growl, or in a thrilling, deep ballad style derived from Soulful Smoothie #1, Jesse Belvin. He displayed every part of his talent on a series of records released with the Flairs, a group of guys he'd performed with in high school; under his own name; and with a variety of other groups, both famous and obscure. Richard also sang background parts, from tenor to bass, though usually the lower ones. Best of all, Berry could be a great dramatic foil, as he'd proven on two of the most important Los Angeles hits of the rock'n'roll era: The Robins' "Riot in Cell Block #9," where his stoic basso lead thundered threateningly, and Etta James's "The Wallflower (Roll with Me, Henry)," in which Berry convincingly portrayed Henry as so hot-to-trot he was willing to agree to any demand Annie dreamed up. Berry totally rearranged "The Wallflower" during the session. One reason Berry wrote a song to Touzet's Latin beat was that he needed material for an upcoming session of his own.

In other words, "Louie Louie" was created about as amateurishly as the atomic bomb.

Los Angeles's original rock and R&B singers would have been shocked by the nineties idea of their town's rock heritage: wimp-harmony acts from the Beach Boys to Wilson Phillips, glitzoid bands like Warrant, pompous production puds like Richard Marx, soft-target satirists like Randy Newman, and arch singer/

songwriters like Ricky Lee Jones. The doo-woppers, shouters, and R&B teams of the fifties—from Don and Dewey to Little Esther to the Cadets—would spit in the eye of all this trash, kick 'em in the balls, then open their mouths and show such imposters how to *rock*.

Most histories of early rock'n'roll center on either New York, the home of Allan Freed, greaser doo-wop, and the biggest record labels, or Memphis, the home of the constellation of half-cracked rockabillies and bluesmen—Elvis, Jerry Lee Lewis, Ike Turner, Howlin' Wolf—around Sam Phillips's Sun Records.

Yet Los Angeles had more record labels in the early fifties than any other city in the country. Its rhythm and blues record companies were especially prolific and significant: Modern/RPM/Flair, Specialty, Aladdin, Dootone, and Imperial Chief among them, but also dozens of smaller outfits like Max Feirtag's Flip, Leon Rene's Class, and Gene Norman's GNP.

L.A. benefited from artistic migration: Little Richard, Lloyd Price, and Fats Domino among others arrived in Hollywood on a pipeline from sweet home New Orleans, and many of their most able backing musicians, like the great drummer Earl Palmer, followed. The first great independent record producers, led by Jerry Leiber and Mike Stoller—and perhaps the greatest of all fifties studio engineers, Abe "Bunny" Robyn—came from L.A.

In Hunter Hancock, "Huggy Boy" (Dick Hugg), and Tijuana's quarter-million-watt wildman, Wolfman Jack, Los Angeles had its answers to Alan Freed. At its peak, the South-central ghetto's main drag, Central Avenue, roared with live R&B blazing from churches, schools, and night clubs like Johnny Otis's famous Barrelhouse—the stud barn of the local R&B scene—and from taverns, living rooms, and storefront shops.

L.A.'s R&B blossomed out of the city's stature as trail's end for the "territory bands" that traversed the Southwest in the jazz and swing eras. The booming wartime shipyards and aircraft factories gave black immigrants from the Deep South industrial jobs (and industrial wages). After World War II, when economics and dance fashion forced the big bands to downsize, the city became home to stomping combos led by Wynonie Harris (originally from Omaha), Roy Brown (another New Orleans native), T-Bone Walker (who grew up in Texas), Roy Milton (an Oklahoman), Amos Milburn (a Texan), Joe Liggins (from Oklahoma), and Johnny Otis (a native Californian but, then again, a son of Greek immigrants passing for black). L.A. also spawned the cool suavity of the piano trio led by the immortal Nat "King" Cole (from Chicago) and the innumerable imitators that Cole's group inspired, most famously Johnny Moore's Three Blazers, featuring Texas-bred crooner Charles Brown; the genius Ray Charles of Georgia, via Seattle; and Percy Mayfield, a Louisiana native.

Southern California also produced some of the most cataclysmic gospel music ever made, especially at Specialty Records, which had the Soul Stirrers, Dorothy Love Coates and the Original Gospel Harmonettes, Brother Joe May, Professor Alex Bradford, and the Pilgrim Travelers. Reverend James Cleveland, prophet and popularizer of the mass choir movement, made his base in Los Angeles. The town was flush with jazzmen, too, including Charles Mingus, Dexter Gordon, Don Cherry, Eric Dolphy, and Art Farmer. And there were hordes of Latin bands, playing mambos, cha-chas, boleros, and corridos.

> First I started out as a singer with the Flairs. My first tune was "She Wants to Rock." After this came numbers and numbers of tunes until I wrote one which created some action. The Tune was "Truly," which was Rhythm and Blues and was recorded by Mercury, Coral, and a few other Pop Labels. Then I recorded "The Wallflower" with Miss Etta James. Later I wrote her next tune which started me on my way, "Hey Henry" and "Be Mine." And now "Good Rockin Daddy" which is breaking big for Etta and myself. So that's my brief but long story. I am still singing and writing and hope to keep it up.
> —RICHARD BERRY, career description, BMI Publicity Questionnaire (ca. 1955)

Richard Berry was born in 1935 in Extension, Louisiana, near New Orleans. He told L.A. R&B historian Steve Propes that he'd been brought to Los Angeles a year later, to live with an aunt. "When I was eight, my aunt bought a piano for her son and I learned a few songs by ear. The first song I played was

'The Honeydripper' by Joe Liggins. The I learned a few boogie songs."

Richard's father and mother soon came west, too, part of a vast migration out of the South that transformed all of America, especially its music, in the decades after World War I.

Berry's father got a job in the South Bay shipyards; his mother went to work in a laundry. They settled in on Central Avenue, on what was then the west side of the city's black residential area. The neighborhood was just beginning to integrate, on its way to new segregation: John Muir, the junior high school Richard attended, was 95 percent white; Jefferson, the senior high, 95 percent black. (Los Angeles never did truly integrate; even the American Federation of Musicians maintained separate black and white locals until 1953.)

As a child, Berry suffered a hip injury; he doesn't say how. Jim Dawson, historian of Southern California R&B, says he contracted polio. One person who went to school with him claims that Richard leaped off a garage roof "during the *Superman* [comic book] craze." Either way, he was left limping for life. "Through all the Xrays they found out that as I was growing, my bones were growing shorter than [they should have]," says Richard. "So it produced this fracture and they had to insert a pin." He wound up a frequent patient in the Crippled Children's Society on Adams Street, which sent him to a "camp for handicapped kids."

"I met a counselor up there. His name was Bill (I can never think of his last name) and he taught me how to play the ukelele, of all things. I used to walk around junior high school playing the ukelele, you know, and doing the talent shows and everything." This while he was at Muir Junior High, which fed its students to Jefferson High School.

Richard couldn't wait to get to "Jeff," whose music program—"the best, the best in the world"—included a swing group that at one point in the late forties featured Cherry, Dolphy, Farmer, and Sonny Criss, later turning out Big Jay McNeely and Chico Hamilton. Jeff was also famed for its a capella choir, which produced O. C. Smith and numerous heroes of Hollywood doo-wop. Most important, its alumni included Jesse Belvin.

In a just world, Jesse Belvin's name would resonate with the power of Sam Cooke's. After all, when RCA signed Cooke in 1960, it was seeking a singer who could fit the crossover marketing plan it had in mind for Belvin, who'd just died in a car crash.

Belvin is remembered as a crooner because his nationwide hits were "Goodnight My Love," "Guess Who," and "Funny." But in L.A., he's recalled as a rock'n'roller, not just a Three-Hit Wonder. He's also the guy who sang lead in 1955 on the Sheiks' "So Fine," the next year on the Cliques' "Girl of My Dreams," and a year after on the Shields' "You Cheated." In addition, Belvin made dozens of other records for John Dolphin's Recorded in Hollywood, the Bihari brothers' Modern/RPM, and Art Rupe's Specialty labels. Most importantly, perhaps, Belvin wrote the seminal parts of "Earth Angel," which the Penguins turned into the first R&B-to-pop crossover hit.

Jesse and his high school buddies learned the music business the hard way. Their studies taught them that a young black man's songs were worth everything and next to nothing, that he would be cheated out of the money for the songs he created even if he wasn't also robbed of credit for writing them, and that the dough went to the (mainly white, always adult) owners of the record labels who published the songs. Belvin and his boys also came to understand that record royalties were an equally silly charade. The companies would nickel and dime you to death with phony expenses and undercounts. Since you generally saw exactly as much money as you got on the spot when you sold or made the session, and never a red cent more, you snatched the cash and ran off to the next label down the block, paying no more attention to the "exclusive services" clause of your contract than the bosses did to the clauses about royalties due.

Jesse Belvin got next to nothing for writing and singing all those hits, local or national, perhaps an average of $50 or (once he became a semi-celebrity) $100 a side. Sometimes he got less than that. Belvin had to fight a long, costly lawsuit for even a tiny slice of "Earth Angel," though the song had its genesis on one of the shirt cardboards on which he scrawled lyrics and song ideas. This kind of crap made the black teenage R&B singers budding into rock'n'rollers a band of teenage cynics, with Belvin, the most talented, also the most contemptuous of the system.

So Belvin boldly walked into a small-time record company with half a dozen lines that he bluffed into a "song," selling them the tune on the spot. They could have it outright, just so long as he got his cash *right now*. Again and again, Jesse got away with it. He could "hypnotize them with his voice because he had such a strong effect on people when he sang," Gaynel Hodge of the Hollywood Flames told Jim Dawson. "But after he left with his money, the people would realize the song had been all Jesse and all they were left with was smoke."

When Richard Berry arrived at Jefferson High in 1950, Belvin, who was three years older, was already making records and touring full-time. Berry and his buddies studied harmony with Thurston Frazier, a choirmaster at a church at 46th and McKinley, but still "Jesse was our mentor, our idol. Everybody had to sing or record like him. . . . The inspiration was Jesse. We'd go to his house and we'd listen to all his songs."

That first semester Richard was banned from Jefferson High's choir for being a bad-ass. "I had to feel like I was gonna be a gangster, 'cause I had a handicap, and so I had me a knife. Didn't really like to fight. . . . But I had to take on that stance because I felt that everybody'd see me walk with a limp, so I had to establish a character: 'Well, yeah, the cat walks with a limp, but he's a bad nigger. Watch out for him.' But when I got to Jeff, there was just as many bad guys over there as I was.

"Then I learned about the a capella choir and I wanted to get into it. But you had to be of extreme character to get in the choir. And when I asked my music teacher about it he said, 'Well, you'll never get into the choir because you got a very bad attitude.' He told me, he says, 'If your attitude ever changes, maybe we could.' And I went through a whole semester with an attitude that was gonna get me in that choir. And I got in that choir, and after I got in that choir, he used to take me around, even after I graduated. He used to take me around, and he let me perform before the choir, go up and sing my songs and everything. I mean, I was the best thing in the world in that choir."

Jefferson High, like all Los Angeles (the temptation is to say *American*) high schools from that day to this, had its own bad attitude, about young black males. Jefferson's faculty and administration were all white: "I think out of the whole school there were about four black teachers." Consequently, "there was not too much emphasis on education for black kids. I had a vice-principal who always used to tell me, 'Why you wanna go to school? Why don't you join the service? What do you want an education for? You ain't gonna be no doctor, you ain't gonna be no lawyer.' It was always like a little snide thing, like an undercurrent of remarks."

Before his freshman year ended, Richard was singing with the Flamingos, a crew of friends who'd met in choir class: Gaynel Hodge, Cornelius Gunter, Curtiss Williams, and Joe Jefferson. Hodge had brought the others together a year or so earlier at Carver Junior High. This was the group of kids that hung out with Belvin at his house on Long Beach Boulevard. "We'd go over to his house and sit around and listen to him on piano before he went into the Army," Berry told Propes. "He had a refined voice, he was the total balladeer, and if you could sing like Jesse you had the girls."

The Flamingos at first sang mostly at parties, then took to singing Sundays at the weekly talent show at the Lincoln Theater. "We always won," Richard told Propes. "We thought we were big!"

The Flamingos changed their name to the Turks when Chicago's Flamingos broke nationally. Then John Jefferson left the Flamingos to join an early version of the Platters, which featured Alex Hodge, Gaynel's brother. Around the same time, Curtiss Williams left to help form the Penguins. Richard started singing with a new group that included Gunter, Obie "Young" Jessie, Pete Fox, and Beverly Thompson, all from Jeff High. Jessie said this group was called the Debonairs.

They acquired another name, the Hollywood Blue Jays, in the summer of 1953, when they made the mistake of auditioning for John Dolphin in the studio at the back of Dolphin's Hollywood record shop at Vernon and Central.

Big John Dolphin was a cigar-chomping, ghetto empire builder as ruthless in his own way as any of L.A.'s early land and water robber barons. He promoted releases on his Recorded in Hollywood and Cash labels with a KRKD radio show featuring a deejay (initially Charles Trammell, later Huggy Boy) who broadcast late at night from the store's front window.

Dolphin didn't think much of the group's audition (Berry admitted they were nervous) but, unbeknownst to them, he ran a tape while they sang. Richard took the lead on "Tell Me You Love Me," Cornell Gunter on "I Had a Love." Dolphin passed on the act but kept the tape.

The group next tried Modern Records, L.A.'s most important rhythm and blues record company. Founded in 1945 by Joe, Jules, and Saul Bihari, three white brothers, the Modern group (it labels included RPM, Flair, and Rhythm and Blues) cultivated a web of talent scouts and small producer associates, including Ike Turner, that brought it such blues stars as Lightnin' Hopkins (from Houston), John Lee Hooker (from Detroit), and B. B. King (from Memphis). Modern's roster also included Johnny Moore's Three Blazers with Charles Brown, Etta James, Rosco Gordon, Johnny "Guitar" Watson, Jimmy Witherspoon, Floyd Dixon, the Cadets (a/k/a the Jacks), the Teen Queens, Elmore James, and Marvin and Johnny (a duo that sometimes included Jesse Belvin). Although the company didn't record much gospel or be-bop, it was involved in every other area of black music and, in the early fifties, even recorded some country and western.

Joe Bihari heard the music behind their nerves and told them to go home and rehearse. A week later, they came back for a session at Master Recorders in Hollywood. Maxwell Davis arranged and led the band; Bunny Robyn engineered. The songs were "I Had a Love" and a new song written by Richard, "She Wants to Rock."

"The Biharis wanted to do something with 'She Wants to Rock,' so they introduced me to these two young guys named Jerry Leiber and Mike Stoller, and they came in and added gunshots and sound effects," Berry told Propes. This was the first example of the gimmicky style that Leiber and Stoller, with much assistance from Robyn, perfected with the Robins and the Coasters.

Bihari named the group the Flairs and released "She Wants to Rock" backed with "I Had a Love" as Flair 1012, the label's twelfth single, second in its R&B series. This probably happened in late July or early August because Bob Rolontz wrote in his "Rhythm and Blues Notes" column in the August 15, 1953, *Bill-*

board: "Flair Records' new vocal group, the Flairs, is composed of five 16-year-old high school students, who will make their first professional appearance at the upcoming Gene Norman jazz concert at the Shrine Auditorium, Hollywood." Rolontz noted that they had been signed to a two-year contract, and wrote their own material, an unusual distinction among vocal groups.

"I Had a Love" showed up in the September 19 *Billboard*'s "Coming Up in the Trade" column, devoted to records "selling well but not yet strong enough to make national . . . charts." But on Dolphin's KRKD show, Charles Trammell was playing a second version, released by Recorded in Hollywood. Although it was billed as being by "the Hollywood Bluejays with Pee Wee Crayton's Orchestra," it turned out to be the one that Dolphin had surreptitiously taped during the Flairs a capella audition. As Berry told Propes, "It was just that kind of crap that later got [Dolphin] killed."*

The Flairs went belligerently to Dolphin and demanded he pull the record off the market. He refused, but the RIH version flopped because it lacked "She Wants to Rock," which hadn't been written when the "Bluejays" session took place. Although the Modern release never broke beyond California, its two-sided appeal established the Flairs as a significant local attraction.

The Flairs became Modern's all-purpose vocal ensemble. "I did so much stuff with Modern, I've forgotten it all," Berry said. They cut records under their own name (the second, "Tell Me You Love Me," came out in November and they had releases about every two months for the next few years), as the Chimes, the Rams, the Howlers, the 5 Hearts, and individually—most notably Richard Berry (the first of a dozen, "I'm Still in Love with You"/"One Little Prayer" came out in October) and Young Jessie (who made the mighty "Mary Lou," among others).

Richard cut more records than any of the others, because he could sing so many different parts, from falsetto to bass, because he was so close to Davis, and because the crippled youngster without so much as a driver's license was almost always willing

---

*Dolphin was shot to death in January 1958 by songwriter Percy Ivy, who was enraged over unpaid royalties.

to make a session: "I'd sit up there in the studio all day and walk around, play the piano, think of songs to write. If I write this song and we record it, I know I've got some instant money.

"It was great, because we were in school, everybody knew us. We were kings on campus to everybody except the administration. . . . Of course we always wore our Flairs shirts with our names written on them. We were hot shit, you know. We'd stand up against the wall. 'I'm cool, man, I'm cool.' "

They toured as far east as Denver, as far north as San Francisco. "Matter of fact, I almost didn't graduate because I stayed gone all the time. 'Cause where was you gonna find a buncha black kids that could go out and make fifty bucks a night apiece, singin' four or five songs. We'd work five or six nights in a row. That was more than my old man could make."

Richard argues persuasively that the Flairs were the first important teenage vocal group on record: "There was no Frankie Lymon. The only groups around were Sonny Til and the Orioles, the Ravens, and the 5 Royales. And those were guys that we kinda patterned ourselves after, but our music was still different. 'Cause you know the 5 Royales had the gospel-type things."

This teenage quality is precisely what made the rawer, harder-driving L.A. doo-wop so special, what made it rock'n'roll. "In terms of arrangements and music, I think that the East Coast stuff—like the Flamingos, the Swallows—was a little bit more refined. The edges are much smoother," said Richard.

Los Angeles never produced a harmony record as beautifully complex as Richard's favorite, "Golden Teardrops" (which was East Coast only on the premise that Chicago might as well be New York to a Californian), but it developed its own doo-wop style. As back East, the rhythm has a Latin accent, there's a lot of deep-voiced moaning and a whole lotta high-voiced wooin' goin' on, and almost all the wailing has to do with the tragedy of teen romance. But in L.A. doo-wop there's a singular drive and bounce, a salacious craziness, a willingness to go for any effect so long as it works. Even on relatively smooth tracks like the Jacks' "Why Don't You Write Me," this madness is pronounced and it reaches true glory on slurry stuff like Marvin and Johnny's "Cherry Pie" and the Penguins' "Earth Angel." This places

L.A. doo-wop closer to the blues, and at its best—on "Death of an Angel," Donald Woods' ghostly, ghastly anthem of lovelorn deprivation—it reaches close to the delirium blues of Rabbit Brown's "James Alley Blues," a 1928 record so grandly poetic that Allen Ginsberg lists it as his all-time favorite.

The Flairs never hit that level. But Richard Berry did.

In February 1954, Leiber and Stoller (now well known for writing Big Mama Thornton's huge 1953 hit, "Hound Dog") and their mentor, song publisher Lester Sill, formed Spark Records. Spark immediately signed the Robins, with whom Leiber and Stoller earlier had recorded "That's What the Good Book Says" for RPM. (The Robins first recorded for Savoy in 1949.) For the group's first Spark release, Leiber and Stoller wrote "Riot in Cell Block #9."

Leiber and Stoller wanted a vehicle for their song more than they wanted to create a long-lasting group, so they felt free to tinker when Bobby Nunn, the Robins' bass singer, didn't seem very dangerous. This upset the Robins, since Nunn was the group's featured singer. But Leiber and Stoller nevertheless called in Richard Berry, whom they remembered from their session with the Flairs. "They got me to do 'Riot in Cell Block #9,' 'cause they knew I used to sit around the piano and do all this Willie Mabon stuff. They knew that I had that nasty type singing voice."

The result was unforgettable. As Robert Palmer describes it in *Baby, That Was Rock'n'Roll*, his account of Leiber and Stoller's career, "The record's rhythmic underpinning was a Delta blues riff lifted from Muddy Waters, but everything else about it was several years ahead of its time." Richard didn't just do a guest shot; he was virtually a solo voice, the most prominent instrument in the music, save Gil Bernal's vicious sax.

Berry's portrayal of a tough black convict narrating a prison riot had its comic side, but he dealt in dangerous double entendres. "Pass the dynamite 'cause the fuse is lit," he intoned and thirty years later you understand this as a possible code for the emergent civil rights movement or, for that matter, a metaphor about the rise of a rock'n'roll itself, which three decades later gave birth to a crew of "gangster rappers" (mainly L.A.—

based hustler/artists like N.W.A., Ice-T, and Ice Cube), whose own bad-ass anecdotes used sound effects (sirens, tommy guns) descended from Leiber and Stoller's. The genealogy is not at all farfetched. In July 1954, CBS banned "Riot" from Peter Potter's "Juke Box Jury" network radio show and from Larry Finley's local KNXT TV shows. Berry knows it, too: "What I was doin' in 'Riot in Cell Block #9' was rappin'. It was rappin' with music."

Spark's weak distribution outside the West Coast prevented "Riot" from becoming a national hit, but after its release in June 1954, it sold about 100,000 copies and even made noise on the burgeoning rhythm and blues radio shows back East. The Robins cut a series of such spoofy dramas, notably "Framed" and "Smokey Joe's Cafe," before the whole shebang moved to New York, where Leiber–Stoller became independent producers for Atlantic Records, which *did* have effective coast-to-coast distribution. Leiber and Stoller later wrote many of Elvis Presley's most important hits (including "Hound Dog" and the scores for *Jailhouse Rock* and *King Creole*), charted a dozen hits ("Charlie Brown," "Yakety Yak," "Young Blood") with the Coasters, launched Phil Spector, and played a significant role in early sixties girl-group music.

For Richard, the success of "Riot" had more complicated results. "The Flairs weren't too pleased about me doin' it with the Robins. The *Robins* weren't too pleased about me doin' it with the Robins," he said. "Of course, Modern Records knew. They said, 'We know that was you.' I said, 'Nah.'" He had to say that; Richard was signed to Flair exclusively. But the Biharis weren't exactly living up to the contract themselves. Berry's songs were being copyrighted under the family's pseudonyms, "Josea," "Ling," and "Taub," thus depriving him of publishing royalties, and their royalty accounting was, to say the least, subjective. In the archetypal style of the independent record business, the Biharis grumbled briefly then set to exploiting Richard's achievement on "Riot." Joe Bihari even suggested Richard quit the Flairs.

"We had like a camaraderie that was there, that you didn't break. So I pondered over it. And I liked the idea but it kinda scared me too. 'Cause you always find shelter in a group. But they finally convinced me to do it and the guys in the group weren't too pleased about it. But in the back of my mind I could see the handwriting on the wall, because we could see the enthusiasm starting to die off in the record company."

The Flairs were flickering. Of the group's half-dozen singles, only "Love Me Girl" got any action outside of L.A. In April it was a *Billboard* "territorial tip" from St. Louis. After he hit with "Mary Lou," Young Jessie also quit; Pete Fox joined the new group that scored first with "Why Don't You Write Me" as the Jacks, then as the Cadets with "Stranded in the Jungle," a playlet as bizarre as any of Leiber and Stoller's. Cornell Gunter formed the Ermines then packed for the East to join the Robins as they became the Coasters. (Ironically, Bobby Nunn was one of only two original Robins who made the move.) Still, they'd really accomplished something: "Out of that group of five guys, there were four guys that went separate ways individually and [are] still in the music business."

After a late summer shot with the female quintet the Dreamers on "Bye Bye," Richard's post-Flairs solo career began with Bihari demanding a "Riot" sequel. In October he gave them a rewrite called "The Big Break" (Flair 1055), in which "Riot"'s deep-voiced con and his pal, Snake, decide to get out of stir once and for all. This droll but somewhat less felicitous follow-up got little attention in Los Angeles. Richard's next record, the riotous "Next Time" (another stop-time blues novelty, in which he's hauled into "district court, room 299" for failure to pay his rent) is far funnier and less derivative, but it sold less than "The Big Break." (The song later made some noise for Sam Butera and Louis Prima.) Over the next two or three years, Richard recorded Little Richard–like wailers such as "Mad About You" and "Yama Yama Pretty Mama"; "Crazy Lover," a rewrite of Muddy Waters's "I'm Ready" with Big Mama Thornton on harp; "I'm Still in Love with You," in the Fats Domino mold; Chuck Berry–style hard-rockers like "Rockin' Man"; and "Oh! Oh! Get Out of the Car," which combined a Leiber–Stoller style of narrative with the car-song trend kicked off by Chuck's "Maybelline."

Meantime, his work as sideman and sessioneer continued. "I was on maybe 50–60 percent of the records that came out" of Modern in the mid-fifties, he claimed. Berry sang, wrote, and

arranged with Arthur Lee Maye (Lee Maye, as the National
League knew him, was then a bonus baby with the Milwaukee
Braves) and the Crowns, incuding the great "Gloria." After Shirley and Lee made mixed duos popular, Berry teamed with Jennell Hawkins as Ricky and Jennell.

But the next major notch in the Richard Berry legend was
carved "on a foggy Thanksgiving eve in 1954," Berry told
Propes. "Hank Ballard was having a big hit with 'Work with Me,
Annie' and everybody was doing answers to it. Maxwell called
me about 11 at night and said he needed me over at the studio.
I drove through that thick fog over to the Biharis' new studio on
Washington Avenue in Culver City.

"Etta was there with four girls [the Peaches] who couldn't
sing too well. She already had the basic song, but we reworked
it, she and I, there in the studio. It was called 'Roll with Me,
Henry.' Etta wrote most of the words and I helped her a little,
but Johnny Otis, who was there on the session, beat her out of
the writer's credit." In the end, copyright infringement suits
were filed by Valjo Music on behalf of Otis (who, whatever his
role in creating the music, undisputably was the first to air the
song, playing it on his radio show in January, causing a sensation
even before the tune was officially released); Armo Music, Hank
Ballard's publisher; Lois Music in New York; and a writer named
Frank Kelton in Hollywood.

As the voice of Henry, the uncredited Richard Berry kicks off
"Roll with Me, Henry," shouting "Hey, baby, what'd I have to do
to make you love me?" then answering Etta's instructions
throughout the first verse. And it's Berry's interplay with James,
especially at the end, when he meekly accedes to her imperious
commands, that makes the disc a classic.

The record business of the 1950s was no less ruthless than it
is today. By February 5, after less than two weeks in distribution,
Billboard called "Henry" an R&B hit in New York City, Baltimore, Nashville, Durham, Cincinnati, New England, upstate
New York, Detroit, and St. Louis, as well as Los Angeles. But
James didn't have a chance on pop playlists, where a strict color
line remained in effect. After "The Wallflower" (the new title
under which it appeared on the *Billboard* chart) topped the black
chart, it was immediately covered by Georgia Gibbs, a semi-re-

formed big-band singer who made millions by glomming onto R&B hits by such R&B greats as James and LaVern Baker, whose records racist radio programmers wouldn't air. (Baker finally got so mad after Gibbs hit #1 on the pop charts with a genetically identical cover of "Tweedle Dee," that she wrote her congressman about theft of song styles. The complaint was made public but nothing came of it. To this day, singers have few legal remedies against such stylistic poaching.)

Gibbs emasculated "The Wallflower." Her Henry was asked not to "roll" but to "dance." Gibbs just tried to get that ol' Hank out on the floor to cut a rug, rather than try to get him to do his stuff right on the carpet. But the white audience hadn't yet rebelled against such bland evasion, so Gibbs still had a million-seller. Soon, the "Annie"/"Henry" fad faded. So Modern's sequel, "Hey, Henry" (issued in May with Richard credited as Etta's partner), stiffed. But James did return to the R&B Top 10 with the Berry-written "Good Rockin' Daddy."

By late 1955, though, Richard was fed up with Modern Records. "I didn't have any animosity against the Bihari brothers. I think they did business on the scale that everybody else was doing on," he later said. "They treated their artists with a little bit more humanity than some of the other record companies did." But Richard had little to show for two years of dogged work at the label.

"Fifty bucks was good money around 1953, 'specially for kids," Berry said. "Those fifty bucks bought me a car and stuff, where I never woulda been able to afford even a bicycle. So the opportunity was there. But after being in the businses for four or five years, then you started gettin' these little things like, 'The guys in the record company's doin' you guys out of your money,' bam bablam bablam bablam. And then you go through your awakening period, where you say, 'Yeah, you know, like, how come every time we get a statement we owe the record company money?' We always were in the red, or whatever you wanna call it. We always owed them money.

"Then it dawned on me. I said, well, I know how the record companies do this. Even if you had royalties, you could have $50,000 up there in royalties, and they could take you in the studio and record you five or six days, and they would charge you for it, even though they wouldn't release the records. They still charge you for the session, the studio time. So when you look up, you say 'Man, what happened to my fifty grand?' 'Well, you know, we went in the studio and we recorded.' And of course, we didn't have access to lawyers and managers like the kids comin' up today. *They* got four or five lawyers before they even go to a record company."

"I could almost at any given time go to Joe [Bihari] and ask for an advance and get it," Richard acknowledges, but he received no performance royalties, no songwriting royalties, and many of his songs had been published with co-writer credit, and royalty money, assigned to the Biharis. You don't get rich at fifty bucks a night, but after a while, it became clear that if the singers and musicians weren't getting rich, *someone* was. The Biharis had prospered so mightily that in May 1954 they announced a move to a newly completed 5,000-square-foot Culver City recording studio and office building next to their Cadet Record Pressing.

"We were all young and ignorant. We didn't have a lawyer, never had a manager, didn't know that as minors our money was supposed to go through the courts and go into a fund until we were 21," Richard told Propes. "I didn't know anything about BMI [which collects money for broadcast performances, *if* the songwriter is registered with it] until Maxwell Davis told me about it in 1955. Modern was collecting my royalties and keeping me ignorant. When I finally asked them, 'What's this Josea shit?' the Biharis told me the distributors would promote my records more if they saw that name on it!"

So Richard filed a lawsuit for back royalties ("It took me five years to get about $1,800 out of a suit that started at $50,000") and cut out to record for a variety of labels, doing one-shots as Ricky, or Ricky and the Pharoahs, for little labels like George Motola's Empire (with a batch of tunes written by Belvin, who told him, "These people be giving away a lot of money") and Leon Rene's Class. Each of his records was good, but still none hit outside L.A.

"We had what you call regional hits. You'd have a top selling record in New York, but nobody heard of you in Buffalo. You had a #1 record in Philadelphia, but nobody heard of you in Pittsburgh. You could have a hit record in Kansas City, but nobody knew of you in St. Louis. It went on and on and on." After "Earth Angel," this began changing, but Los Angeles didn't become the center of the recording universe for another decade.

In January 1955 *Billboard* wrote that "Max Feirtag, formerly associated with Imperial Records, last week disclosed formation of a new independent label, Flip Records. Firm will specialize in R&B and a line of authentic Latin American music."

Feirtag, listed as secretary/treasurer on the 1946 incorporation papers of Lew Chudd's Imperial Records (a key L.A. R&B label that released Fats Domino, among others), ran his new venture out of an apartment on Sixth Street near LaBrea Avenue, just south of West Hollywood. Feirtag had been around the record business for years; his wife, Lillian, says that he made his first releases "about 1948." Nobody remembers him as especially musical, but Flip still came up with three of the most important Los Angeles R&B records: Donald Woods's "Death of an Angel" in the summer of 1955, the 6 Teens' "A Casual Look" in the summer of 1956, and in the summer of 1957, Richard Berry's "Louie Louie."

Berry signed with Flip at the end of 1955, but his Modern contract hadn't expired. Modern continued releasing Richard Berry material through "Angel of My Life"/"Yama Yama Pretty Mama" (RPM 465) in June 1956. Richard had begun working with a new vocal group, the Pharoahs: baritone Noel Collins, first tenor Godoy Colbert (replaced by the time it came to "Louie" by Stanley Henderson), and second tenor Robert Harris. Berry occasionally supplemented them with Gloria Jones (about whom he wrote Arthur Lee Maye's doo-wop classic) and Jennell Hawkins (his erstwhile duet partner, for whom he wrote "Moments," a 1961 R&B hit).

"The Pharoahs were already a group. They were young guys into Jeff High just as I was leaving. They weren't really doo-wop, which was fine with me 'cause I was getting into a Latin thing. They had a funkier sound. The Flairs always had access to a piano when we went over to Pete Fox's house and rehearsed, but with the Pharoahs we'd rehearse at my house, get loaded, turn the lights down, and start singing. In the darkness, that was when I could really hear the harmony that I wanted and that's what made my music change, 'cause we didn't have the piano to work off of." Richard didn't work with the Pharoahs exclusively. His days of exclusive musical association ended with the Flairs. He still sang session dates and he still worked dates with the Rhythm Rockers.

After Richard figured out that "El Loco Cha Cha" was the right record, he began to rework its opening and closing riff and a chunk of its melody to fit the lyric idea he'd scribbled down on the paper bag in the Harmony Park dressing room.

This doesn't mean Richard Berry *stole* "El Loco Cha Cha" any more than the Rolling Stones stole the half-dozen of their most famous songs that indisputably owe their origins to Chuck Berry—because Berry owes Louis Jordan, T-Bone Walker, and Charlie Christian equally. Lawsuits about such issues were and remain common, from the cycle of litigation around "The Wallflower" to U2's 1991 attack on the punk band Negativland's sampling of its wares. But that's never prevented boasting about the provenance of one's material: In October 1956, *Billboard* reported, "Publisher Goldie Goldmark took the prize this week for finding the most unlikely source of R&B material yet reported. He maintains that the background figure in Screamin' Jay Hawkins's Okeh release 'I Put a Spell on You' is from Haley's opera *La Juive* (written in 1835). Who could prove that it isn't? It's doubtful if even Haley could." Anyway, since the copyright on *La Juive* had long expired, Goldmark had no fear of litigation. Yet to this day Richard Berry must be circumspect about the origin of "Louie Louie," even though the "El Loco Cha Cha" revelation is hardly fresh.

Anyway, by the time the Kingsmen made "Louie" famous, and valuable, it no longer had a Touzet beat. For that matter, even Richard Berry and the Pharoahs' "Louie Louie" is *not* "El Loco Cha Cha." *Duh duh duh. duh duh* isn't uncommon in Latin music; you could sing "Louie Louie" to "El Loco Cha Cha," but you could also hum that other great 1963 hit, Ray Barretto's "El Watusi."

The biggest, or at least most readily apparent, difference between the two songs is the lyrics. Touzet's are in Spanish and have nothing to do with sailors, the sea, Jamaica, or the moon above. Berry's is an account of a homesick navvy explaining to a barkeeper why he pines to renew his dalliance with the darling he's left on his home island. (In Richard's song, "Louie" is the name of the bartender the sailor addresses, not the singer. Richard says that the sailor "didn't have no name.")

What Richard Berry wrote is not without antecedents. By far the most important was Chuck Berry's "Havana Moon," the flip side of his 1956 nonhit, "You Can't Catch Me." Chuck sang "Havana Moon" to a calypso beat, using a Jamaican accent. "I wanted to write a song like 'Havana Moon' all my life," Richard says, "and I was working with a Mexican band, the Rhythm Rockers." The Rilleras (whom Richard sometimes calls "the Riveras") aren't Mexican; they're Filipino-American. But they played for Mexican audiences.

In "Havana Moon," Chuck Berry sings a forlorn calypso about a Cuban sailor who waits up all night, accompanied only by a jug of rum, for the American girl with whom he's fallen in love to arrive and take him away to live in a New York City highrise. But the sailor, fearing she'll never come, anxiously sips too deeply from his jug so when, at dawn, she does arrive, he's out of sight, comatose on the dock. He awakens to bright sun and blue skies just in time to see the boat carrying his weeping girlfriend "head for hor-i-zon." The connection to "Louie," where a pidgin-speaking sailor moons into his glass about his girl and sweet home Jamaica, couldn't be clearer. But Chuck Berry's shaggy dog ballad lasts half a dozen verses; Richard Berry's three verses are far more concise and elliptical.

"Louie" 's other lyrical inspiration was Johnny Mercer and Harold Arlen's standard, "One for My Baby (and One More for the Road)," also known as "Set 'Em Up, Joe," first sung by Fred Astaire in *The Sky's the Limit* (1943) and popularized by Lena Horne in 1945. But the version generally regarded as definitive is Frank Sinatra's somber but swinging 1958 Nelson Riddle arrangement. Richard knew the song because its 3 A.M. self-pity made it a staple for every saloon singer.

In "One for My Baby," an anonymous lovelorn sot drops in on Joe, the bartender, just before closing time and fills him in on

his romantic woes, a scenario all but identical to the one con-
fronting Berry's Louie. Richard had to be careful here. In rock
or R&B, Johnny Mercer's scenario would be absolutely insup-
portable: The singer is already drunk and suggesting he have
"one more for the road" would have earned any black or teen
songwriter instant condemnation then as now. But it was understood that white-collar drunks of the kind portrayed by Astaire
and Sinatra posed no social threat. Berry evaded the issue of
drunkenness—his protagonist may have poured his heart out for
a bartender but not a drop touches his lips.

"Louie Louie" 's pedigree extends further. "One for My
Baby" comes from a grand tradition of late-night drinking
songs, all of them saturated in abjection and remorse. "Havana
Moon" was as derivative of Nat "King" Cole's 1949 "Calypso
Blues" as "Louie" was of "El Loco Cha Cha." "Calypso Blues,"
in which a Trinidadian sailor presents his plans to cut out from
the cruel USA for home and honey, is closer lyrically than *any*
other song to "Louie Louie." Also, in picking a name for his
forlorn sailor, Louis Jordan's 1946 hit "Run Joe" might have
crossed Richard's mind; not only is the lyric similar to some of
Leiber–Stoller's comic tales of a man on the lam, but the track
opens with the Tympani Five chanting "Louie, louie, louie," an
invocation of their leader's name that becomes, like the latter-
day reiterations of "Lou-ee, Lou-ay," a hypnotic nonsense
phrase.

After Richard finished writing "Louie" in April 1956, he and
the Pharoahs, with Gloria Jones adding the feminine touch, immediately recorded it at Hollywood Recorders on Santa Monica
Boulevard, using a band led by pianist/arranger Ernie Freeman.
The band also included drummer Ray Martinez, Irving Ashby
on guitar, Red Callender on bass, and a horn section featuring
Plas Johnson, Jewel Grant, and John Anderson.

The same group also recorded in late 1955 and earlier in
1956, but Feirtag didn't issue any records because he didn't want
a legal problem with the Biharis. By April "fresher" material was
wanted. So Richard cut "You Are My Sunshine," "Somewhere
There's a Rainbow," and "Sweet Sugar You," plus "Louie."

Freshness didn't seem to be the real issue: Richard's first Flip

release featured "No Kissin' and Huggin'" b/w "Take the Key,"
recorded at the 1955 session. But "No Kissin'" flopped and
"You Are My Sunshine," the Governor Jimmie Davis country
standard, came out as Flip 321 in April 1957. The B side was
"Louie Louie."

Berry chose "You Are My Sunshine," a song he remembered
from childhood: "We used to sit up in the living room quite a
few nights with the red light on and we'd be singing 'You Are
My Sunshine.' I thought that if I was ever gonna have a hit record it was gonna be off of 'You Are My Sunshine.'" (Not a wild
idea: In 1962, Ray Charles put an R&B version of "You Are My
Sunshine" in the pop Top 10.)

"Louie Louie" was an afterthought. "I didn't think 'Louie
Louie' was gonna be a hit. I just thought it was a good song that
I wrote," said Richard. "But everybody that I ever talked to had
a preference of 'You Are My Sunshine' over 'Louie Louie.' Even
now people that used to follow me and still know my music always tell me, 'Well, yeah, man, "Louie Louie" was great but
"You Are My Sunshine" was greater.'"

Hardly. But what Richard did with "You Are My Sunshine"
was akin to what he'd done with "El Loco Cha Cha": "I dis-
sected it and put it together with the harmony and stuff, and
even added my own little bridge in the song. . . . I just made that
up, you know, 'cause you always had to have a bridge in a song
in those days. In those days, if a song didn't have a bridge, it
wasn't a song. I mean, you just can't have this thing goin' on and
on. You put in the bridge." Technically such alterations to a song
should be done only with the writer and publisher's permission
but "nobody ever bothered us about it," since the record never
hit.

The restructured "You Are My Sunshine" yawped bolder
than anything Richard had recorded for the Biharis, but "Louie
Louie" was bolder yet, though not so bold as he'd hoped. "When
I heard this song I envisioned all the timbales and the congas
going and me singing 'Louie Louie.'" In his dreams Berry made
the song a thorough mixture of Latin and R&B accents, perfect
for a moment when *Billboard* was writing about the converging
tastes of R&B fans and "record buyers of Mexican and Spanish
descent."

Max Feirtag might have been interested in "authentic Latin American music," but he didn't want any part of Richard Berry's hybrid. "We don't want that crap," Richard remembers Feirtag saying, "We want a good R&B-sounding record." So the song's Latin accoutrements were deleted, "which," Richard now thinks, "mighta been a good thing when the Kingsmen got it. You often wonder what woulda happened if I had recorded 'Louie Louie' the way I had it envisioned in my mind."

Richard Berry could sound like the most dangerous man on the cell block, but his original version of "Louie Louie" isn't even raucous. As the Pharoahs chant their *duh duh duh. duh duh,* they sound less threatening than jaunty. Berry made a dozen records you wouldn't want to meet in a dark alley, but "Louie Louie" isn't one of them. Turn his "Louie Louie" up as loud as you please; it thunders not, neither does it shatter eardrums, speakers or consciousness. It's an R&B dance tune with a hint of cha-cha, a vehicle for a beat, and Richard's vocal is imploring but ultimately sure of itself—"me gotta go," he seems to be telling that barkeeper, because what's waiting for me is *fine.*

Records sell by word of mouth, which builds best and quickest through radio airplay. Because there are many more records released than there is time to broadcast them, whoever gets to pick which ones get played—and played, and played—becomes a powerful shaman. In the 1950s—though, alas! no longer—the men making radio's musical decisions were mostly deejays. Those deejays were myth-mongers, projecting a convincing personality on the thinnest possible evidence: a sheet of sound composed of nothing but a human voice, a few taped jingles, and a bagful of musical mist. For a time in the 1950s, deejays were at least rock stars' equals in fame and wealth.

The king of Los Angeles rhythm and blues record-spinners was Hunter Hancock, who possessed a high-pitched voice, a self-deprecating avuncular streak, and a penchant for bad (sometimes leering) jokes offset by a gift for spotting new hits early. Hancock first hit Hollywood in the early 1940s; he claimed to be the first white man in America to air black music, but whether or not that was true, by 1948 he'd worked his way up to a daily show that made must listening for R&B and jump-jazz fanatics.

Hunter Hancock's sonic self-image became an entire world, all of it based around Negro jive music. "Huntin' with Hunter," his KGFJ show (on KFVD it was "Harlem Matinee") opened with a bugle call. "Let's go a-huntin' with Hunter," said a staff announcer, "huntin' around for some of the very best popular Negro musicians, singers, and entertainers in the world. You'll hear music that runs the gamut from be-bop to ballads, swing to sweet, and blues to boogie, records that are the tops in popularity around the country along with some of the newer records, whose popularity will be determined by you, the listeners." Then you were off into the deep depths of R&B with a heavy emphasis on local Los Angeles favorites.

Maybe Hancock didn't know much about R&B until he got Todd Clothes of Watts as a sponsor, but by the fifties he knew all that was necessary about how to spot what was then known as a "sepia" hit. He staged talent contests and amateur shows at the fabled Barrel House and Club Alimony; he even had his own record labels, Swingin' and Magnum. By 1954 "Ol' H. H." was a legend—when he went to the Rockies on his regular hunting trips, or performed as tenor soloist at the Hollywood First Methodist Church, or got a new sports Mercedes, it was news in the industry trade papers. In 1956 the local CBS affiliate gave him a television show, "Rhythm and Blues"; Maxwell Davis led the house band.

"Hunter used to play all our records," Richard said. "He would play your record and then, after a while, flip it over and play the other side. And he never asked for any money or anything. He had record hops and stuff, where you were always glad to do something for Hunter because he played the local guys."

Hancock wasn't only good; he was smart and tough. When the morality types began the first anti-R&B witch-hunt, he stepped to the music's defense more aggressively than any other disc jockey then or since. "It is my contention that most of the criticism being leveled against R&B is unwarranted," he told *Billboard* in May 1955. "True, some rhythm and blues has objectionable lyrics, but so do many of the top-selling records in the popular and Western fields. Actually, R&B is the music that

to the average Negro is his pop music." By August 1956, when
the clamor, inflamed by the Tin Pan Alley songwriters being put
out of business by popular demand for rock'n'roll and R&B, still
hadn't been quelled, and promoter Hal Zeiger was threatened
by the El Monte city council with a ban on all rock shows, Hancock called forth an industry group, including Speciality's Art
Rupe and bandleader Johnny Otis, to counteract the witch-hunt.
(Zeiger lost in a decision clearly based more on anti-black and
anti-Latin racism than any threat to public safety, and the legend
of the shows at El Monte Legion Stadium—which led to Frank
Zappa's first great song, "Memories of El Monte"—began.)

Leaving Modern Records may have been a necessity but it didn't
improve Richard Berry's living conditions. Feirtag proved
cheaper than the Biharis ever had. While Richard was going to
school and living at home, he'd been prosperous, owning a huge
1949 Buick convertible with a Continental kit (and employing a
cousin as chauffeur because he still couldn't drive). At 21, living
on his own, money got so tight he had to think twice about marrying his girlfriend, Dorothy Adams (who later recorded as
Dorothy Berry and toured with Ray Charles as a Raelette).

Without even a local hit since the Flairs broke up, recording
and singing live couldn't support him anymore. So he went to
work as a stock clerk and general laborer at Monarch Records,
a record pressing plant. "Max got me the job 'cause, I guess, he
got tired of me hittin' on him for advances. . . . I used to call him
my Jewish father because he's, 'You gotta have a job, Richard.
You can't depend upon this business. You gotta have a job.' "

Richard was working at Monarch one afternoon when
Hunter Hancock made a special announcement. "He says,
'We're gonna do something we never did before. We got this
record by Richard Berry, it's the flip side of 'You Are My Sunshine.' We've got so many calls for it, we're gonna play it every
hour on the hour.' For a week, he played 'Louie Louie' every
hour on the hour."

This only made things worse at Monarch. "Every time the
song came on, the guys would say, 'Hey man, they're playin' your
song.' This Japanese guy was my foreman. He says, 'Whadda
you want this job for?' He says, 'You gotta hit record.' I says, 'No,

I don't have a hit record.' I says, 'Even if it was, I don't have no money, man, I'm not working.' 'You oughta give this job to somebody else.' I said, 'I *need* this job.' He was really off the wall. I think he was a racist, too. Because he put me outside, breakin' up returns. Like seven o'clock in the morning in November—it's *cold* in November, you know—and I'm out there with a hammer and the guys are inside where the heater is. So one morning I just threw the hammer in the barrel and I walked in and I walked over, and I said, 'Fuck it, you know, that's it.' "

"Louie Louie" was a full-fledged regional hit, popular to some extent all the way up the Pacific Coast, especially in San Francisco. "I used to work up there every weekend, I'd make anywhere from three to four hundred dollars, five hundred dollars a week." Serious bucks for those days, but it didn't last. Sometimes Richard regretted leaving Modern. Feirtag never cheated Richard—but he couldn't deliver hits either. "Max told me we sold 40,000 records at the beginning of 'Louie Louie.' I said, 'Well, if you sold 40,000 how come you can't sell a hundred and forty thousand?' Well, that's all it was gonna sell.

"At that time I was always second banana to the Six Teens. He would always be telling me about this guy, Ed Wells, who wrote ["A Casual Look"] for the Six Teens. 'Oh, you know, you gotta do like Ed, you gotta save your money, blah bablah bablah bablah.' But when 'Louie Louie' became *the* hit for Flip Records, then all of a sudden, now everything was 'Louie Louie.' It wasn't the Six Teens anymore. Then he started asking me to write for the girls in the Six Teens, and so on and so on."

Max Feirtag and Richard Berry shared no musical vision. "I had this song called 'No Room,' which I figured was the greatest song I ever wrote. I told Max, I got this song that's got so much soul in it, make you cry. He says, 'Well, I don't give a fuck about your soul. I just want to sell records. I want another "Louie Louie." ' Oh man, that pissed me off so *bad*, you know. So I said, okay, I'm gonna write a piece of shit. Well, at that time they had "Have Gun, Will Travel" on TV, so I just wrote, [he sings] 'Have

love, will travel' and put 'Louie Louie' behind it. And five years
later, after 'Have Love, Will Travel,' he calls me and says, 'I'd
really like to do a song with you that has some soul in it.' " To
be fair, "Have Love, Will Travel," musically a "Louie Louie"
rewrite, is fabulous, recorded definitively by the Seattle garage-
punk group the Sonics and still performed by everybody from
Paul Revere and the Raiders to Bruce Springsteen.

But none of Richard's Flip follow-ups hit. As the "Louie
Louie"–related live work petered out, Richard briefly worked
the docks with his dad. But with his bad hip that job couldn't
last.

In 1959 Berry and Feirtag suffered a complete falling out.
Part of it stemmed from Feirtag taking off on his annual trip to
Europe at a time when Richard felt he should have been making
new records. But Max was also angry about Richard's outside
recording ventures. "He refused to pay me royalties 'cause he
said I had violated my contract," Richard said without a hint of
bitterness.

"Things got kinda tight and then I wanted to get married. I
always knew that you could go to record companies and ask for
a hundred, maybe a hundred and fifty, but when you started gettin' up to two and three hundred dollars, they don't want to give
it to you. And I wanted seven hundred and fifty dollars; I really
wanted a grand but I settled on seven hundred and fifty.

"I knew with Max there was no negotiation. He was one of
those tight, tight, tight jeans types," said Richard, apparently
without exaggeration—he told Steve Propes that once, asked for
a $400 advance, Max took him to the bank and withdrew four
hundred one-dollar bills, which he counted out into Richard's
hand one by one. "I mean, I could go and ask Joe [Bihari] at any
given time, 'Man, I need two hundred bucks.' Maybe he'd tell
me, 'Well, I can't give it to you now. Can you wait for about a
week?' But with Max it was always like you wanna ask your dad
for some money."

So Richard decided to sell his share of the publishing and
songwriting rights to "Louie Louie" to Feirtag's publishing
company, Limax Music, which already controlled the other half.

"I figured, what the hell, I wasn't getting my royalties anyway. I just thank God that I kept my BMI rights." Richard got his $750.

For the next 28 years, except for small semi-annual airplay, checks from BMI, that was the only income "Louie" would bring its creator.

4

"Louie" in Limbo

Richard Berry And The Pharoahs—
"Louie Louie". . . . 70
Okay reading of sprightly calypso, but flip
is side to watch. (Limax, BMI)
— Billboard, April 13, 1957

By 1959 "Louie Louie" wasn't even a has-been item, it was a dead song, a corpse whistling past its own graveyard, every bit the nonentity *Billboard* claimed it was, a relic for ten-cent bargain bins and prepacks of a dozen 45s you've never heard of sold for 89 cents just to get rid of 'em. Flip 321 was nothing more than another disc that failed to click, a slab of vinyl that rested only in a few attics and garages and in the mossy collections of low-riders and oldies freaks. No more than a couple hundred thousand people—at most—have ever heard it, even though it was reissued in 1986 on a Swedish collectors album compiling some of Richard Berry's 1950s work (*Richard Berry/"Louie Louie*," Earth Angel JD 901). Perhaps that many more *think* that they've heard it on the Rhino album *The Best of 'Louie Louie'* (Rhino RNEP 605, 1983), but that's a re-recording, made because Max Feirtag refused to issue a license permitting Rhino to use the Flip master. The Rhino remake intentionally replicated the original so closely that Feirtag called producer Richard Foos to complain.

When stuff like that starts to happen, questions outweigh answers. Like, what is this "Louie Louie"—a song, a record, a property, an artifact, a memory? How come the guy who prevented Rhino from using Richard Berry's old tape couldn't keep them from using the song, which he also owned? And if "Louie Louie" as Flip 321 by Richard Berry and the Pharoahs was moldering away in the dustbin of history in 1959, how did it come to pass that, by the beginning of 1964, this hunk of R&B junk had become the #2 song in the entire nation, according to the self-same *Billboard*'s Hot 100?

"Louie Louie" is all five things: a song, a record, a property, an artifact, and a memory. It became a song when Richard Berry wrote it. It became a record when Richard Berry first brought the Pharoahs and Ernie Freeman's combo together in a studio and Max Feirtag agreed to press and distribute it.

That's where things get complicated. The copyright law regarding music is a peculiar thing, and in 1957 it was even more peculiar. In the first place, the law—which supposedly protects creators of artistic works from being deprived of the fruits of their labors—provides a statutory ceiling on what the songwriter may receive for a recording: At that time, the amount was two cents per record sold, a figure that had been established in 1909 and wasn't changed until 1976. The reason it took so long for composers to get a raise is that whole industries—juke boxes, record companies, and song publishers—based their economic livelihood on the copyright law and a change benefiting one or the other of them was bound to adversely affect at least one and maybe a lot more of the others.

In those 67 years the center of the popular music industry shifted. A song-based business became a record-based business; an industry devoted to works that could easily be written out as sheet music became an industry devoted to works that were performed in ways that have never been properly annotated. Song publishers in 1909 were the equivalent of record companies today. By 1957 (let alone 1976) song publishers were banks or, more accurately, siphons — capable of tapping a major portion of a recording's income by virture of statutory quirk and industry custom.

In the early years of the century, song publishers performed an indispensable function: They printed and sold sheet music, and they sought out performers to publicize the song by singing it in shows, concerts, or — as time went on — in the movies and on the radio. For this work the publishers took 50 percent of the song's income unless the tune was sold outright, the way Richard sold his, in which case they took 100 percent. (The BMI payments that Richard continued to receive were for broadcast airplay only. BMI doesn't allow writers to sell their share in a song's performance rights. ASCAP [the American Society of Composers, Authors and Publishers], which was formed by established Tin Pan Alley songwriters, most of whom also happened to be song publishers, will let you sell the whole thing. But this didn't matter much to R&B songwriters, because in the fifties ASCAP advocated segregation, both racial and stylistic.)

By the fifties most songs sold as records, not sheet music. At first that didn't matter much, because record company A&R men came to publishers for material. But as R&B and rock'n'roll took over, more and more performers began crafting their own tunes. Song publishers still had a useful purpose to perform, at least so long as the color line held — *somebody* had to collect the money from Georgia Gibbs's version of "The Wallflower." Theoretically, the publisher sought out such "cover versions" and remakes. But in reality it didn't work that way for black writers. Their record companies set up publishing companies that were in most cases little more than passive collection agencies, although their rake-off was still half the song's income. As often as not, these publishers simply diverted more income into the record label, sometimes outright swiping credit from writer/performers and giving it to the record company owner, the A&R man, or an influential disc jockey. (What are the odds that Alan Freed really co-wrote "Sincerely" or "Maybellene"?)

You'd think the last thing that Etta James and Modern Records would want was for Georgia Gibbs to snatch a song like "The Wallflower," and as far as Etta is concerned, you'd be right. But Modern might have had other ideas, because its Modern Music subsidiary would collect a huge check either way. The Bihari brothers were certainly not in business to challenge the separate, unequal status of black recording artists. Of course, if Etta James instead of Georgia Gibbs had gone to #1 on the pop charts, Modern would have collected two big checks, so probably they would have tried to stop Gibbs. But that would have been illegal.

While no other writer can take these sentences and paragraphs and put his or her name upon them and claim them for their own, songs and songwriters lack such protection. For music the 1909 law devised something called the "compulsory mechanical license," a provision that says once a song has been recorded by one performer, anybody else who thinks they're capable of singing it can also record it, provided they pay the writer and publisher a reasonable fee (if two cents per side is a reasonable fee which it was in 1909 and wasn't by about 1929).

Of course, two cents was the *maximum* anybody would have to pay; record companies often negotiate the price downward, especially now that the maximum is more than seven cents per side. But if the negotiation fails the record company knows that it'll never have to pay more than the statutory fee—it's a ceiling, not a floor, on what songwriters can earn. In 1909 the compulsory mechanical license prevented a few big songwriters, publishing companies, and star performers from monopolizing all the good tunes. But by 1957, compulsory licensing meant that black performers had no hope of keeping the mitts of white interlopers off their hits. Thus, Perry Como's version of Gene & Eunice's "Ko Ko Mo," may it rot in hell.

And that's why Max Feirtag couldn't keep Rhino Records from making the *Best of 'Louie Louie'* album and paying his Limax Music subsidiary a passel of dough.

At this point it's pretty easy to see why and how "Louie Louie" ceased to be just a song or just a record and became that most hallowed of cultural objects, a capital-generating property. (Copyright issues have become known, in one of today's more outstandingly ugly neologisms, as debates over "intellectual property.")

But how did a piece of R&B tripe like "Louie Louie," a mere B side worth nothing more than a mediocre 70 on *Billboard*'s rating scale, become a cultural artifact that sustained itself across another three decades and grew into one of the most recorded and performed songs ever?

While calling "Louie Louie" an important cultural artifact might be enough to make Adorno puke, that is exactly what it became. Except for a few pachucos and their acolytes, the song hadn't achieved such status even in 1959, but it was on its way. And it was on its way because its memory lingered on, long past what preachers and schoolteachers, moms and pops, congressmen and music critics (including, sad to say, *rock* critics) would ever predict. This occurred because Richard Berry's "Louie" was the real thing, a record whose groove refused to let go. If this makes "Louie Louie" sound like a kudzu of the spirit, well, okay. But remember, you're going to have to follow that prejudice straight down the doomed gullet of John Belushi.

The reason folks up and down the West Coast remembered "Louie Louie" even after it stopped appearing on "Huntin' with Hunter" isn't so hard to figure out. Richard Berry knows why: "It was an R&B dance song. And it was still a cha-cha. At that time, everyone was doing the cha-cha-cha."

And then again, it was a rock'n'roll song and even though most of the people who sold and marketed and promoted it at the time thought the stuff was rubbish, rock'n'roll (as an idea, at least) really *was* spiritual kudzu, or as the Showmen's great anthem, "It Will Stand," put it in 1961: "It swept this whole wide land / Sinkin' deep in the hearts of man."

From a purist standpoint this makes no sense at all. No *Billboard* critic of 1957 or 1959 or even 1963 would have identified Richard Berry's "Louie Louie" as rock'n'roll, because neither song nor record has anything like a rock'n'roll beat. But rock'n'roll shook off all definitions that tried to limit it or any other narrow musical form. Rock'n'roll became a *concept*, an idea, signifying spirit more than sound.

Ironically, Max Feirtag, with his gaze firmly attached to the bottom line, figured this out sooner than Richard Berry, and this is probably why he figured that "Louie Louie" was worth the whopping sum of $750. Richard was ready to make the transition from R&B to soul music, because he'd been exposed to

Bobby "Blue Bland out on tour. "It was like I had gotten the Holy Ghost," Berry told Propes.

Yet "Louie Louie" remained the most unavoidable fact of his career and somehow Berry knows, "That song made me a rock'n'roll artist. When I went out on the Bobby Bland–Junior Parker tour up to the Northwest in 1957, I was there to attract white audiences." Not only that, "Louie Louie" continued to sell. Eventually the Flip version of the song may have sold as many as 130,000 copies, which was as many as a far bigger hit like "Death of an Angel."

Why? What made people remember this piece of Afro–Latino fluff? Easy:

Duh duh duh. duh duh.

Put it in your brain and it won't come out. It's not hypnotic exactly, but it's as mesmerizing as anything anyone's dreamed up in five decades of this stuff we now call rock'n'roll. *Duh duh duh. duh duh* is a mnemonic so powerful that even Adorno would have had to be dragged gibbering away from his desk if ever he'd caught wind of it.

And so, lost though it may have been to history, "Louie Louie" hung on, persisting in common memories, waiting like a virus for the opportunity to erupt.

Up in the Pacific Northwest the kudzu that was "Louie Louie" found its spiritual home. By the time those guys were done with it, "Louie Louie" was no damn cha-cha anymore. It was a rock'n'roll song, forevermore.

5

"Louie" Unleashed

Puyallup, Washington, September 1957

Little Bill Engelhart and his buddy Buck Ormsby had spent the day strolling the fairgrounds in Puyallup, the little farm town where everybody—hipsters and squares, tough guys and geeks, moms and dads, toddlers and teens—went in mid-September for the Puyallup Fair. The summer's-end celebration probably even featured the adolescent Jimi Hendrix walking the dusty midway; Hendrix was a student in Seattle. Lots of folks came to Puyallup from farther away than that, eager for the season's last chance to hit the rides and sideshows.

Engelhart and Ormsby made an unlikely pair. The short, feisty Buck personified cool-as-tough. Engelhart stood even shorter; he'd had polio as a child so he dragged his way through the fairgrounds because of the braces on his legs. Yet Buck and Little Bill were best friends at Tacoma's Stadium High School and after school, too. They led Tacoma's only rock band, Little Bill and the Bluenotes, one of the first groups in the whole Pacific Northwest. Engelhart turned out to be a better than passable rhythm and blues singer. Ormsby played bass, but he was also the Bluenotes' motive force, the one who didn't just dream about the big time but actually dared reach for it.

They'd gone to the Puyallup Fair to hunt girls and kicks, not to meet aspiring Elvises. But as dusk was coming on, Buck and Little Bill rounded a corner and saw a crowd gathered round a bench. Upon it stood a four-eyed young man yelling his head off. Buck and Bill strolled over to see what the guy was haranguing about. As they drew nearer their ears told them that this was no ordinary crackpot heralding our Savior and the End of Time, but a crackpot whose speciality was singing rock'n'roll, mainly Buddy Holly songs.

"Wait a minute! I know that guy," Buck said to Bill. "That's Robin Roberts."

"You mean the bookworm?" said Bill to Buck (or words to that effect), for the Robin Roberts of Tacoma's Coliseum High was a full-fledged, slide-rule-bearing, pencil-pocketed geek. "People kinda harassed him once in a while. But he actually was a Buddy Holly–lookin' kinda guy," Buck remembered many years later.

Roberts didn't just look like a bookworm; he was a college-bound math and science wiz with a palpable future. That made his singing display that much weirder. Rock'n'roll was for misfits, outcasts, delinquents with bad grades. Maybe they weren't quite losers, but the kids who latched onto the music were certainly among the least likely to succeed.

But as they watched and listened, Engelhart and Ormsby could not deny the evidence of their ears. Robin Roberts not only had the guts to get up on a park bench in the middle of the only state fair in western Washington, he not only had the sheer nerve to sing Buddy Holly in broad daylight without a band in the summer of 1957, when to do such a thing was to risk your reputation as a sane human, let alone a scholarship candidate, Robin Roberts was actually damn good. So when he finished singing and strolled on his way as the impromptu audience tried to figure out what it had just run into, Buck and Bill called out to him.

"Hey, that was great! You wanna be in our band?"

He did. Thus was born Rockin' Robin Roberts, one of rock'n'roll's great lost wildmen.

Every kid listened to rock in 1957 but it was a lot harder for kids—any kids, let alone white kids in the whitest part of the nation—to take the bold step of publicly affiliating themselves with the renegade music. To participate in rock'n'roll back then was to associate yourself with all the undesirable elements: juvenile delinquency, hoodlumism, sexual degeneracy, and the spectre of racial mongrelization.

Maybe it was a mite easier for Buck and Bill, working-class kids without much future to risk, when they put together their first band in 1956. Little Bill, with withered legs too wasted even to wear tennis shoes, certainly had nothing to lose. He heard dreams of a better world played out in the R&B music beginning to ooze out of late-night radio. More typical of the rocking class was Buck, who bore an unmistakable chip on his shoulder but kept himself always ready to go the limit for a friend. Ormsby, years ahead of his time, dreamed of the rock band as an idealized noise-making community.

Buck started out mainly playing pedal steel guitar. Pedal steel came from country and western bands. At the time all the white bands in the Northwest specialized in C&W. Given the huge number of transplanted Southerners who'd worked for the aerospace industry, lumber mills and shipyards, and the ones who were based at McCord Air Force Base and the Army's Fort Lewis, playing country music made the most economic sense. (Loretta Lynn, among others, began her career in Washington for this very reason.)

But as in L.A., the Southern migration imported all kinds of music. Seattle also became a new home to black Southerners (not many but enough) and with them came black blues and R&B. Somewhere in between fit the sped-up renegade C&W called boogie. Seattle also possessed its own big bands and the smaller combos that played jump music as the big bands splintered.

If Los Angeles had the nightlife of an anything-goes boomtown in Richard Berry's youth, Seattle—at least by reputation—was even more wide open. In the early fifties, Seattle and Tacoma were every bit as tough and wild as big cities on the Western frontier ought to be. Seattle, the bigger of Puget Sound's not-quite-twin cities, was full of bars and after-hours joints like the Rocking Chair, the Esquire, the Palomar Theatre, and a blues joint called the Washington Social Club, where B. B. King and Muddy Waters—having strayed as far from the Delta as it was possible to get (in several senses)—occasionally held forth. Little Willie John, Hank Ballard and the Midnighters, and Clyde McPhatter brought their salty, sassy, slow-grooving music to the city, playing the joints in the central district for black Service-men, and what few black workers there were, then in joints north of Denny Street for mixed audiences as their music—with its heightened eroticism typified by Ballard's "Work with Me, Annie," Willie John's "Fever," McPhatter's "Honey Love"— caught hold of whites. Seattle also hosted the West Coast brand of blues, derived in equal measure from the jump bands and from the blues musicians typified by Lowell Fulson and his huge hits, "Three O'Clock Blues" and "Reconsider, Baby."

The Bluenotes—despite Buck's odd instrument—wanted to rock those rhythm'n'blues like what they heard on the radio and saw on weekends at the Evergreen Ballroom: "Little Bill knew about these things and he took me out there," Buck recalled. "He was the guy who had the car. I didn't have a car; I was 16 years old. So I go out there and I'm standing in a sea of black people and there's two little white heads sticking up there, and that was Little Bill and me. And we were catching all these black acts—you know, Little Junior Parker, Little Willie John. We used to go up and talk to 'em. B. B. King'd sit on the stairs and talk to Little Bill. It was like casual, no big deal. Bobby Darin came through with Little Richard and the Upsetters once, singin' 'Splish Splash.' He sat down and talked to us.

"It was just, the show was over, okay, let's go home. But we'd be little guys who'd go back and talk to 'em, find out more about 'em. 'How'd you get that idea? Where'd you come up with that?' And they were real nice people, excellent people. I never met any nicer people. 'Hey, I'll go get my guitar and show ya.' I re-member B. B. King doin' that with Little Bill. 'Hey c'mon.' "

In Seattle big bands and country stars played at roadhouses like the infamous Spanish Castle out on U.S. Highway 99, just past the Tacoma city limit. Some of these acts were locally based, like Oscar Holden's big band, and the early groups formed by the great Bumps Blackwell, who in the mid-fifties linked up with Specialty Records in Los Angeles and became the maestro be-hind the hits of Little Richard and other rock'n'roll stars.

Long before it spewed out the loathsome banality of Kenny
G, Seattle was home to such substantial jazz talents as pianist/
educator Billy Taylor and Quincy Jones, who got his start in
something called the Bumps Blackwell Junior Band after a stint
spent living next door to Ray Charles. Most of the local jazz players were trained by Oscar Holden, a music teacher who'd grown
up in New Orleans and—legend held—played riverboats down
there with Louis Armstrong, then toured with Cab Calloway's
big band before settling in Seattle in the mid-thirties. During the
war and just after, Holden's band was enormously popular. "My
dad would even do gigs at the Seattle country clubs," recalled
his son, Ron. "We were solid black middle class."

All this music didn't come in separate packages. As early as
1951 saxman Billy Toles, an Illinois Jacquet sound-alike who'd
done a stint with Louis Jordan, was running what's been called
Seattle's first rock'n'roll group. A couple of years later, about the
time that Bumps Blackwell headed south, organist Dave Lewis's
trio was installed as the house band at Birdland, the most prominent of the after-hours joints. Lewis scored with three instrumental records—"J.A.J.," "David's Mood," and "Little Green
Thing"—which became local standards for the white bands that
sprang up in his wake.

Toles and Lewis were both black. They inspired dozens of
kids, both black and white, to make music for themselves. As
groups like Little Bill and the Bluenotes began appearing, Birdland also featured back-up bands and intermission acts manned
by teenagers, some of them white.

Even though the city's residential areas and even music
unions were segregated, its club scene never was. "At that point,
the black population was not a threat," Ron Holden says. "The
military was the difference. The reason my dad's band was so
popular during World War II was that Seattle was a port of em-
barkation—it's where they left from, it's where they returned
to—Fort Lewis, Bremerton Naval Shipyard."

Not that the Pacific Northwest was free of racism, as any of
its Asian and Native American residents could attest. But because there were so few blacks, the degree of discrimination
against them was relatively small—as Ron Holden discovered
the minute he left to tour behind his 1960 hit, "Love You So."

In Seattle Holden had never played in a band that wasn't integrated, but he got no further than Los Angeles when the bad news slapped him in the face: "In Seattle in the fifties black wasn't about blacks—there were no niggers or anything like that. There was no ghetto. That was my rudest awakening of all when I came to L.A. The Indian population was replaced by Chicanos. Then I went to New York City and then out on the chitlin' circuit, behind the Cotton Curtain, where our first stop was North Carolina and I got slapped right in the face with discrimination and racial prejudice."

Seattle wasn't paradise, but in the days of Jim Crow it was at least liveable—the price you paid was that your horizons were limited, because the city had no music industry, only a few rinky-dink studios, and not enough of a black community to support black-oriented institutions like radio stations and newspapers. So while Seattle had a role to play in the careers of Ray Charles, Quincy Jones, Loretta Lynn, Buck Owens, Little Richard, Billy Taylor, and Larry Coryell, the city eventually had to be abandoned by each of them lest a major career stagnate.

Nevertheless, it's worth considering an article called "Why Did the Northwest Have a Different Sound," written for a 1964 edition of *The University of Washington Daily* by young Coryell, then a journalism student at the University of Washington and a guitarist with local rock bands:

> The Seattle bands have by and large stuck to the blues and turned a deaf ear toward the Beatles, the Beach Boys, and Al Hirt. Hence, Seattle bands like Dave Lewis and the Dynamics have developed original and natural styles of playing that are welcome alternatives to the pop music that is packaged and peddled by Madison Avenue and shoved down the ears of gullible subteens as "music of today."

Whether Dave Lewis's style was "natural" or simply less mannered than the stuff Coryell (who within two years became nationally famous as one of the pioneers of jazz-rock) derided is open to debate, but Seattle's resistance to trendiness is a prime characteristic of its rock scene from the late fifties straight through to the grunge of the early nineties. In fact, the best Pacific Northwest bands did not reject anything at all, including what Coryell believed to be "Madison Avenue pop," but maintained an elastic attitude that incorporated everything it heard in idiosyncratic ways: This is as true of Jimi Hendrix as it is of Quincy Jones and, for that matter, grunge bands like Soundgarden, Seattle's rap kingpin, Sir Mixalot, or even that poor ol' hack, Kenny G.

Out of this stew of influences a Pacific Northwest rock aesthetic began to emerge. It boiled down to a willingness to try anything, make any unlikely noise, adapt all available resources in the service of shaking the spirit.

Outsiders thought of Seattle as wild, but locally Tacoma was regarded as the genuinely tougher place—smaller, more industrialized, more working class, more militarized, and more ethnic than Seattle, suffering beneath the noxious "Tacoma aroma" produced by the city's mills, a Northwestern Nazareth from which nothing good could come. It was in Tacoma that the great rhythm and blues singer Little Willie John stabbed a man to death and wound up spending the brief rest of his life at the state pentitentiary in Walla Walla. The secret of Pacific Northwest rock is that the best bands of the fifties and the sixties—including the Wailers, the Sonics, and the Ventures—all hailed from Tacoma, not Seattle. Buck and Bill may have been rock'n'roll loners, but not for long. The area's most important band of the fifties was not the Bluenotes but the Wailers, a group whose members were drawn from several different Tacoma high schools, including Coliseum.

In 1956 and 1957 nothing that could be called a "rock scene" existed. The Wailers came together as a fundamentally instrumental combo drawing on the light jazz styles professed by Dave Lewis and the then popular "cool" West Coast jazz style. The Bluenotes, a Caucasian version of an R&B revue, were out on a limb. It wasn't until Buck scraped together the cash for the first Fender Precision electric bass that showed up in a Seattle music shop in early 1957 that the Bluenotes became a recognizable rock'n'roll group.

"There were other bands: kinda country, rockabilly bands," Buck remembered. "But they didn't have rock instrumentation—we had sax where some of the other groups didn't have sax. We just thought that the natural configuration for a rock band at that time would be bass guitar, lead guitar, drums, saxophone, piano, organ. So we had a Wurlitzer, which was our piano, we had an M3 organ—that was our configuration. And eventually what we did in the Bluenotes was, we added another tenor and a baritone sax and we had that real rich sound. No brass, all saxes. Warm, hard. So the Bluenotes was like an R&B show—you know, current R&B of the time and some originals."

Their breakthrough came from winning a talent show. "It was held at the Crescent Ballroom right down in the middle of Tacoma. They had jugglers and dancers and we happened to win. So they put us on a half-night with this country band. At first, the audience was 25 percent rock'n'roll people and 75 percent country. Then 50–50. Then 75 percent for us. Then 100 percent. The owners couldn't believe it, that people would come out and pay to see this stuff."

Like Richard Berry and the Flairs, the Bluenotes found themselves high school heroes. And they were at what might have been the most beautiful high school in North America, for Coliseum High overlooked the full sweep of Commencement Bay from a hilltop perch that held on one side a natural amphitheatre—the Coliseum—where football games were played in full view of what seemed to be the entire north Pacific. No miracle that such a school produced more than its share of dreamers.

Yet American working-class high schools consider it their mission to stamp out dreaming in favor of students who follow orders and get down to business. This is nowhere truer than at working-class American high schools abutting military bases, pulp mills, sawmills, and aircraft factories. You didn't have to be a bookworm to understand that, you just had to be alive enough to grasp the dehumanizing futility of what the faculty passed off as success. Perhaps this accounts for the eventual status of that fine chemistry student, Rockin' Robin Roberts, as Seattle rock's prime wildman.

"We sort of *discovered* him," Buck remembered. "I mean, he'd already discovered himself. He had a lot of nervous energy and he let loose with it wherever he was. He was a genius, really. He was a chemist, eventually got a master's degree. And he was the greatest natural-born entertainer I've ever seen. He was alive." In places like Tacoma at times like that, being alive could get you in a lot of trouble. It could also make you a star.

But first you had to make the leap. The way Buck remembered it, "You had the city fathers, the city mothers, trying to protect the kids from this rock and roll music. It was only going to last a year anyway. It wasn't even called rock and roll then. There wasn't really a name for it until somebody coined the word: *rock and roll*. It was rhythm and blues then, or rockabilly in the Southeast. Then hey, that rocks, that rolls. It was black talk, old blues guys rapping.

"There weren't really any places to play then. You had to find your own places. We'd play parties and once in a while we'd go out and rent a hall, a grange hall or fire hall or Norwegian hall, you know; and get four, five hundred people to come out. You couldn't do the teen dances. The only teen dances were the ones the high schools put on—chaperoned, ballroom situations—with an old band playing foxtrots and so on."

Even when you found a place to play, dangers abounded, as Ron Holden found out the hard way, when he began working with his first really popular band, Ron Holden and the Playboys. It was 1959. Holden was about 19; none of the other band members were yet 18. "One night, I was out in the band car, smokin' and drinkin' I. W. Harper. The cops came by and I was arrested for contributing to the delinquency of minors." He wound up doing six months in the local jail. There he wrote his big hit, "Love You So," whose lyrics started out as part of a letter he was writing to his girlfriend. Sitting in his cell with nothing better to do, Holden improvised a doo-wop melody to the poem.

"I came out and I had no band—the Playboys went off by themselves. But my brothers, Oscar Jr. and Dave, were all-state athletes and this sheriff's deputy, Larry Nelson, was a friend of my brother David. He heard my 'letter' in jail and asked me to come and see him. So I sang it for Larry and his wife, Mary. She had this label, Nite Owl, with Chuck Margolis. She loved the song, so Larry Nelson recorded it; he put together the Thunderbirds for me to record it with."

According to what Holden told Steve Propes, it took a marathon 20-hour recording session, disrupted by a barking dog and general lack of technical competence, to finally get the master take, which was still crude, shaky on matters of pitch and tempo, and filled with distortion (the saxophonist's major influence may have been that barking dog). But with its pledge of "true love for all eternity" and its ghostly melody (whose mildly dissonant origins are in Little Bill and the Bluenotes' "I Love an Angel" of the year before, and resurfaced four years later in J. Frank Wilson's Top 10 "Last Kiss"), its clunky wood-block accents and its rhumbafied rhythm, "Love You So" finally transcends ghastly to become haunting.

Holden's vocal was the one part of the record that stood out clear and strong. What he'd written encapsulated every awful teen love song cliche, so much so that the song could have been penned by a rock-hating parodist like Stan Freberg or Steve Allen as a gag. But it wasn't a gag, and that was the catch: These bombastically corny lyrics were what every girl longed to hear her guy say just before they leaped into the backseat—or maybe those words said plainly what few guys had the guts to utter: "Always remember, my love is true / No matter, what I may do / You'll stay in this heart of mine / Until the very end of time." "Love You So" doesn't swing or soar, but when a song has expressed the clumsy banalities at the heart of teen romance so completely, it doesn't have to.

First the Northwest, then the nation responded: "It was a hit in Seattle and then Bob Keen [of Donna/Del-Fi Records in L.A.] came in. Actually, a lot of record labels came in—Liberty, Warners. But they all said, well, we'll take the singer and do a five-year development plan, but this record is a piece of shit," Holden said. "They all wanted to know, what was this wildcat record keeping their records from being #1. Bob Keen was the only one who came in and said, 'Here's some money. Let's go.' "

"Love You So" cracked *Billboard*'s Top 10 in the summer of 1960, reaching #7, right alongside "Cathy's Clown" and "Alley-Oop" and Elvis's "Stuck on You." It wasn't the first Seattle-area rock hit. The Northwest had turned out a variety of good records that were also strong sellers in recent years, the best of which might have been the wimp-perfection of the Fleetwoods' "Come Softly to Me" and "Mr. Blue," each of which hit #1 in 1959. Among Northwest rock bands, the Wailers got there first with the instrumentals "Tall Cool One" and "Mau Mau," followed by the equally unsung Frantics with "Straight Flush," "Fog Cutter," and "Werewolf." Little Bill and the Bluenotes finally made it with a vocal, their self-penned sax-driven, nasal ballad, "I Love an Angel." All these hit in 1959 and early 1960. "Love You So" was one of the biggest, eclipsed by only the Ventures, who hit #2 a few weeks later in that same summer with another guitar-based instrumental, "Walk Don't Run."

If "Love You So" was neither first nor biggest among the Northwest's first batch of rock hits, it was and is the most mythic, the most inexplicable, the one record that could not have become a hit except in an era where the virus of rock'n'roll was in the street and poised to take over.

Nevertheless, even "Love You So" is not the most important reason Ron Holden's name ought to be sung—well, at least hummed—in the Rock and Roll Hall of Fame. His accomplishments include something far more significant than putting a crude anthem of puppy love, no matter how definitive, into the Top 10. For it was Ron Holden and the Playboys who introduced the dormant "Louie Louie" to the Pacific Northwest.

The least surprising thing about Ron Holden's "Love You So" was its Latin rhythm. Holden's bands always had an unconventional lineup. "It was nothing like the structure of a band," he said of the Playboys. The group had drums, piano, two horn players, and Holden himself sitting on a stool (as Richard Berry often did) with bongos between his knees, leaning forward into the mike to sing. A rhythm and blues quintet with no bass (the pianist added what bass the baritone sax did not supply with his left hand) and no guitar would have been unorthodox even in the pre-rock'n'roll jump-band R&B period, especially since the Playboys' tenor and baritone saxes served as rhythm rather than lead instruments.

The Playboys featured Johnny Francia (a Filipino-American, like Richard Berry's pals, the Rillera brothers) on alto and tenor saxes. But their most important member—in some ways eclipsing Holden himself by the singer's own account—was Carlos Ward, who played baritone, alto, and tenor saxophone, flute and "all woodwinds." It was Ward who taught Holden to play bon-

gos; he later went to New York and became a co-founder of BT
Express, whose "Do It ('Til You're Satisfied)" and "Express"
were two of the mid-Seventies' biggest disco-funk hits.

Holden first heard "Louie Louie" on late-night R&B radio
programs in 1957 while it was still a hit, but it wasn't until well
into 1958 that he decided to perform it. "When I brought it to
rehearsal, Carlos knew exactly what to do to arrange it for our
sound."

Holden and the Playboys' "Louie" had a specific purpose.
Seattle/Tacoma's budding rock scene featured intra-city battles
of the bands. These would pit the Playboys in a face-off against
the Wailers, or the Wailers against the Frantics, or one of those
against Little Bill and the Bluenotes, or one of the dozens of
other new bands now cropping up.

The aim of local promoters may have been to pit the new
wave of rock bands against each other like so many low-level
club fighters. Sometimes it worked out that way: "They were
almost like gang wars—inasmuch as they were inter-city rival-
ries," setting bands from Seattle against those from Tacoma, the
way both Holden and Ormsby remembered it. But the bands
thrown into competition at ballrooms like Parker's, the Encore,
the Eagle, Tacoma's Crescent Ballroom, and the Spanish Castle—the jousting arena between the two biggest towns—failed to
feud. Instead, those groups "became a fraternity that will last
until we die because we went through so much together as budding rock'n'rollers," as Holden put it.

"The records gave people the idea that, gee, these people are
growing—maybe we can do this too," said Ormsby. "So there
were other little bands startin' to sprout here and there. To me,
it started to create a healthier scene. And the Wailers were sorta
the hub of that. Because with a hit record right out of the chute,
it just gave people incentive—God, we can do that too.

"And these shows where like Little Bill and the Bluenotes
and the Wailers would get together, that's a pretty powerful impact, you know, on people growing up, learning to play instruments or just being awed by the fact that anybody could get up
there and actually do that, with these little tiny amps. Sometimes
you'd have two guitars plugged into one amp—I mean, that was
the way it was." It boiled down to a brotherhood of musicians,

one that leaked out into the audience, for sure, but whose basic solidarity was on the bandstand itself.

This brotherhood encompassed not only the big-time bands but dozens that never hit the charts and would be forgotten except for collectors. Or except for the fact that one or another of such a lost band's members—for instance, Larry Coryell of the Dynamics and the Checkers, or Jimi Hendrix of the Rocking Kings—went on to careers outside the Northwest, in the big-time music world that believed (in its predictable ignorance of its own origins) it had nothing to do with the territory up around Puget Sound.

In that world inhabited by the music business, rock'n'roll wasn't even an issue; rock faltered and "died" in 1959 and 1960. You probably know the autopsy findings: Elvis went into the Army, Chuck Berry was sent to jail, Little Richard sent himself back to church, Jerry Lee Lewis was banned for marrying his 13-year-old cousin, the plane carrying Buddy Holly and Ritchie Valens and the Big Bopper went down, and (perhaps most damaging of all) Alan Freed and a host of other deejays were ruined in the payola scandal. So the Big Beat ceased to dominate the airwaves—until 1964, when the Beatles and the blessed British Invasion arrived.

It didn't happen that way. Don't take my word for it. Ask Berry Gordy and the gang at Motown. Ask the Beach Boys. Ask the Four Seasons. Or trust the ghost of Casey Stengel, and get off your own lazy butt and go ahead and look it up. The facts are right there in the charts. The post-plane-crash hits of 1959–1963 included "Stagger Lee," "Kansas City," "Only the Lonely," "Quarter to Three," "Heat Wave," "What'd I Say," "Da Doo Ron Ron," "The Wanderer," "Shout," "Party Lights," "He's So Fine," "Duke of Earl," "Stay," "Surfin' U.S.A.," "Blue Moon," "Hit the Road, Jack," "Do You Love Me," "Green Onions," "Wipe Out," "The Loco-Motion" . . . and that's without dipping below the Top 10 or including any posthumous smashes for Buddy and his brethren, or any of the absentee best-sellers copped by Elvis and Chuck and Richard or, for that matter, any disc whose tempo is less than indisputably rockin'. In places like Motown or the Pacific Northwest, beat music still kicked hard as ever.

Rock'n'roll didn't roll over and die in those dismal days when it was supposedly ruled by pompadoured pinheads named Bobby. That may have been what the serge-suited record and radio executives of America hoped had happened; it may have been the result that the united martinet vice-principals of U.S. education prayed for. But in reality, the music prospered and took on new forms.

The teenage rock bands of the Pacific Northwest built a great lost rock'n'roll scene in those years when the Big Beat wandered in the wilderness and, not only that, without the help of a single Brit, they created one of the first great *modern* rock scenes, one in which spirit and community were central for both musicians and audiences.

The dancers on the floor and the players on the stage came to enact a ritual to the call of *duh duh duh. duh duh*, taking their cues spontaneously from one another's dances and postures. Nothing mystical about it (necessarily); perhaps they were doing nothing more than trying on gestures that might give some lift to the lives they were leading at school. And maybe afterward, when it turned out that high school never ended, that the hallway hierachies and locker-room bullying only got worse in college and at work, maybe *duh duh duh. duh duh* was what they heard while they dreamed of a way out. And maybe some of them, deciding that enough was enough, simply danced to *duh duh duh. duh duh* and *duh duh duh. duh duh* and *duh duh duh. duh duh* again for all their days. Maybe it was just that and nothing more.

Or invent your own explanation. But much as many hated it, rock'n'roll did not die and, somehow, *duh duh duh. duh duh* was at the heart of why it could not be stamped out.

At the battles of the bands, Ron Holden said, the hip kids did the dirty boogie and the bop, competing for a prize. "The real cool ones knew a dance called the chalypso," in which the cha-cha met the calypso. "It was minus two steps from the cha-cha: 1-2-3, 4 instead of 1-2-3, 4-5. I gave them the perfect song for chalypso—'Louie Louie.' That was my battle of the bands song. It gave us victories because it crossed all lines with its rhythmic pattern and its sensuous beat and the message that it sent."

Holden, no stranger to myth himself ("I did the original lyrics, did it as a love song," said the author of the world's corniest love lyric as if "Louie" really had some other set of words to sing), knew how to milk the drama from Richard Berry's lines: "I sat on a chair, with the bongos between my knees and bent into the mike and sang [ultra softly], *'duh duh duh. duh duh, duh duh duh. duh duh.'*

"After a while, all the other bands picked it up: Little Bill and the Bluenotes, the Wailers, the Frantics, Tiny Tony and the Statics, Merilee and the Turnabouts. And the rivalry became broader and bigger, especially with the development of the Wailers, and especially when the Wailers got Gail Harris and Rockin' Robin Roberts."

Holden, though, went off to Los Angeles soon after "Love You So" and remained there, emceeing oldies shows like Dick Clark's twice-annual events and working for the oldies deejay Art Laboe at his annual Ritchie Valens Memorial Dances at El Monte Legion Stadium.

With Holden out of town, "Louie Louie" went up for grabs. Every band in the area played it. Crowds loved it, often demanding to hear it several times a night. But nobody owned it. It was just a song that "everybody"—the Wailers, the Bluenotes, the Frantics, and the new bands that sprang up in the wake of their success—played, like a Buddy Holly or Chuck Berry song. In fact, a lot of people say that it was the Frantics who did the best version of the Richard Berry/Ron Holden arrangement.

The Bluenotes split up. After "I Love an Angel," there were no more hits and Little Bill headed out of town with a road band. Rockin' Robin and Buck held the group together only a few months.

The Wailers had also failed to continue the streak begun by "Tall Cool One" and "Mau Mau." Their lineup needed an overhaul and it seemed logical to look to their only significant Tacoma rivals for new parts. After all, Orsmby pointed out, the two groups had often swapped personnel: "The Bluenotes would open for an artist like, say, James Brown. And after our slot in that show was over, I'd go out and sit in with the Wailers for the last half of their night. Sometimes I'd start with them and then

I'd leave and go play with the Bluenotes, however it worked out. It didn't happen every night but as often as I could."

In late 1959 or early 1960, after the departure of John Greek, one of the group's original guitarists, Buck became the Wailers' full-time bassist. Around the same time, Rockin' Robin started singing with them, although he was only one of three vocalists (the others were the Orbisonesque Morrill and the extremely teenage belter Gail Harris, whom Buck remembered as "a 13-year-old white girl screaming rhythm and blues rave-ups").

Rock shows proliferated throughout the Northwest from local gigs down to Portland, Oregon, and through the Cascades, west to Boise, Idaho, and east to Wenatchee. The Wailers and their mates and imitators played in hamburger stand parking lots and on the rooftops of drive-in theatre concession stands. They played to preppy high school kids and greaseballs in car clubs, to servicemen barely ready to shave and workers spoiling for a new kind of honky tonk, every weekend and all through the week once school let out.

The toughest crowds came from the car clubs, groups like the Stompers or the Roman Wheels, who weren't the low-riders of East Los Angeles but, Ormsby remembered, "a bunch of people in hot cars, drinkin' beer, havin' a good time, goin' out to dances. And they all had these real hot cars and they'd go toolin' around. Fifty of 'em would show up at a drive-in restaurant after the dance." But even *they* weren't that rowdy. "You could pack 2,000 of those people in there and maybe have one fight," he said. But the car clubs were only the edge of a scene whose emotional essence one observer described as "a rough, remote cool." You could feel it in the music, which was wired with trebly electric energy.

Though their hit record made them regional stars, the Wailers still toured like the small-time show band they were. "I couldn't believe how we'd get all of our equipment and five or six guys in a four-door 1948 Chevy. This was a regular auto, just a car. And nothing on top, unless we had a couple of bags; then we'd get one of those baskets, we'd put our suitcases on top, and the car would sit about one inch off the ground, you know," said Ormsby. "Then I remember we got a van, a Ford van, one of the first ones, you know, those little square boxes, to haul our equipment in."

Seattle hadn't yet built its freeways, so if they had a gig in Bellingham, up at the north end of Puget Sound, it meant going straight up Highway 99, past the Spanish Castle and radio station KOL (where "Tall Cool One" broke), traveling two-lane blacktop through dense traffic and tons of small towns, hitting stop lights all the way, so that a trip that might take two hours today could be accomplished only by leaving at 3:30 in order to arrive by 8:30 and set up for a show that began just after 9. Five hours to go a little more than a hundred miles, then "Just set up and go—that was before the union thing"—seems so primitive by today's standards that the Wailers might as well have been moving around by Conestoga wagon. To prepare themselves, they practiced in garages in their little working-class neighborhoods of single-family one-story frame bungalows on small city-size lots.

The group's sound equipment was as primitive as its transportation and rehearsal space. They had "two mikes running through an amp—like little contact mikes. And we never had any PA system. So a little later when we played for 2,000 people with a Bassman four-speaker amp and maybe a Standell with two 12s [12-inch speakers] in it, it was loud. It was. And maybe a Bogen amplifier with two University horn speakers. They were big metal horns with drivers on the back—that was our P.A. amp.

"It was real funny because, the way people play today, it's real loud. Then you could create energy just with not a whole lotta sound. It was electricity, you know, it was energy. And you just learned how to do it. It wasn't power because it wasn't any powerful amps. It depended on how you played it and how you mixed yourself. Jazz guys did the same thing, how they worked off each other. So it was a real good way to learn how to create that energy because you never really had anything that was distracting you or giving you a false impression of how you were really mixed in with the band. I mean you actually had to do it to get the strength."

The kids "didn't know where we got the material from," said Ormsby. "It was white boys playin' black music. And doin' it real good. You know, fusing. You know, the idea of what people *thought* white music was. Because they really didn't know. I always thought that maybe Dick Clark just fed people a lotta music. Chubby Checker doing 'The Twist'—that was really Hank Ballard and the Midnighters. Or Pat Boone doing Fats Domino. And that's what white people thought it was. But when they heard us do our own versions of those songs they went, 'Holy mackerel! Where'd this come from?' "

Now younger kids turned up regularly, and not all of them on the fringes of teenage society by any means, though the music was still just outlaw enough, with the bands onstage not only cranking out beat, but doing steps, putting on an R&B-style show, not laying back cool like jazzbos, but not yet immersed in the T-shirt and Levis anti-fashion of hippie bohemia either. "There'd be carloads of kids coming. It was okay then to go to a dance if you were 15 and 16. 'Cept that parents weren't really approving of it. 'Cause it was still the devil's music," said Ormsby. "I mean, we were still kinda straight-lookin' guys. We wore suits. We all dressed alike—had uniforms, sort of, but they were normal suits. We wore ties and stuff. I look at pictures of the Beatles and they got the same drift goin', y'know?"

Had the music business been paying attention, the Northwest scene might have exploded or, at least, its talent might have found a national showcase. Had labels like the Wailers' New York–based Golden Crest or the Bluenotes and Fleetwoods' locally-owned Dolphin (later Dolton) possessed either vision or development capital, the whole story might have turned out differently. Or maybe if some sharp-eyed promoter with a sense of what all this weekend furor portended *had* turned up, the whole Northwest scene would have burned itself out in six months, and all that talent and energy would have gone to a fate more tawdry than the mere obscurity that awaited it. But one way or another, the verve and invention that bands like the Wailers possessed were displayed in isolation. Records leaked out and, because nobody thought of a "career," because the record label was on to the next good sound or the guitarist's girlfriend wanted to get hitched and settle down or the Army drafted the drummer, the show stopped.

By the end of 1960 the Wailers were through with Golden

Crest, a label to which their connection had never been more than third-hand anyway. As Kent Morrill told Lisa Lancaster-Barker of *Goldmine* magazine, the Wailers had been together only about three months when they acquired a manager named Art Mineo (the uncle of actor Sal Mineo). Mineo put them in touch with some recording industry types from New York.

"I don't know who they were; they were like mini-mafia, or something. Anyway, this guy flies out at 2:00 A.M. to the Knights of Columbus hall with a tape recorder. He set up a microphone on a 12-foot stand, pointed at the stage, and said, 'Play.' " The group played its regular set: a couple of original tunes—"Tall Cool One" and "Dirty Robber"—and rock'n'roll standards like Bo Diddley's "Roadrunner" and Little Richard's "Lucille." "The guy then turned off the machine, went back to New York, and about three or four weeks later we had a hit record." (According to a bill reproduced in Dan Rogers' *Dance Halls, Teen Fairs and Armories*, a history of Pacific Northwest rock, the group first recorded "Scotch on the Rocks" [a/k/a "Tall Cool One"] on August 28, 1958, at Commercial Recorders in Seattle during a two-and-a-half-hour session that cost $64.30. But maybe that was just a demo date—"Tall Cool One" didn't chart until the following May.)

"We honestly didn't know any better. We thought that's how you did it. . . . We got a call from Dick Clark in Philadelphia, and he said, 'You boys come out and be on my show.' So we went out and bought a Plymouth station wagon and drove to Philadelphia, did the show, toured for two months. We were like the Three Stooges; we didn't know what we were doing. We were missing half our gigs."

Then "Mau Mau" was pushed out as the group's second single, at the insistence of guitarist John Greek, the group's nominal leader. The rest of the band wanted to put out "Dirty Robber," which featured a Morrill vocal. "Mau Mau" made the charts, but then stations in Chicago banned it because of the title. That was the end of John Greek and the beginning of Buck Ormsby's Wailers' tenure. By late 1960, the Wailers had renounced their contract with Golden Crest (most of the band members were only 16 years old when it was signed) and had begun looking around for a new opportunity.

Buck was anything but overawed by what he'd seen of Bob
Reisdorff's locally-based Dolphin/Dolton operation as a member of the Bluenotes; the Wailers all knew the labels in New York
and L.A. just hustled bands out of their money. So Ormsby convinced Kent Morrill and Rockin' Robin that they should start
their own record company, and the three of them formed Etiquette Records, which consisted of not much more than a hand-
shake among themselves and a red and black label logo. To
make it more, they needed another Wailers hit. Casting about
for material, they heard the siren call of *duh duh duh. duh duh.*

The myth has it that Rockin' Robin Roberts discovered "Louie
Louie" in a bargain bin, the place where old records, hits and
nonhits alike, go to be scooped up by those infested with the
vinyl collector bug at a fraction of their true worth, presuming
they're worth anything at all. If Rockin' Robin came by his personal copy of Richard Berry and the Pharoahs' greatest musical
moment so haphazardly, though, he knew what he was buying
the instant he read the label.

The Wailers definitely had a copy of the Richard Berry record, because even though other bands around town played it,
once Holden left, nobody was sure *exactly* how "Louie Louie"
went. "Robin was really aware of it," according to Buck, "but he
needed to know the lyrics, because nobody really knew what the
lyrics were. So he went and got the real lyrics off a record."

Until Rockin' Robin went to work on it, "Louie Louie" was
a laid-back song with a story to tell. The versions by Richard
Berry and Holden and even the Frantics have not much more in
common with the "Louie" loved and loathed today than chords
and syllables. After Roberts and guitarist Rich Dangel spent a
couple of afternoons rearranging it, every lick and lyric meant
something drastically different. In a sense, the song born at the
Harmony Park Ballroom didn't fully spring to life until Roberts
and Dangel found the true madness lurking inside it.

Their new arrangement toughened the song, stiffened the
rhythm, attacked every beat. The languid Latinisms of Berry and
Holden vanished, and "Louie" immediately felt faster (though
it wasn't) and harder. In short, it rocked more.

The Wailers' "Louie Louie" opened with a honking sax

bleating *duh duh duh. duh duh,* then said it again with backing by the guitar. At that point, Rockin' Robin arrived. His timbre matched precisely the shrillness of a wood rasp on steel, his intonation infused that poor Jamaican tar with breathless desperation, his phrasing groped for every word and having found it, nearly bit it in half. What Rockin' Robin Roberts sounds like on the Wailers' "Louie Louie" is nothing less than a guy who really does see that Jamaican moon above while sailing all alone for three nights and days without respite, who really can see and smell the one he loves, no matter the distance. In other words, somebody who's telling this story because his life depends on how it turns out, a man willing to do just about anything to see that it has a happy ending in which he holds that girl (and for the first time, you have to wonder, what's *her* name if she's so all-fired important?) and promises he'll never leave again (even though he must know he can't possibly be telling the truth unless he plans to leave the sea). Rockin' Robin Roberts and his bandmates understood the story of "Louie" as it might have applied to them: It was a song about a man crazed by hot pants and maddened with itching desire.

To drive the point home, as he came to the end of the second verse and approached the song's bridge, Rockin' Robin raised his squeak-perfecto voice to the point where you thought it was going to run out of hormones and break completely, and uttered for the very first time in human history a line heard 'round the world:

"Let's Give It to 'Em, Right Now!"

At that moment Rockin' Robin Roberts entered the lists of true rock'n'roll immortals, as sure as the guy who convinced Leiber and Stoller that it was better to write a song about a hound dog than a stray cat, as definitely as whoever told Little Richard to sing about tutti-frutti rather than Neapolitan. His cry is pure inspiration—*"Let's give it to 'em, right now"* yowled breathlessly and, what's more (and better), totally out of context. Here the guy goes singing about lost love and separation from home and, all of a sudden, his misty remorse and nostalgia curdles into a cry for vengeance: *"Let's give it to 'em, right now."*

Richard Berry never thought of inserting that line because it had nothing to do with what he was singing about. But Berry and his Pharoahs told a fictional story, and Rockin' Robin Roberts and the Wailers were spilling their guts.

Give 'em what? Rich Dangel knew and he gave it to 'em before Rockin' Robin's yelp had faded: a guitar solo that raced pulses in its simple emblematic urgency, ripping the cover off that cool chalypso before returning to the glories of *duh duh duh. duh duh.*

In that swift interpolation, Rockin' Robin Roberts did way more than breathe new life into "Louie Louie." He made it a song that everybody who'd claim it without nicknaming it *had* to know. It's too mystical to say that the Wailers' "Louie" made the Kingsmen's version inevitable—or maybe not mystical enough, since inevitability suggests that there are no miracles—but they did more than prepare the way.

All this took place on stage long before it took place on record. But the crowds immediately let the Wailers know that their new "Louie Louie" was beyond the common currency of dance songs. They'd invented—or stumbled across, or been given by the Muses—an anthem.

"Louie Louie," released as by Rockin' Robin Roberts (though everyone referred to it as the Wailers' version), didn't exactly explode on Seattle radio, but it got airplay there—and down in Portland—and it claimed a place on jukeboxes across the region. It made enough noise for Liberty Records to reissue it.

Cashbox gave it a B+, commenting, "Fine blues vocal by the songster on a catchy ditty that was an awhile-back success by cleffer Richard Berry (his reading is available again on the Flip label). Roberts receives striking combo support. Date could move again in R&B-pop circles."

According to a local Seattle newspaper many years later, "The company explained to Buck that it was one thing to have their promo men going to radio stations pushing Bobby Vee's latest hit, but they were simply afraid of going in there with something as raw and wild as 'Louie Louie.' " Further evidence to Buck and the boys that starting their own company wasn't a

luxury but a necessity. So the Wailers returned to the circuit playing professionally—meaning full-time, without day jobs—but
abandoning much hope of hitting the big time.

Their shows were legitimately legendary in the sense that
dozens of people eagerly told stories about them decades later.
The shows at the Spanish Castle became mythic, especially after
Jimi Hendrix (a Castle regular who always came prepared with
guitar and spare amp in case the headliners would give him a
chance to sit in) wrote about the place in "Spanish Castle
Magic" (and, if you ask me, in "Castles Made of the Sand"
about the joint's demise).

"It was but one of many old ballrooms on the NW circuit,
like Parker's, Lake Hills, and the Crescent; but the Castle was
the place to play," wrote Art Chantry twenty years later, in the
Rocket, Seattle's music magazine. "In the daytime it looked like
a cartoon version of a medieval fortress that stood for decades as
a roadside attraction on old Highway 99. But at night it transformed into a classic nite spot/dance palace offering big bands,
R&B, blues, jazz, and the main staple of country western/folk
dancing."

Seattle native Keith Abbott gave the best description of the
faded pink-and-white Castle in his short story "Spanish Castle,"
collected in *The First Thing Coming* (Coffee House Press, 1987):
"Surrounded by marshland, blackberry brambles, and swamp
alder, its name came from the false front of notched parapets
and a square tower. On top of that tower sat a smaller tower with
a flagpole. Originally a club for swing bands, Spanish Castle
changed briefly into a roller rink, then evolved into a country
and western beer joint, before it was ruined enough to finish its
days as a rock'n'roll dance hall. Once rock'n'roll dances moved
in, a cyclone fence was built from the northeast corner out to the
highway embankment to cut off any hot-rod traffic and prevent
drive-by bottle throwing or any other hoodlum routines," Abbott
wrote. "Over the front entrance the marquee sported a neon sign
with *Spanish Castle* written in loopy flowing green letters under-
lined by two yellow bars. Sections of the neon tubes were burnt
out. A skeleton frame for a canvas canopy stood over the sidewalk leading into the foyer. A few frayed pieces of black and
white canvas hung down from the top of the frame's spine. In

front a dirty strip of canvas remained, with the words *New Mangemen* in red, the letters *a* and *t* hidden under triangular strips of ripped canvas."

You could cram maybe two thousand kids into the Spanish Castle, and for especially important gigs, the owners did. By 1961 the Wailers were so identified with the place, they decided to turn it into a recording studio: "It was the legendary gig, that was it, the Spanish Castle. You couldn't record an album and call it the Castle, unless you recorded it at the Castle. So that's what we did." Thus *The Fabulous Wailers Live at the Castle*, Etiquette's first LP release and one of the wildest sessions of its era, rock'n'roll flat out and unadulterated, featuring all the group's hits and misses, not—needless to say—omitting the siren thump of *duh duh duh. duh duh.* The album is a true document, no matter how much of it might be overdubbed: a great band absolutely in its element, a championship team playing a home game.

But that album was about the crest for the Wailers, for the Castle, and for the Seattle part of the Northwest's Sixties scene. The Wailers made no noise outside of the Northwest; by 1963 or so Rockin' Robin had left the group and gone down to San Francisco to ply his trade as a chemist. Ormsby, Dangel, and Morrill kept the Wailers and Etiquette going, but about the time that Robin left town, Buck discovered a new gaggle of Tacoma kids called the Sonics, who picked up where "Louie Louie" left off and made great garage-punk music. It was all two chords and a cloud of dust with a great raucous "Louie Louie" thrown in and an even more shattering take of "Have Love, Will Travel." But even the Sonics never broke out of the Northwest.

No band from that Seattle/Tacoma circuit did. Ormsby blames the area's lack of a powerhouse entrepreneur. "There were chances to be like Bill Graham and Dick Clark here for some people. They had gold in their hands and they didn't take advantage of it. Neither did the bands. I mean everybody had an opportunity and . . . they weren't thinking big enough. And when they did think big, it was when the Beatles or the English came in and they thought 'That's where we're going to make our money. Let's go for it.' "

At best, that's partially what happened. The biggest reason

Seattle rock wasn't mass merchandised stemmed from its content. Listening to the Wailers, the Sonics, the Frantics, and the
rest involved direct and dangerous encounters with madness,
poison, the edge of criminal lunacy. The best Seattle records
sound like they were made by people involved in an occult ritual—in short, they appear as a prophecy of nineties grunge.
Song titles like "The Witch," "Strychnine," "Shanghaied,"
"Out of My Tree," and "Mind Disaster" suggest the terrain,
borne out in the music—huge distorted guitar, voices that
sounded like they'd been chemically abraded just before the tape
started, rhythms that careened with all the discipline of a hyper-
thyroid metabolism. Most likely, Liberty couldn't sell "Louie
Louie" because it frightened them, and some fans of Pacific
Northwest rock swear that stacked up against the area's truly
wild discs, the Wailers' "Louie" sounds wimpy. When you saw
these bands onstage or met them in your record company or
radio station office, the impression just grew stronger. Hell, the
Etiquette *Christmas* album contained songs as goofy-furious as
the Sonics' "Don't Believe in Christmas," and maybe those guys
thought it was a gigantic joke (obviously, they did) but if you
didn't share their particular sensibility, it must have seemed like
a threat. It didn't matter much. Northwest rockers adopted the
attitude of all rebel rock cults: If you get it, great. And if you
don't, fuck off. Maybe you could merchandise that some day—
Nirvana's "Smells Like Teen Spirit" proved you could—but not
in 1963 or even 1965.

The irony is that this singular scene crashed in trendiness.
On the numerous reissue albums of early Sixties Northwest rock,
the pre-1964 playing is distinctive in its energy and the way that
the groups balance guitar noise and soulfulness. After the British
Invasion and the advent of the Dylanesque, Seattle/Tacoma
wasn't that different from other places in the Midwest and the
Southwest that had large but derivative garage-band scenes.

The city eventually tore the Castle down. Legend has it that
it happened after six kids were killed one Friday night doing 80
mph on Old 99, which had become known as the "Bucket of
Blood." Drunk out of their skulls, they turned left into the on-
coming traffic, sealing their fate and the Castle's.

"It was a classic building. Perfect," said Ormsby mournfully

as he drove past the site one day in 1990. "But then, wood build-
ings get old if you don't take care of them, if there's not any
activity going on. People are still sick about that. It shoulda been
a landmark." The place is now a parking lot in what's called
Federal Way, the remaining part of Old 99 that runs alongside
Interstate 5.

The Wailers hung on through the early psychedelic era,
though the membership changed many times. In 1968 they
headed to Hollywood "for one last shot," as Morrill put it, and
when that petered out, they split for good. "We were used to
having the semi-star treatment in the Northwest, and in Hollywood we couldn't get arrested," Morrill told Lancaster-Barker.

Buck stayed in Seattle, still trying to get the area's musicians
the respect they deserved, still struggling to bring his rock'n'roll
dream to life. Dangel never left either, except for some road
work here and there. He played in three or four club bands to
make his living. Morrill split, did some studio production work,
and made a couple of solo albums in Los Angeles, then went to
Vegas and began doing a very well-regarded Roy Orbison "tribute" show that cashed in on their close visual/verbal resem-
blance.

Maybe it would all have turned out differently if Rockin'
Robin had stuck around. But he stayed in San Francisco, and in
1966 he was riding with a woman who somehow managed to get
on the freeway going the wrong way. Roberts was killed instantly,
dying without honor except among those who keep their memories in the grooves.

6

Spanish Castle Magic

Any fact becomes important when it's connected to another. The connection changes the perspective; it leads you to think that every detail of the world, every voice, every word written or spoken has more than its literal meaning, that it tells us of a Secret. The rule is simple: Suspect, only suspect.
— Umberto Eco, Foucault's Pendulum

The Wailers' "Louie Louie" is a full immersion in rock'n'roll possibility. It's as if Rockin' Robin had discovered in some musty backroom at the university library a passage from the gnostic *Gospel of Thomas* that brought him close to the holy heartbeat of his music:

> Jesus said, "If you bring forth what is within you, what you bring forth will save you. If you do not bring forth what is within you, what you do not bring forth will destroy you."

And so rather than risk self-destruction, Rockin' Robin and his band just poured it all out: "Let's give it to 'em, right now!" While we cannot say that the Wailers and their fans were saved truly and eternally by means of sacred *duh duh duh. duh duh,* it's undeniable that in the moment of playing and listening to this song they were free. Undeniable because this freedom is a gift they and "Louie Louie" offer to every listener or, at least, every listener who, upon hearing the magical incantation "Let's give it to 'em, right now," is willing to open a heart and not ask too damn many questions. For, after all, if it is details connected that add up to Secrets, details too long examined tend to extinguish Mystery, and without mystery, without *duh duh duh. duh duh,* there is no secret left.

"Louie Louie" made Richard Berry feel proud as a matter of craftsmanship and guile: He had written a good song, one that used unlikely elements, like calypso and cha-cha, and it had been—at least, on a small scale—a commercial and popular success, furthering his career goals. If it made him feel a better, more successful person, that was a pleasant by-product. But any such emotion had absolutely *nothing* to do with the content of the song. Nor did anyone who heard the original "Louie Louie" extract such emotion from it. There was no need to cry "Let's give it to 'em, right now." The essential mystery at the song's heart remained unsuspected and thus unconnected.

What becomes clear in listening to *The Fabulous Wailers Live at the Castle* is that Rockin' Robin Roberts and his merry men transmuted Berry's song so radically in part because they did put such personal feelings into their music. For the Wailers, as for so many up-and-coming rock bands of the early sixties (not excluding the Beatles of Hamburg and Liverpool), expressing and exploring these emotions was central to the rock'n'roll experience. The Wailers weren't alone, even in Seattle, where the Frantics were making records whose very titles now feel psychotropic. Out in Detroit none other than Berry Gordy, auteur of the cynical "Money," would also write: "Do you love me / Now that I can dance?"—which may be the clearest expression ever penned of the theology behind "Louie Louie." And all that the Wailers (or the Contours or anybody else who got down to the root of the issue) simply suggested, the Kingsmen drove home.

It would be dangerous to be too definite about where this new kind of rock'n'roll spirit originated. Maybe it came from the bandstand, maybe from the crowd, maybe from what the musicians, singers, and songwriters were putting into their music, maybe from what the audience started feeding back. Certainly, a big part of it came from the times themselves, from the atmosphere that spawned the civil rights movement and the planned obsolesence of cherished totems, from the first blush of electronic media frenzy and the total crackdown of the McCarthyite Red scare, the thrill of space exploration, and the ecosocial catastrophe of military-industrial expansionism. One way or another, the command "Let's give it to 'em, right now!" was heard and obeyed throughout that great beleaguered time.

It's easy—and fun!—to spin theories about what was happening in those days of supposed innocence. Doc Pelzell, a high priest of "Louie," once told the *Wall Street Journal*, "Everything had been so, shall we say, straight. Any hint of something raw and possibly obscene was eagerly glommed upon by the postwar baby-boomers who were just getting into their pre-pubescent period."

There is a dryly factual and not altogether inaccurate way of looking at why this happened. Robert C. Toll discusses it in *The Entertainment Machine*: "The record business was the first of the new media to target its entertainment to specific groups. Records combined the economy of mass production and national distribution with great flexibility because they were designed to be bought and played by *individuals*. Like sheet music—but unlike stage, radio, or movies—recordings were essentially consumer goods that could be produced in great variety and marketed selectively to people who controlled their use. Unlike movies and network radio, then, the record business could continue to appeal to the general pop audience as its major market while at the same time producing entertainment for limited special-interest groups."

But that's too drab and sociological for even a materialistic fool such as I. Those cold facts—all true, all irrelevant—just do not come close to what I feel about it; and not because I know, but because I don't know, you don't know, the people who were doing it at the time *couldn't* know. In a way, it's important that the answer never be spoken, lest such an essential and essentially hopeful miracle be perverted and sold back as a shell of itself. Breweries and sneaker manufacturers can buy rock'n'roll, wine cooler companies can pay big bucks to use "Louie Louie" its own bad self; but until science becomes truly, totally and ir-retrievably evil, none of 'em will ever be able to cry with the requisite openess of spirit, "Let's give it to 'em, right now!"

I say this not to summarize, but because this is the last ripe moment to pause and reflect: What happened next, thanks to the Kingsmen and that great Irish Catholic secret society, the FBI, took "Louie Louie" into another dimension entirely. It went from mystery to mystique, from fable to fantasy, from a song that captured—no matter how—the force of its moment to a song whose legend discorporated the facts of its birth and up-bringing.

In this context you could say that the "Louie Louie"myth took shape and blew the lid off the show-biz structure at just the moment when one of Toll's special-interest groups achieved a position of such dominance that it could sneer at anybody who didn't grasp its jargon, no matter how high and mighty that per-son might be. Neither the Governor of Indiana nor Richard Berry "got" the Secret of "Louie Louie," because neither of them spoke the new crowd's special, somewhat sneering, esoteric lan-guage. On the other hand, every random, apparently dimwit bobby-soxer who wandered half-lit into the Spanish Castle on a Friday night grasped it completely.

But then, the language of *duh duh duh. duh duh* is booby-trapped, always revealing more than is ever intended. Here is Geoffrey Stokes writing the sixties portion of *Rock of Ages: The Rolling Stone History of Rock'n'Roll* in 1986:

> *It's almost embarrassing to speak of "significance" in any discus-sion of "Louie Louie," for the song surely resists learned exegesis.* It did, however illustrate a significant music industry trend that the coming rock hegemony would nearly erase: the discovery and national licensing of regional hits. . . . When the economic orientation of the industry subsequently changed from singles to albums—and when one group could mean tens of millions of dollars of income—the licensing system faded away, emerging again in modified form only in the days of American punk. [my emphasis]

Everything in that quote is pretty much true (except that it was disco, not punk, that provided the vehicle for licensing's reemergence—but then you, or at least I, wouldn't expect *Rolling Stone*'s version of musical history to get that part right), but it is also rendered totally and crashingly irrelevant by the revelation that *Stokes is embarrassed by "Louie Louie" and its claim to significance*, which means (to put it bluntly) that he (and his version of history) is out of touch with the only question that matters. Because even though you might think so, given the amounts of cash and crassness involved, rock'n'roll isn't about marketing. If that's what you want to talk about, shoes or sour cream offer far more useful general cases. Rock 'n' roll—the whole damn "Let's give it to 'em, right now!" shebang—is about something else: The mystery of why items like "Louie Louie" (call them totems, call them trash) are learning's true reward.

Anyway, in the world shaped by the academic study of the magic and majesty of *duh duh duh. duh duh,* "Louie Louie" and stuff of that nature has become the *most* appropriate vehicle for learned exegesis (which is part of why that world sucks).

Consider University of Florida professor of film studies Robert B. Ray, who also serves as songwriter and vocalist of the Vulgar Boatmen, a much-beloved rock group of the late 1980s. The last thing one would say of Professor (or even guitarist) Ray is that he is anything so debauched as a "rock critic," and yet in "The ABC of Visual Theory," "an encyclopedic essay describing the inter-relations between typography, language, and thought, [which] connects the 'paraphernalia of the text' with every cultural association which can be brought to bear on these practices," published in the rarefied academic journal *Visible Language,* Vol. XXII No. 4 (Autumn 1988), we find, as entry "L":

"Louie, Louie" The Kingsmen's 1963 hit version depended enormously on the evasion of printing. By not reproducing the lyrics on either single or album cover, the group ensured that a confused but imaginative listener would hear as vaguely salacious what in fact was a clumsy attempt to imitate Calypso's pidgin English ("Me catch the ship across the sea"). In doing so, the band had intuited a classic strategy of all intellectual vanguards: the use of tantalizing mystification. Lacan's "Imaginary" and "Symbolic," "the mirror stage," "The unconscious is structured like a language"; Derrida's "deconstruction," "grammatology," "differance," "There is no outside the text,"

etc.—these terms and phrases, while committed to writing, remained elusive, inchoate, quasi-oral charms. As such they en-
ticed, beckoned, fostered work. Lacan explicitly pointed to the
paradox: at one moment in his year-long seminar on "The Pur-
loined Letter," knowing full well that almost no one in the enor-
mous lecture hall had actually *read* Poe's story (for, by that time,
Lacan himself had become a celebrity, provoking curiosity
among many people who had little interest in his subject matter), he turned and addressed his audience:

> We find ourselves before this singular contradiction—I
> don't know if it should be called dialectical—that the less
> you understand, the better you listen. For I often say to
> you very difficult things, and I see you hanging on my
> every word, and I learn later that you did not understand.
> On the other hand, when one tells you simple things,
> almost too familiar, you are less attentive. I just make this
> remark in passing, which has its interest like any con-
> crete observation. I leave it for your meditation.

My own meditation tells me that what Ray's claiming is
mostly hogwash and that the Kingsmen, in particular, had about
as much in common with anybody's vanguard as did the first
lounge singer to use a synthesizer because he didn't want to pay
a drummer (quite a bit less, come to think of it), but that's hardly
the point. The point is that *Ray is not embarrassed.* Not at all.
And that his lack of embarrassment is something that "Louie
Louie" helped bring into the world. Or in other words, "Let's
give it to 'em, right now!" And it was given.

In his book, *Mystery Train,* itself a totem erected to certain
aspects of termite trash, Greil Marcus comes closer to describing
what took place: "A joke in the late Sixties, when bands like the
Mothers of Invention would play it to make fun of the old-fash-
ioned rock'n'roll they had transcended, by the late Seventies and
in the Eighties the tune was all pervasive, like a law of nature or
an act of God."

Yet even agreeing that God or the gods were at work in the
history of "Louie Louie," you also have to agree that he, she, or
they chose for a vehicle characters cut from strange cloth indeed—*deus ex cartoona*? Perhaps this was inevitable or necessary; perhaps no god would play such a strange joke as "Louie

Louie" except by using damaged goods—a crippled rhythm and blues singer connected via a convicted contributor to the delinquency to a four-eyed, bookworm rock'n'roll genius connected via jukebox to a teen-scene rock band that instantly severs its tie to the singer who made it famous.

But the mystery remains: What did Richard Berry hear in *duh duh duh. duh duh*? Why did "Let's give it to 'em, right now" strike Rockin' Robin Roberts as just the right incantation? And how was it that the Kingsmen, with the least adept version of all, were the group who brought all this home to millions of listeners around the world?

Each of these avatars of "Louie Louie" was not only unlikely but outright weird; none of the song's incarnations was anything like logical (hard as Stokes might try to extract from the story some nugget of commonsensical analysis), and the minute that "Louie Louie" became explicable by any such process, you and I both would lose all interest in it.

But suppose for one instant that a Secret unconnected and unsuspected is a Secret nevertheless. Suppose, more importantly, that there are Lost Secrets, Secrets once pursued, their charms actually put to work, but now abandoned, discarded, or forgotten. Wouldn't such Secrets leave a residue in the places of their begetting? Would not such a Secret retain its power and, while perhaps changing shape a mite, seize any opportunity to come back to life?

The Pacific Northwest held such a Secret, perhaps, in the tradition of its original Native American residents, called the *potlatch* (because forked tongues have so much trouble with the Nootka *patshatl* and the Kwakiutl *P!Esa*).

The potlatch, developed by the richest tribes in the Northwest (clans that lived amid abundant fish and game and vegetation and in a climate more mild than the latitude suggests), was a giveaway, the Indian equivalent of winning one of TV's ten-minute fill-your-shopping-basket-with-all-you-can-grab greed sprees. Except in the potlatch, instead of receiving, you gave—gave everything you had: your food, your clothing, your house, your name, your rank and title. Marcus reports in *Lipstick Traces* that tribes competed in potlatching, each trying to give on the next higher plane of value, so that eventually a whole village might be burned to the ground in order that the rules of the ceremony could be properly honored. But even if all that the potlatch meant was that a great chief "always died poor," it violated every moral and legal tenet of non–Native American civilization, encumbered as it was with the even stranger socioreligious assumption that God most honored men by allowing them to accumulate possessions beyond all utility in this life, let alone the next.

There exist few modern parallels to this "insane exuberance of generosity," as it was called in 1885 by a Canadian legislator successfully bent on criminalizing it. But one, certainly, is the Battle of the Bands, those shows at the Spanish Castle and elsewhere in which the Northwest rockers were set at each other's throats like gladiators and developed (like gladiators, too, if *Spartacus* is to be credited) a sense of community that Ron Holden, Buck Ormsby and everyone else who participated, on or off the stage, describes by using terms like "brotherhood" and "fraternity." And it is in the context of this sort of modern-day electronic potlatch, set to the beat of *duh duh duh. duh duh,* that we can make a kind of sense of the cry Rockin' Robin Roberts brought forth to save his soul: "Let's give it to 'em, right now!"

This doesn't solve the Secret of "Louie Louie." But at least it identifies it, gives it its proper name, and in the naming of things (or so we are told), there is great power. It would, of course, be going too far to suggest that the development of the "Louie" folk-devil, with its overtones of obscenity and government surveillance, was a logical response to the recurrent force of the potlatch on the world of capitalist accumulation frenzy. But if J. Edgar Hoover had any purpose in life, it consisted precisely of visiting the plague of federal surveillance upon any revival of the potlatch mentality. The G-men had to bust "Louie Louie," the breathing antithesis of all they stood for.

7

"Louie" Come Home

The Pypo Club, Seaside, Oregon,
Summer 1961

The Kingsmen finished their set, which consisted of 45 minutes of Little Richard and Gene Chandler songs interspersed with current hits, guitarist Mike Mitchell doing a couple of Buddy Holly tunes, and drummer Lynn Easton's vocal on the Olympics' "Big Boy Pete"—left their instruments on the stage, and drifted to the dressing room at the back of the little club, a hangout for college kids and water rats who "surfed" up here, where there were no workable waves, by using round "pypo" (*pee-po*) boards to skim over the four or five inches of water scudding at the shoreline.

On their break, the Kingsmen (singer/rhythm guitarist Jack Ely, drummer Easton, lead guitarist Mitchell, bassist Bob Nordby, and organist Don Gallucci) watched as kids pumped dimes and quarters into the Pypo Club's jukebox. But the kids weren't playing a variety of records. They punched the same button over and over—the one that spat out the Wailers' "Louie Louie." As *duh duh duh. duh duh* filled the room, the crowd danced avidly, shingalinging themselves into a frenzied sweat.

The Wailers were among Jack Ely's rock'n'roll idols: "To me,

they were *men*. There was a huge age difference—when you're
that age, a couple of years is big. And when I was 16, the guys
in the Wailers were in college. I used to go to their shows and
stare at Robin Roberts, Kent Morrill, and all those guys." Their
on-stage antics and mean cool were everything Ely wanted his
band to emulate. So he proposed adding "Louie Louie" to the
Kingsmen's set list. "Let's everybody get copies and learn the
song by rehearsal on Wednesday," Jack said.

"But the song's more in Mike's range," someone else suggested. "He should sing lead, not you, Jack."

"That's all right," Ely replied. "But let's get it together by
Wednesday."

The Kingsmen were just a semi-pro combo. Ely, the oldest,
was 18, preparing to start college at Portland State in the fall;
the others were a year younger, now entering their senior year of
high school, except for Gallucci, still a mere 15 years old, but so
talented the others couldn't resist having him in the band. Although Jack had just moved into his own place, everybody else
still lived at home. They held their weekly practices in the garages, basements, and rec rooms of the members' houses—but
never at Jack's. His stepfather wanted no racket.

The following Wednesday Jack turned out to be the only one
who'd learned "Louie Louie." "I was the only one who even had
the record, probably because to get it you had to go to the section
of town where none of the others would have dared to go," he
said, meaning downtown Portland, which had the only record
shops likely to carry a record on a little Seattle-based label like
Etiquette. So Ely was the only band member who knew the
song, and it was Jack who taught "Louie Louie" to the rest of
the group, and it was Jack who dropped a beat from its cadence.
So no matter how more ably Mike Mitchell's voice might have
fitted the tune, "Louie" became Jack's song to sing.

Thirty years later the Kingsmen's story is tough to get
straight, largely because of Lynn Easton's fabled August 16,
1963, coup, which resulted in the expulsion of Jack Ely and con-
siderable turmoil among the band's personnel throughout the
rest of its unconscionably long career. The Easton putsch resulted in a revisionist history of the band, much of it invented by
latter-day band members who spread all manner of unlikely

apocrypha about the group, its origins, and the history and contents of its claim to glory, even though the major tale-spreaders weren't even a part of the band when the epochal "Louie" made it to wax.

As a result, the story told here mainly conforms to Ely's version of events as he told it to me and in the slightly variant but excellent history of the group compiled by Robert Dalley, who interviewed both Ely and Easton, for *Goldmine* in 1981.

Why Jack Ely's version? Well, for one thing, Jack Ely will not try to persuade you that the magic of *duh duh duh. duh duh* resulted from his dropping a beat when the Kingsmen learned the damn song. He did get the rhythm wrong, of course: "I showed the others how to play it with a 1-2-3, 1-2, 1-2-3 beat instead of the 1-2-3-4, 1-2, 1-2-3-4 beat that is on the [Wailers'] record," he told Dalley. "It turned out to be a much faster version of the song, but we liked it." The song now went faster because what Ely's memory had eliminated was the rest after the third *"duh"* (as if he were eliminating the period from the written phrase *duh duh duh. duh duh*). However accidental, the change accentuated an undercurrent already in the song. But Jack Ely knows that the secret of the highest expression of Spanish Castle Magic lies far deeper than the merely dropping a beat.

"A very wise person once told me, 'The spirit of love is in that record,' " Ely said late one night in 1991. "At that precise moment the six people involved were in love with that song and you can hear that on the tape.' " Told that this seems a very precise definition of what's going on within the grooves of the fabled Wand 143, Ely sighed and even on a transcontinental telephone line, you could feel his face squinch up somewhere between a smile and a grimace. "That was my mother," he said.

Jack Ely's mother and stepfather were best friends with Lynn Easton's parents. The boys grew up in different neighborhoods and went to different schools, but they came together at Sunday school and a dinner at one another's houses at least once a week. The families sometimes even took vacations together.

Nevertheless, their lives were quite different. Jack grew up in southeast Portland, near Mt. Tabor. Lynn's folks lived further out in the exurbs, "halfway to Gresham," back east along the Co-

lumbia River. Jack grew up tougher and more knowing, a city
kid who loved the rhythm and blues becoming known as
rock'n'roll. Lynn grew up sassier and more middle-class, the
paragon of the frat-party style the Kingsmen helped pioneer.

Portland and Seattle are separated by only a couple hours'
drive, but the two towns are very different—and in the late Fifties the discrepancy was greater. Seattle was a rising industrial
city with a seaport and military bases. Although it also had an
active port, Portland was a river city and, thus, a comparatively
sleepy regional center. Even today Portland's population is
barely half of Seattle's, and it has never come close to Seattle as
a cultural metropolis.

Seattle's relative lack of anti-black discrimination stood in
sharp contrast to Oregon, which was ruled by the Ku Klux Klan
through most of the twenties. Oregon's state legislature didn't
even ratify the Fifteenth Amendment, granting black Americans
the vote, until 1959. In Portland, an R&B-loving kid like Jack
Ely was likely to find his ambitions, if not utterly thwarted, at
least more easily diverted than Seattle's Rockin' Robin, Buck,
and their buddies. Ely remembers that at Washington High
School only the infinitesimal minority of black students played
rock'n'roll. But that minority made a big difference: Suburban
David Douglas High School, where Easton and the others went,
was lily white and that absence of contact meant that for a long
time no one at all played the basic teenage music there, even
though everybody listened to it.

Portland was big enough to support two daily newspapers,
the *Oregonian* and *The Oregon Journal,* and provincial enough
for each of them to support its own troupe of kiddie vaudevilli-
ans, the Oregonaires and the Journal Juniors. These featured
kids from grade school up to age 18 exhibiting various kinds
(and degrees) of entertainment talent, as they traveled the state
in old Greyhound buses to put on shows at VFW halls, Shriner's
hospitals, old-age homes, and the like.

The newspaper troupes represented show biz at its most ru-
dimentary: "We didn't get paid in money, we got paid in experience," said Ely. In his feature spot with the troupe, Jack played
guitar and sang a couple of songs by his hero, Elvis Presley. The

rest of the time he was in the stage band, "backing up circus acts." Lynn Easton played drums with the Journal Juniors.

Jack Ely's musical ambitions descended from his natural father, Ken Ely, an opera and semi-classical singer of such promise that in 1943 when Jack, his only child, was born, Rudy Vallee sent him a congratulatory telegram. But Ken Ely died young, and though Jack studied piano beginning when he was just five (and gave his first recital at seven), his stepfather was unremittingly hostile to music as an enterprise. In 1956, when he was 13, Jack, bored with formal piano study, had the standard conversion experience upon seeing Elvis Presley on "The Ed Sullivan Show." He knew this was something he could do and that pursuing it would radically alter and improve his life. Soon after, Jack began to play guitar and sing. But no matter how much it mattered to the kid, his stepfather's disdain remained firm: "My band was *stupid*. 'Don't practice when I'm around. I don't want to hear it.' " On the other hand, Jack's quick to point out that he derived his perseverance from his stepfather: "He worked me like a slave, but he didn't beat me, and he did teach me a lot of the values that prodded me to push the band as hard as I did." Still, with his mother also unsupportive because hedonism and joy didn't conform to her religious values, Jack felt "I was in music despite my parents."

The Oregonians and the Journal Juniors worked only during the school year, taking the summers off because no schedule-maker in the world could have coordinated that many different family vacations. So it must have been about the autumn of 1959 when Jack's mother received a call on a Thursday from Lynn's mother. The Young Oregonians had the weekend off and the Journal Juniors lacked a guitarist for a show at a downtown Portland hotel—could Jack fill in? He had the time and, for once, his mom's encouragement. So he took his "$13 Woolworth guitar" and played the date.

"After that night's show, we were sitting at this table drinking our Cokes and cramming our faces full of sandwiches and stuff," Jack recalled, "when Lynn asked me, 'Do you ever do any playing with anybody else?' I said, 'No,' and that was as far as it went."

A few weeks later, though, Lynn called Jack about another of

Mrs. Easton's ideas. The Easton family belonged to a yacht club, and the club needed entertainers for a party. Would Jack be willing to appear with Lynn as a duo? That sounded fine and they made the gig, doing their solo routines from the newspaper troupe shows. It went over so well that they cooked up a few more numbers and over the next six months began performing "duo stuff as many places as we could." The pair was billed as Jack Ely, because he did the singing. It still wasn't a rock'n'roll combo—with only one guitar and a drummer, it couldn't be. But there were those Elvis songs mixed in.

"Then Lynn found this guitar player at school named Mike Mitchell and he joined as lead guitarist, which was great. I'd never played lead guitar. I just used the guitar to back myself up singing." (Mitchell's father was a country and western guitarist and Mike had played since childhood.)

Shortly after that they ran across Bob Nordby playing stand-up acoustic bass in the Douglas High band, and after Jack and Lynn's mothers convinced Nordby's "incredibly religious" parents that playing pop music for profit and pleasure was not necessarily a path beyond redemption, he was allowed to join. "We'd hang out at lunch time and after school. By now we were doing a lot of R&B—Dee Clark songs, Gene Chandler's hits," said Jack. Mitchell, drawing on his country roots, added a rockabilly influence.

Now that the Ely/Easton combo had become a full-fledged band, it needed a name. Dalley says Lynn Easton's mother saw a local newspaper article about a band called the Kingsmen that was breaking up, and that Easton's parents then went to the club where that band was doing its final gig to get permission to pick up the name. But Mike Mitchell has since claimed that he named the group after his favorite after-shave. One way or the other, by 1960 the Kingsmen was their monicker, and Lynn Easton and his mother had gone to the local courthouse to register the name on everyone's behalf. (According to Dalley, the Easton family always took a strong interest in the band and, in fact, Lynn's father's name was on the group's business card as manager "so nobody would think they were dealing with a bunch of high school kids.")

Don Gallucci joined in 1962 after being discovered playing

with a group called Jim Dunlap and the Horsemen at a teen club called the Headless Horsemen. The Kingsmen had sought an organist since Booker T. and the MGs hit with "Green Onions" and, in Ely's words, "this kid was an incredible wiz on the keyboards. He had a Hohner electric piano and played it through a Sears Alamo amplifier." Gallucci, who was just starting out at Cleveland High, grabbed the chance "to be in a more music-oriented group, where he could play a few instrumentals." Despite his age, Gallucci joined as an equal—the band's financial structure was share-and-share-alike, economically if not necessarily always creatively.

Nordby's parents weren't the only ones who had religious reservations about rock'n'roll. Until Jack finally turned 16, their parents totally controlled which jobs they took and which ones they turned down, because an amplified rock band cannot travel by bicycle. Even after they began driving themselves, "our parents wouldn't let us play in bars," said Jack. "So we used to play the weirdest shows you could ever imagine: junior fashion shows on Saturday afernoon at theaters in downtown Portland, Red Cross fundraisers, supermarket openings."

They got the supermarket gigs because business-minded Lynn Easton took an after-school job as a stockboy in the warehouse of Fenimore Pacific, the local food broker, gaining the Kingsmen an "in" for promotional grocery bookings. "We'd play at promotions for a pancake mix or a biscuit mix, for mayonnaise or a particular brand of milk," remembered Jack. At those shows, they had to downplay their rock and R&B numbers. "We did a lot of thirties and forties songs, vaudeville-type material. We'd play whatever the people in our audience wanted to hear—at the grocery store, you had to play whatever the *parents* wanted to hear."

Around 1960 the band met Ken Chase, program director of KISN ("kissin'"), Portland's main Top 40 radio outlet. Chase ran a new teen club—which meant a nightclub where no liquor or beer was served, just soda-pop cocktails with names like real drinks (Singapore Slings, for instance)—in suburban Milwaukee, Oregon, and he offered the Kingsmen a slot as house band, five nights a week, Thursday through Monday. They took it and began packing the 150-person-capacity teeniterie. Eventually

Chase became their manager, which meant that the Kingsmen started hounding him for the chance to make a record.

In early 1961, before lining up their house-band residency at the Chase, the Kingsmen went on their own to a local studio and made "Peter Gunn Rock," a rockified version of Henry Mancini's TV theme (working off Duane Eddy's rocked-up 1960 hit rendition, no doubt). It didn't take long for even the band members to understand that "Peter Gunn Rock" just wasn't very good. "It sounded terrible, so we just made a few acetates for ourselves and forgot about it," Jack said.

But they didn't forget the ambition to make a record, to make their mark. Gradually, as they learned that "if you wanted to fill the dance floor, all you had to do was play 'Louie Louie,'" they decided that was the number they should wax. Chase agreed but kept telling the boys that the time was not yet ripe.

Finally, one Friday night in April 1963 at the Chase, the Kingsmen decided to try an experiment. They would play, one time only, a double-length set—an hour and a half—consisting of nothing but one long "Louie Louie." Ninety minutes of *duh duh duh. duh duh.* If one doubts (as one must, given the later evidence of elephantine post-Ely trash like "Annie Fannie" and the world's most hapless rendition of "Money") that the Kingsmen with Jack Ely and Don Gallucci were a great band, this first of all "Louie" marathons confirms some weird kind of incipient rock'n'roll genius stirred within them.

Ken Chase had not become a Top 40 program director without being able to recognize inspiration when it festered to life. As the band emerged sweatily triumphant from the marathon, (even the normally state-silent Bob Nordby having sung his lungs out for a few choruses), Chase told them, "Okay, that's it. You're ready to record. We're going into the studio tomorrow morning. I've made all the arrangements. Meet me at the studio at 10 A.M."

To ask veterans of the early sixties Seattle scene about the Kingsmen is to court sneering derision: They were small-time, of no consequence—in fact, nothing from that little Podunk down where the Columbia rolled into the Willamette mattered.

Even in Portland the Kingsmen weren't the most important

band. Their rivals were Paul Revere and the Raiders, a group
that originated in the wilds of Boise, Idaho, and wound up in
Oregon only because its leader, keyboardist Paul Revere, was a
pacifist Mennonite who did his conscientious objector service by
serving as an orderly at a mental hospital in nearby Wilsonville.
Though their mid-sixties' residency on Dick Clark's "Where the
Action Is" once caused them to be dismissed as teenybopper fod-
der, the Raiders possessed musical skill, relentless personality, so
much confidence that it became audacity, shameless flamboy-
ance, and an outrageous sense of humor, all applied with extraordinary promotional vigor. Although rock historian William
Ruhlmann may go too far in calling them "the most underrated
[band] in rock history," today critics and musicians respect the
Raiders. Even the Wailers, who worked from a summit so high
that they barely deigned to notice a batch of upstart high school
brats like the Kingsmen, considered the Raiders comrades. "We
used to go down to Boise and play down there," said Buck. "And
I remember Paul and Mark Lindsay used to come up [to the
bandstand]. They were the same to us as we were to those black
people that I was tellin' you about. They'd come up and say,
'How'd you do this? What'd you do?' Same damn thing, you
know."

It was in a Wilsonville coffee shop in March 1963 that KISN
deejay Roger Hart met up with Paul Revere. Hart was looking to
promote a show with the Raiders. Revere asked for $150 for the
night. Hart gulped. Paul told him he knew how to make promoting such a midnight ride highly profitable, especially with
the assistance of the most important drive-time deejay in town,
and Hart agreed to give it a shot. They put on the show at the
Trocadero Club across the Washington state line in Vancouver.
It went well—well enough that they stayed together for the next
decade, with Hart serving as the group's manager.

Revere and his fellow crazoids emerged out of the wilds of
the Rockies, places so remote they made Seattle and Portland,
let alone south-central L.A., look as cosmopolitan as Berlin's
Alexanderplatz. Paul Revere was born in 1938 in Harvard, Ne-
braska, to parents with enough guts and enough wit to actually
put that name on his birth certificate. Revere grew up in Caldwell, Idaho, just west of Boise, poor and ashamed of it: "I was

ashamed of where I lived, I was ashamed of my family. I was ashamed of the car that wouldn't run that they tried to drive, I was ashamed of the house that the wind blew through, I was ashamed of everything . . . I don't think that is abnormal for a teenager, especially a poor one. You have a tendency to worry about what other people think, to the point where it gets out of hand. Whatever's happening, man, you've got to be part of it."

In Caldwell Paul Revere wasn't just part of it; he took charge of it. Paul heard only church music at home, where his mother played the battered piano she talked her impoverished husband into buying somewhere between second- and fourteenth-hand. But as he entered his teens a few R&B-type songs began floating over the airwaves. Particularly, there was the living, breathing hellfire of the great, the one and only, the totally flamboyant flash from Ferriday, Louisiana, the scariest fire-breathing rockabilly of them all: Jerry Lee Lewis, with his golden locks flopping and his knees knocking as he romped and stomped fingers, face, and feet all over the baaaaaddest piano ever displayed on "American Bandstand," growling and yowling through "Whole Lot-ta Shakin' Goin' On."

"I can do that," said Paul Revere. So he began to, holding jam sessions at his home, playing the wildest R&B tunes by the Clovers and Hank Ballard and Bill Haley's Comets, while at the same time starring as an end on the Caldwell High football squad; leading a gang called the Nemos; sculpting one of the area's few significant waterfall pompadours; and dragging Main Street in an ancient low-rider, "whose underside scraped every railroad track in Southern Idaho." Graduating from high school, he "went where all dumb kids go if they have no talent or ambition . . . hairdressing college." A "long-lost relative" died, leaving him $500, and he bought a barber shop, which prospered. He bought two more.

"So at the age of 18, I was a businessman and piano player. I wanted to do both, so I sold the barber shops and bought a drive-in restaurant." He called it the Reed'n'Bell. Despite its hideous trade name, the Reed'n'Bell became the Boise area's #1 teen hangout (no, we do not want to imagine #2), especially after Revere decided to promote it by renting a hall (for $200), hiring a couple of rent-a-cops and a PA system, buying some spot time on local radio, and putting on a show for seventy-five cents a head. Teens flocked to hear "Idaho's only rock'n'roll band," and next time the price soared to a buck. The Downbeats did their shows wearing farmland chic outfits of coveralls and jeans, giving way with prosperity and experience to white shirts, black trousers, and rust-and-black vests.

"I was 19 then and thought I had it made—I did," Revere said. "Piano playing was an obsession, and I started playing rock in local halls with some other musicians." The Downbeats, as he called this aggregation, cleared as much as $600 a night, a seeming fortune with no middleman to cheat the band. After a few months Mark Lindsay—a flour-covered kid in the bakery that made the Reed'n'Bell's buns—joined up as lead singer, and the band began to cut a groove deep and wild across Idaho's Treasure Valley with leaps into eastern Washington and Oregon.

Even if they hadn't been good—and they were a little better than that—Revere and his bandmates might have left a large scar anyway, because they were such expert self-promoters. Lindsay hooked a PA onto the top of his little gold Valiant and drove through high school parking lots, broadcasting news of each upcoming dance while a turntable inside the car blared rock'n'roll.

Like the Kingsmen, the Downbeats got ambitious early. Unlike them, in Revere they had a leader with the business instinct to figure out what to do about it and a pianist who made recording worthwhile. Revere took a cheaply but competently made demo tape of the band's material to Los Angeles. There he nearly got hustled into a bad deal with an executive at a major label. Revere dodged that dagger, then left Hollywood and found John Guss, who ran a pressing planet in suburban Gardena, California.

Guss told Revere he was crazy not to use his real name, although the name Guss suggested—Paul Revere and the Nightriders—sounded too country to Paul, a major issue because Idaho teens *hated* country. But Paul Revere and the Raiders wasn't just euphonious; it was descriptive.

Guss picked the right track off the demo tape: an overaccelerated boogie-woogie "Chopsticks" that he renamed "Beatnik Sticks" for no better reason than that beatniks were in vogue.

Revere headed home; he didn't bother telling his band its new name until the first shipment of records arrived.

"['Beatnik Sticks'] became a regional hit, mostly because Paul walked into nearly every station of more than 250 watts in the Northwest with the record under his arm and a one-liner on his lips," according to Tim Woodward of the *Idaho Statesman.*

"No one in Idaho had ever made a record," Revere said. "The radio stations thought they'd found a hero and played it. Little towns would jump on it because they were impressed that you'd stop by."

Guss's Gardena Records wound up putting out three instrumental singles by Paul Revere and the Raiders through his Gardena Records: "Beatnik Sticks," "Paul Revere's Ride," and "Like, Long Hair." The latter, a takeoff on Rachmaninoff's "C Minor Prelude" produced by the notorious L.A. record producer / termite scavenger Kim Fowley, combined rockified classical pianistics that anticipated B. Bumble and the Stingers' 1962 "Nut Rocker" (or, hate to say it, Emerson Lake and Palmerisms) with a tough surf guitar solo, and it reached #38 on the *Billboard* chart in the spring of 1961. Guss hired PR man Irwin Zucker, who brought the band to Hollywood, where they appeared on Wink Martindale's pseudo-"Bandstand" TV show and played a gig at the Santa Monica Pier. On the real "Bandstand," kids gave it a 95.

But there was no leap to stardom, not even a follow-up hit, because Revere got drafted, and although his Mennonite background kept him from drowning as a frogman or some similarly cruel fate, he spend the next couple of years clanging bedpans in the Wilsonville asylum. The debacle was quick and complete: Paul also lost his drive-in because he was not longer there to run it; when the lease expired, so did the Reed'n'Bell. The other Raiders split up and Lindsay went to southern California, from whence Revere summoned him upon the canny piano pumper's release from CO duty in late 1962.

The transplanted Idahoans began to assemble a new band, starting with drummer Mike "Smitty" Smith, found playing guitar at the Headless Horseman (the same teen club where the Kingsmen located Don Gallucci—it must have been like Birdland with Clearasil standing in for smack). Smith brought along bassist Ross Allemang and guitarist Steve West, although by January 1963 Dick Walker replaced Allemang. The new Raiders promoted a few local gigs, with the unremitting devilishness that passed for savoir faire in the potato country. This caught Hart's attention.

"I had told Roger the very first time I ever met him . . . 'There's this place that we can rent, the D Street Corral,' it's a big old dance hall in Portland," Revere told Ruhlmann. "I promoted all my own dates. I bought the advertising. I did it *all*: hired the policemen, counted the money at night, paid everybody. I was a promoter that happened to get onstage, also. So I told him, 'We can do this thing,' 'cause I knew he's on the #1 radio station and he's got the #1 time slot, and I thought hey, man, you can sneak in lots of ads that we don't have to pay for, and we'll do this promotion. So I said, 'We'll split this thing.' We did it, and it was a killer success. I got a circuit going, and he was a great partner because of his situation with KISN radio."

The Raiders had reached the outer limits of rock'n'roll stagemania. "[When] we started the band again in Portland," Lindsay told Ruhlmann, "I said, 'Paul, we can't do it the way we did before. I've seen how it works down there [in Hollywood], and you've got to involve the crowd, you've got to be showmen, it has to be a show band.' Before, everybody just did what they did. Paul played piano, I played sax or jumped up and down, but it was totally disorganized and no focus on anything and no flow."

"The music in Portland, Oregon, at this time was all folk music," Lindsay claimed. "It was like the Brothers Four and the Kingston Trio. There was no rock'n'roll there. And our repertoire had changed. We had added some things. Over a period of time I'd been exposed to a lot more R&B in Los Angeles, so when he got together we were doing 'Oo Poo Pah Doo.' We [were] basically a white R&B band and they'd never seen anything like it before. We had skin-tight pants [that] I'd gotten from the drummer, who'd done some work in Vegas. He said, 'Man, you got to be sexy for the girls.' We had these pants that were so tight, my pants had been sewn so many times on the seams that they just had rope down the seams!"

According to one account, the Raiders even set their hair on fire. Paul bought pianos for fifty bucks or so and destroyed them onstage, anticipating the Who's guitar-bashing antics by a good two years. "Mark would jump on the piano and scream, yell, and kick," Revere said. "We were nasty, bizarre, and the rowdiest, rockingest, craziest group that ever stepped on a stage. We were animals. We had the worst reputation in the Northwest."

In a town as small as Portland, up-and-coming bands have few secrets from one another. The Kingsmen and the Raiders got to know each other well, primarily because the Kingsmen also played The D Street Corral. Both bands also played the circuit of clubs on the coast; Ely told Dalley (though not me) that the Raiders and Kingsmen were playing the Pypo Club *together* when they first ran into *duh duh duh, duh duh* on the jukebox. Jack remains certain that the Raiders and Kingsmen were playing the same club—the Coaster, a converted roller rink—on the first weekend that the Raiders first heard "Louie Louie."

The Raiders were a little older (Paul was, by these standards, a lot older), but by the fall of 1962 all the Kingsmen except Gallucci were out of high school and the band became more of a full-time project. So the two groups met as something like equals. "Everybody thought we were rivals, but we were all good buddies," said Jack. "We would get to the gigs, set up each other's equipment, and jam for a while before the shows or battles. Sometimes Mark Lindsay and I would get up and sing some Righteous Brothers songs together before the show. We couldn't do it in front of people because our fans wanted us to have this rivalry between us."

"Louie Louie" was already a local phenomenon when the Idaho contingent hit Portland. "We started playing at the Headless Horseman and people'd say, 'Play "Louie Louie," ' " Lindsay told Ruhlmann. "We'd say, 'What's "Louie Louie"?' Nobody knew Richard Berry. Rockin' Robin Roberts and the Wailers had cut 'Louie Louie' and that was the version that everybody played. So I got a copy of it. I think Lynn Easton might have gotten me the copy, as a matter of fact. . . . So we learned it and we had to play it three times the first night."

According to Roger Hart, "Louie Louie" came to Portland under the auspices of disc jockey Ben Tracy, the first to play the Wailers' record. Revere says it was Hart who wanted the Raiders to make a record of "Louie." By 1963 the locals were ready for a new version, and outside the Northwest the song still kept its secret. Revere agreed to do the session only if Hart would pay for it: "I think the song is a piece of junk. It'll never make it," he said.

But Hart had no idea how to be a record magnate. Revere told him, "Hey, I'll just get ahold of John Guss and he'll print you up some records. You can put it on your own label." Hart called his label Sande (pronounced *sandy*). Its first release was the Raiders' "Louie Louie" backed with a version of the Jimmy Forrest / James Brown R&B instrumental standard, "Night Train," also set to the *duh duh duh. duh duh* beat.

Ironically, the Raiders and the Kingsmen went into the very same recording studio, Portland's Northwest Recorders, to make their separate "Louies" *the very same week*. Which band recorded first has long been a matter of controversy among "Louie" scholars, as if there were some musical law of primogeniture that would thereby render the latecomer an imitation or ripoff.

To which the wisdom of "Louie" replies, "Aw, c'mon."

Anyway, different people remember the story differently and not always to their own advantage: Paul Revere has always insisted that the Raiders were first, but Lindsay has repeatedly insisted that during the Raiders session the engineer talked to him about the oddity of doing two sessions featuring the same song in a week. Different Kingsmen also remember differently.

The Raiders were probably first. According to the story Roger Hart told William Ruhlmann for his exhaustive 1991 *Goldmine* history of the Raiders, "There was a disc jockey, Craig Walker, in Portland who did a thing about two years ago and he announced it. He called me on the air. His research said that 'You recorded it on April 11th and the Kingsmen recorded it on the 13th.' " This jibes with the recollection of Bob Lindall, who engineered both sessions, and with Jack Ely's memory that the Kingsmen did their "Louie" marathon on a Friday night and recorded on Saturday morning—the 11th was a Thursday, the 13th was a Saturday. But the records at CBS Records, which eventually licensed the Raiders' disc, show that the Raiders didn't cut until April 25th. But the 25th was a Thursday anyway, and that could still have been two days before the Kingsmen traipsed in. It also wouldn't be terribly surprising if Ken Chase, Roger Hart's boss, decided a little competition with his star air talent was appropriate after learning that the Kingsmen's best number was being recorded by their biggest rivals.

But as Hart told Ruhlman, "It doesn't make a bunch of difference anymore. It isn't going to change history about who sold most."

In the spring of 1963 anybody in Portland would have told you that the Raiders were going to sell the most, the most by a wide margin. In fact, you might have had trouble finding anybody who knew that anybody else had recorded "Louie Louie" recently.

The Raiders' "Louie" session was uneventful, but it turned out a great version of the song. It certainly has a great introduction: In fact, the Raiders' intro to "Louie Louie" is one of the greatest intros of any record in the history of rock'n'roll, ranking with the opening of Elvis's "Milk Cow Blues Boogie," the Jackson 5's "I Want You Back," and the "one-two-three-*fuh*" with which Paul McCartney counts off the Beatles' "I Saw Her Standing There." It's a moment of shock and surprise and outright silliness, the more amazing because it actually pulls off the hoary trick of transferring a stage-act gimmick to a record.

The Raiders' "Louie" opens with a halting saxophone riff, Lindsay playing as if he's not really sure this is such a good idea after all. Then as the guitar chops its way in, ending all doubt with its opening *duh duh duh*, Mike Smith, singing from back at the drumkit, shouts words crafted by a genius of the vernacular in a voice so harsh and rasping it might emerge from a descendant of Walter Brennan:

"Grab your woman—it's-uh 'Louie Louie' time!" It's a barband apotheosis, but undeniably an apotheosis for all of that. So yet one more time "Louie Louie" reached a height of rock'n'roll grandeur. Listening to the playback, the Raiders should have felt satisfied. No semi-pro high school band was likely to top this.

But then how likely was the Spanish Castle Magic of *duh duh duh. duh duh* in the first place?

*   *   *

The Kingsmen arrived at Northwest Recorders that Saturday at 10 AM, the crack of dawn, Rock'n'roll Standard Time. Chase was the last to show up. They went inside and set up their gear as quickly as possible—studio time cost money, and the clock started running when they walked through the door. But then there wasn't that much equipment to set up and Northwest Recorders, while the best facility in Portland, was pretty primitive itself. The band moved a large backdrop curtain and rolled up a rug. Within a half hour, engineer Lindall began placing the microphones.

That was a problem. Instead of having microphones on a stand or a vocal booth in which an overhead mike conveniently dropped right to mouth level, Northwest Recorders' vocal mike hung from a large boom stand, and it was so unwieldy it remained well overhead. Jack Ely was forced to stand on tiptoe. (Additional reasons Ely slurred: He wore braces on his teeth, and the "Louie" marathon had been cord-crunching.)

After he'd made his adjustments, Lindall retreated into the engineer's booth, where he sat with Ken Chase, who observed through the large soundproof window. Easton hit the downbeat and crashed about a third of the way through the first verse when Chase's voice suddenly squawked through the intercom: "Wait! Wait a minute! Gotta change a couple of things in here." The band stood idly strumming and banging while the "producer" and engineer fiddled with knobs and dials.

A couple minutes later Chase called, "Okay, let's just do a run-through, just so I can set the levels." Easton counted the song off and again kicked into *duh duh duh. duh duh.* Ely squalled upward at the mike as hard as he could. The band was nervous; this may have been a rinky-dink setup but it was their Shot. Ely yawped like Donald Duck in a rage on "Okay, let's give it to 'em, right now!" The others' nerves showed, too: Just before the vocal came back in, Lynn Easton clacked his sticks together and cussed, "Fuck!" Although Lynn was off-mike, he said it loud enough to register slightly on the tape, and he never quite recovered the beat, stuttering and stumbling throughout the rest of the take. When they got to the guitar break, Mike Mitchell fumbled his way through his Rich Dangel–inspired solo as if he'd never heard of the song before. By the time Jack yelped his final "Let's go!" they sounded relieved to be finished. Now they waited for Chase to call for the first real take.

Instead, his voice came through the intercom: "Okay! That was *great*! What do you guys wanna put on the backside?"

"Are you *sure*?" the guys wanted to know.

"Yeah. Yeah. That was great, man, you never did that song better," Chase told them. "Now, what're you gonna do for the B side?"

The Kingsmen had one original song, a surfish instrumental called "Haunted Castle" (credited to Lynn Easton, though Ely claims he and Don Gallucci wrote it just before the session), and the bandsmen knew enough to figure that, if they were going to make any real money, they were better off using the flip side for a song for which they'd get composer and publisher credit. So they cut 'Haunted Castle' in what remained of the hour for which they'd have to pay.

As they packed, Lindall asked, "Who's paying for this?"

"He is," the boys said, pointing to Chase.

"No, I'm not," said Chase. And he wasn't, since he didn't have the dough—various authorities cite the figure as $37, $38, or $44, but Ely says it was a whole $50. Lindall made it clear that the tape wouldn't leave his hands until the cash crossed his palm. So the band sighed and each crumpled ten bucks out of his jeans in order to get their masterwork out of hock.

Ken Chase had no more idea how to get a record pressed than Roger Hart, and he didn't even have Paul Revere to introduce him to an out-of-town record presser. So he called a Seattle independent promotion man, Jerry Dennon. Dennon had been around quite a while—he'd actually worked for Flip's Northwest distributor on Richard Berry's "Louie Louie," according to Max Feirtag. Chase had heard that Dennon was starting his own label and might be looking for product. Dennon was doing exactly that, and so the Kingsmen's "Louie Louie" first came to life on the Jerden label at just about the same time that the Raiders' "Louie" was issued on Sande.

According to Jack Ely, Jerden released the record on the basis of nothing more than Chase "loaning" it to him: "The next thing we knew, we got a box of records. No contract, no nothing." Not that it seemed like dividing up a pile of profits was going to be the issue. They had a thousand copies of a disc that sounded to the uninitiated or unconvinced, as Ely put it, "like all bands sounded in those days. There was a lot of buzz, the low end of the bass, a little bit of guitars and keyboards — all kind of running together. We thought it was horrible but Ken loved it. We had a thousand copies. We sold them to our friends, relatives, and neighbors. And we bugged all the radio stations in Portland to play it."

In the life of a rock'n'roll record, radio station airplay isn't everything, but it is the only thing that ensures a certain level of attention, so it's the *sine qua non* of record sales. With two versions of "Louie Louie" competing for regional programmers' attention, the Portland situation shaped up as a classic "cover version" battle between two acts with the same song. There are three possible outcomes: Record A will win, Record B will prevail, or they will kill each other.

The Raiders had made a more conventionally appealing record, but the Kingsmen's raw energy was virtually unprecedented. Their connections at KISN just about cancelled each other out. Chase was the big boss and he must have favored the Kingsmen, but Roger Hart had the station's most popular show and he was clearly going to back the Raiders. With Jerry Dennon in their corner, the Kingsmen had a wily promo veteran, but then, Paul Revere's promotional flair couldn't be underestimated.

The contest seemed settled when local Columbia Records rep Ken Bolster asked Hart for a copy of the Raiders' disc to send to Columbia's Los Angeles A&R (talent development) staff. Bolster made his request after hearing just an acetate, well before the Sande version was even pressed. By May 23 the Raiders had signed with Columbia, the largest wing of CBS Records, the richest record company in the United States and one that was desperately trying to sign up rock'n'roll talent after many years of rejecting all such music as too vulgar. Bolster had been offered a $100 bonus for coming up with a signable act, so when he spotted an acetate on Hart's desk during a promotional visit to KISN, he snatched it up.

"I don't think that we'd have thought of Columbia Records,

'cause Columbia didn't have a reputation of being a rock label,"
Hart told Ruhlmann. "But within a couple of weeks I had a
phone call from David Kapralik [head of A&R] at CBS in New
York." The Raiders signed almost immediately and remained
with the company for the next decade, during which time they
spit out close to a dozen major hits. But "Louie Louie" wasn't
one of them.

Initially, Columbia's West Coast A&R man Terry Melcher
(the 21-year-old son of Doris Day and mentor-to-be of Charles
Manson) thought Bolster had picked a big winner: The Raiders'
"Louie" sold between sixty and seventy thousand copies in the
Northwest alone and the band's restless tour schedule, which
took them as far south as San Jose, California, spread the word.
In fact, Paul claims that in the Northwest, " 'Night Train' was as
big a hit as 'Louie Louie.' It has the exact same beat—on purpose. We did it at the same tempo because it was the perfect
dance beat of the time."

From May, when Jerden released it, through the summer of
1963, the Kingsmen—getting whupped on non-KISN airplay
and with a much more circumscribed touring path—barely sold
six hundred copies of their little gem. The group started talking
about disbanding.

What no one except Jack Ely knew was that Lynn Easton had
some ideas about revamping the Kingsmen. He'd been studying
saxophone "diligently," according to Ely, and wanted to try
making that instrument a more central part of the sound. Ely
knew because he and Lynn were "more than band members. We
did a lotta stuff together: gang fights, double dating, family
things. We weren't just in the band."

At the band's regular rehearsal on August 16, 1963—"a date
I'll remember as long as I live," said Ely—Lynn marched in to
lay out a new plan. "He just came in and said, 'I've been taking
sax lessons and I'm getting good.' He said we needed a stronger
personality up front, so he was going to stop playing drums and
step out front, because Mike and I didn't do enough talking to
the audience. Lynn always focused on what bar bands did—just
like I always focused on what rock stars did. He wanted Vegas; I
wanted Elvis."

Lynn's proposal went much further: Jack, who'd always been

a guitarist, would become the band's new drummer, a bizarre idea because Ely had never played drums except while Lynn sang "Big Boy Pete." "Lynn and I had been talking about making some changes," Ely admitted, "But it had always been that his repertoire [as frontman] would jump from one song to maybe four or five songs a night."

Ely's recollection is that the others were initially "amused. Everybody was amused, because he could hardly sing. He could never sing 'Raindrops,' none of the Dee Clark, Gene Chandler stuff I was singing. The band told him he was nuts."

What happened next remained unmatched in the annals of rock band animosity until John Lennon and Paul McCartney had the little falling out that lead to the demise of the Beatles at the peak of their career: Easton announced that when he and his mother had filed the paperwork for the legal use of the name "The Kingsmen," they'd been told that because all the band members were under 21, not only would each of them have to sign a document, but so would their parents and each signature would have to be notarized. That seemed time-consuming and unwieldy so the Eastons decided to register the Kingsmen in Lynn's name alone. The way Ely remembers it, Lynn said that meant, "If you don't like it, tough shit," or words to that effect.

"Bob and I said, 'Well, up yours if that's the case, Lynn. We're not rehearsing tonight. I'll see you guys later.' We got up and left. Why Don and Mike didn't leave, I'll never know." He drove away mad. "I probably just went out and got drunk."

Jack expected either his or Lynn's parents to intervene. But Ely's parents have never indicated to him that they feel the Eastons did him any injustice. The two couples remained friends: "That's the biggest how-de-do."

After everybody realized that Lynn meant what he'd said, Jack presumed that the Kingsmen would break up. "Louie Louie" had flopped, the core of the group had disintegrated, and unless a life in the lounges of Oregon was your idea of a great future, not much was left for the band to accomplish.

8

Every Termite a King

The record hardly stands up to attention out of context, as it had been recorded with a vocal so muffled that suspicious minds thought they could detect obscene suggestions in the lyric. But it did have those "La Bamba" chord changes rumbling along the bottom and a dumb chorus that was undeniably catchy.

—Charlie Gillett, The Sound of the City

With certain kinds of greatness there can be no trifling. The best thing to do is just 'fess up to the facts. So history's judgment on the Kingsmen's "Louie Louie" ought not to be as stuffy and half-hearted as Gillett's but a review that just plain spits out the evidence: "Really stupid, really great. Not really dirty, but so what?"

A lot of people imagine that the importance of the Kingsmen's "Louie Louie" stems from the profoundly absurd possibility that Jack Ely was singing dirty words. Even the master termitologist Lester Bangs—universally acclaimed as the Greatest Rock Critic in History—led himself down this false path. "This was the one where you can hear the singer start the line 'See Jamaica moon above' too soon, while the drummer crashes into a stumbling roll that must have been accompanied by a wither-ing glare; this was also the version that had all of us destroying our styluses in 1964 as we struggled to figure out whether the garbled lyrics, as rumored, were dirty and if so, what the words actually were. My circle of friends deciphered in one line, 'I felt my boner in her hair'; but debate and doubts persisted, with the Kingsmen disavowing any intentional lewdness, if only to keep the record on the radio," Bangs wrote in "Protopunk: The Ga-rage Bands," a chapter in *The Rolling Stone Illustrated History of Rock & Roll.*

Such assessments of "Louie Louie" miss, or omit, the lim-ited relevance of craft when confronted by absolute transcen-dence. The Kingsmen's "Louie Louie" is the most profound and sublime expression of rock'n'roll's ability to create something from nothing. Like a termite should, it burrows into your con-sciousness only to burst forth at the summit of trash rock to chal-lenge the credentials of any pundit who dares to pontificate on meaning. If you don't embrace it, and embrace it whole, stum-bling beats and all, you've missed the point. To my knowledge only one expert has been able to describe this damnable disc in the right spirit: Seattle rock historian Peter Blecha in his liner notes to a Rhino Records compact disc called *The Best of the Kingsmen,* where he refers to "[t]he Kingsmen's chaotic ver-sion—with its clubfooted drum beat, insane cymbal crashes, ul-tra-cheezy keyboard figures, lead guitar spazzout/solo, and that famous fluffed third verse, as well as Ely's generally slurred and unintelligible vocals. . . ." Blecha describes the mess perfectly and he does so without the faintest odor of condescension.

Don Gallucci may have been a virtuoso prodigy. It hardly matters since he could have played "Louie" 's opening chords if he'd been born with ten thumbs. And yet transferring "Louie" 's opening to a cheap-sounding electric keyboard gave the riff the same kind of escalating tension that Ray Charles found in the similar monotonous-but-relentless opening of "What'd I Say," Which, for all I know, is where Gallucci got the idea—and good for him if he swiped it. The device was hardly worn out.

Lynn Easton's drumming is another matter. Lynn may have refused to run his rock band as a collective entity—so much for mythic teenage democracy, eh, Nirvana fans?—and he was un-

deniably, on this evidence, a pretty shitty percussionist, pound-
ing away as if his limbs were artificial implements he'd only
lately learned to halfway control, and his sense of time perhaps
imported from off-planet. But the stew that Easton makes of the
simple cha-cha-cha of *duh duh duh. duh duh*, exhibits the genius
of the Kingsmen's "Louie Louie" as much as Gallucci's rendition of the riff or Jack Ely's hyperventilations on "Let's give it to
'em, right now" and his awesome, final *"Let's go!!"* Easton's
playing is a great example of why rock'n'roll, which shares so
many roots with jazz, is *not* jazz in the most extreme sense. In
jazz improvisation is of the essence, but the trick is to cause what
you're making up to sound fated and inevitable. In rock'n'roll,
the idea is to make what is actually totally predictable sound like
a surprise. In Easton's case, this meant playing as if he had no
idea what beat might be coming up in the next bar or, if he did
know, lacked any concrete opinion as to exactly which of his several drums and cymbals he ought to smack when he got there.

Playing that way wasn't any kind of technical breakdown or
failure, no matter what an elephantine expert might have you
believe. Rather it is the triumph of the drumming of the Kingsmen's "Louie Louie"—which was forever after, as far as most of
the planet was concerned, if not the *only* "Louie," at least the
only "Louie" that *mattered*—even for the hordes of amateur
musicians, many of them with an even sorrier assortment of
skills than Easton's, the Ur "Louie," the alpha, if not omega, of
termite rock. Lynn Easton had no idea what he was doing that
day in the studio (although he had a very clear idea of what he
was *supposed* to be doing) and it showed, but if that's supposed
to be so all-fired simple, Mr. Marsalis, how come it's been thirty
years and nobody has ever reached that level of inspired incompetence ever again? (Don't tell *me* about "Wild Thing.")

Which is not to say that the Platonic Idea inhabiting Easton's
traps-thrashing died stillborn. There was one drummer and one
drummer only in the history of rock'n'roll who truly grasped the
genius of what "Louie Louie" represented as a monument in
the annals of percussive history: Keith Moon of the Who, a
drummer who made bashing his kit as the fancy struck him,
rather than as orderly musical progression demanded, into an
elegant style—and a drummer who also kept his cymbals going

nonstop in order to cover up any mistakes he might make in a white noise wash. To say that Keith Moon was the most influential rock'n'roll drummer of the 1960s is only, in the early 1990s, to emphasize the self-evident. But to say that Keith Moon's greatest influences as a drummer were *both* Hal Blaine, the supreme technician of Phil Spector and surf music both, *and* Lynn Easton, who stands in relation to Blaine roughly as Jimmy Swaggart to Moses, is to begin to come to grips with the true dimensions of Spanish Castle Magic and its all-but-undetected influence upon the whole story of rock'n'soul music. And this makes sense because, if you'd asked him, Lynn Easton probably would have chosen to sound like Hal Blaine, too. And if you'd asked *him,* Hal Blaine probably would have cocked an ear toward "Louie Louie" and thrown up his hands in despair. Or maybe not—he never put down Ronnie Spector, whose vocal on "Be My Baby" (Blaine's greatest musical moment) is the singer's equivalent of Lynn Easton's drumming on "Louie Louie."

But then for people who are cool and confident, what has rock'n'roll ever been except a cause for despair? And for those of us who are less serene and less certain, what has it ever been except a cause for hope? And isn't such a triumph for termites the most tremendous subversion of all the standards and practices of our society? Isn't the idea that there is something eternal about Jack Ely yawping *"Let's give it to 'em, right now"* like a man whose gonads are attached to a vacuum cleaner, a deep and meaningful threat to our whole way of life as understood on the spectrum from Tipper Gore to Marilyn Quayle?

In short, why *shouldn't* the FBI have tried to prove that "Louie Louie" by the Kingsmen (as reissued on Wand 143) was a piece of filth undermining the values of the nation? Because we know now that even though the G-men were too square to figure out how to prove it, that's *exactly* what the Kingsmen's "Louie" did. Which is exactly why it has endured and will forever deserve our love, devotion, and—most of all—gratitude. As Elvis once put it, "Have a laugh on me. I can help."

9

"Louie" Who?

There is only one thing in the world worse than being talked about, and that is not being talked about.
—Oscar Wilde, The Picture of Dorian Gray

WMEX radio, Boston, October 1963

Arnie "Woo Woo" Ginsburg met with promotion men from Boston's record distributors a couple of days a week in the afternoon before he began his top-rated evening deejay program on WMEX. Ginsburg, whose voice was so unlikely that he sometimes called himself "Old Aching Adenoids," had been the biggest jock in town since Presley was a pup; he'd even survived giving testimony before Congress in the 1960 payola scandal, during which he revealed receipt of money from several record distributors.

Ginsburg didn't just survive. Unlike most post-payola deejays, he still picked his own music. By late 1963 he later boasted, "I was the only guy in town who would play a new record."

On this particular afternoon Woo Woo was visited by Bob

Levinson of Bay State Distributors. Bay State was one of the biggest distributors in New England (and another major player in the Congressional payola hearings, though not one of those that gave Ginsburg honoraria); it carried many of the smaller rhythm and blues labels. Levinson pitched several discs, the least likely of them being the Kingsmen's "Louie Louie."

Ginsburg put Jerden 712 on his office turntable. It hadn't gotten much past the opening *duh duh duh. duh duh* when he looked up at Levinson to say, "Wow, this is interesting. But it sounds *awful*." Levinson looked crestfallen but Woo Woo reassured him. The Kingsmen were perfect for his show's occasional feature, The Worst Record of the Week.

Woo Woo was one of the most gimmicky of the great rock deejays, inserting shamelessly corny bells-and-whistles set pieces between nearly every record and commercial. Ginsburg also possessed a sense of the mythic. When he promoted record hops at the Surf Ballroom at Nantasket Beach, he gave it the monicker "Surf Nantasket." So he was well prepared for Spanish Castle Magic.

Ginsburg played an awful lot of novelty records, and to him "Louie Louie" sounded like the ultimate rock'n'roll novelty. But even though Ginsburg may have thought "Louie" was awful, buggy trash, the wiles of "Let's give it to 'em, right now" did not elude him entirely. In fact, he understood them so well that on that night's show, he played this Worst Record of the Week not the usual once but *twice*.

"The next morning, when I came into the office," he remembered several decades later, "there were maybe 50 calls from record stores, wanting to know where they could get copies of 'Louie Louie.' People were going into the stores and asking for it—on the basis of those two plays."

Something similar had happened in 1961, when Ginsburg became the first disc jockey in America to risk airing a UK hit by the British skiffle star Lonnie Donegan. "Does Your Chewing Gum Lose Its Flavor on the Bedpost Overnight?" made *Billboard*'s Top 5.

Bay State Distributors probably took on "Louie Louie" as a favor to Jerry Dennon, its Seattle colleague. Dennon might not yet have had a contract with the Kingsmen, but he had a release, and in the record business, from that day to this, possession may or may not be nine-tenths of the law but it has always been 100 percent of standard operating procedure. Having failed to break the Kingsmen in the Pacific Northwest, Dennon apparently tried what he figured Columbia Records would not yet do for the Raiders: He took a shot at the national leverage East Coast airplay could generate.

Dennon's chances looked slim. In *Billboard*'s October 5, 1963 issue, the Raiders' "Louie" appeared as a "Regional Breakout," which indicated a record achieving hit status in a single geographic area, in this case not Seattle or Portland but San Francisco. That was just about the same time that Woo Woo received the Kingsmen's "Louie." Within two weeks the Kingsmen's yawp had begun to spread like kudzu through the Northeastern corridor, the most heavily populated and influential market in America. The margin of life this brought the Kingsmen's record was still tenuous. After all, this battle of the bands didn't just pit the Kingsmen versus the Raiders; Jerden had to compete against CBS Records distribution, the mightiest enterprise in the record biz.

Dennon's concept must have been to get the Kingsmen disc started (somewhere, somehow) and then to license it to a larger label—from time immemorial, the favored tactic of the freelance record marketer with a finished master tape. According to one interview with the Kingsmen, he first tried to sell their "Louie" to Capitol Records in Hollywood, but the future home of the Beatles rejected the rock'n'roll masterwork as, according to Mike Mitchell, "the worst piece of garbage they had ever heard." It's not certain how many other shots at a distribution or licensing deal Dennon may have taken (he refused to tell me his story). For certain, he sent Jerden 712 to Marv Schlachter, one of the proprietors of New York–based Scepter/Wand Records, home of the Shirelles, Chuck Jackson, and Dionne Warwick.

Schlachter co-owned Scepter/Wand with Florence Greenberg, who had started Scepter in 1958 in order to promote the Shirelles. When Luther Dixon, the brilliant arranger/producer who also had a piece of the company, discovered the great soul baritone Chuck Jackson the next year, it was decided to place him on an new affiliate label, Wand, in a perfectly understandable chain of reasoning. Throughout its history Scepter/Wand also released novelty rock hits, including the preteen Rocky Fellers' discotheque tribute, "Killer Joe," and the Guess Who's best-ever waxing of "Shaking All Over." So the company was certainly a logical home for the Kingsmen, even if Greenberg later called it "the shame of my life."

"Jerry Dennon sent us a copy of this record, which we had listened to," Schlachter remembered in 1991. "Frankly, we didn't think much of it and so we sort of passed on it. A few days or a few weeks later—I really don't remember which—I was talking on the phone with Bob Levinson, a promotion man with Bay State Distributors in Boston, and I asked him if there was anything particularly hot. He told me about a record that he'd had on some small offbeat label that was selling a ton: 'Louie Louie' by the Kingsmen on Jerden. I reached in my desk drawer, where I kept the stuff I'd rejected, and there it was. 'Oh, *I* know that record,' I said, and I called Jerry Dennon and told him I thought it was a perfectly wonderful record."

Wand re-released the Kingsmen's "Louie Louie" as Wand 143 with the strange (or at least inaccurate) credit, "A Jerden Production by Ken Chase and Jerry Dennon." By October 19 the Kingsmen had their own regional breakout, from Boston. A week later, *Billboard* actually reviewed it, which it never did the Raiders' version, although the review couldn't have been very helpful since the text was one long typo: a comment on an entirely different record.

For a while the contest for chart supremacy stayed even: On November 2, *Billboard* showed the Kingsmen "bubbling under" the Hot 100, at #127, which meant little more than that the Boston airplay continued. The same week the Raiders scored another regional breakout, in Los Angeles. On November 9 the Kingsmen's disc debuted in the Hot 100 at #83, between the Secrets' "The Boy Next Door" and Bobby Vee's "Yesterday and You," but the Raiders' bubbled under at #108, not that far behind. The next week the Kingsmen's "Louie" jumped to #58, between the Beach Boys' legendary "In My Room" and Johnny Tillotson's monument-in-treacle "Talk Back Trembling Lips." This just about killed off the Raiders and three weeks later the race was over when the Kingsmen exploded from #23 to #4, a leap of nineteen positions in a stage of the contest (not the one against the Raiders but the one pitting the Kingsmen against all the other bonafide hits of the day) where a jump of four or five places represented a major gain.

Columbia Records still plugged away on the Raiders' behalf. On December 14, the group notched its final regional breakout, this one in Minneapolis/St. Paul. But the issue was settled: History was now guaranteed to remember *duh duh duh. duh duh* as done by the Kingsmen, if it remembered it at all.

Back in Portland, "Revere was screaming at Roger [Hart], who was screaming at Columbia, who'd done next to nothing with the record. CBS said, 'How were we to know?'" Mark Lindsay told Ruhlmann. Thanks to its long-standing hidebound attitude about the degrading nature of rock'n'roll, CBS was a novice in marketing and promoting any music more rhythmically strenuous or conceptually outre than Steve Lawrence's pedophilic pop tune "Go Away Little Girl," which was *Billboard*'s top tune of 1963 but did not set the company up very well for the beat boom that the "Louie" revival portended.

There wasn't much that could have been done by the most savvy record marketer. The spirit of the Kingsmen's disc transcended the band's bumbling technique, conveying an order of essential wildness that outstripped even *"Grab your woman! It's 'Louie Louie' time!"* According to Peter Blecha, the first week after Wand picked it up the Kingsmen's "Louie" sold 21,000 copies in Boston. The Raiders' popularity in the smaller San Francisco market seemed inconsequential. As radio stations around the country made their decisions, the evidence lay on the Kingsmen's side. Musical competence has never motivated programmers hunting ratings popularity.

There was only one place where the Raiders beat out the Kingsmen: in the Pacific Northwest. According to Mark Lindsay, in Portland "their version sold approximately 600 copies, our version sold 6,000."

By the time Woo Woo Ginsburg made the Kingsmen's "Louie Louie" the most memorable Worst Record of the Week ever, the Kingsmen basically didn't exist. Jack Ely was going to school a

bit and selling vacuum cleaners door to door a lot and considering forming a new group. Lynn Easton, busy at Lewis and Clark
College, hadn't done much since taking control; Ely claims that
the Kingsmen didn't play at all from the August 16 split-up until
the record hit nationally that fall. A sensible development would
have seen the old group revived to capitalize on the hit. But in
these annals, what's sensible?

Easton recruited new players. Drummer Gary Abbot took
Lynn's old spot, while Easton subbed for Ely and Norm Sund-
holm took over on bass. This configuration recorded the album
The Kingsmen in Person, Featuring "Louie Louie" (except for the
title track, of course) but it lasted only until early 1964, when
Abbot and Gallucci split and were replaced by drummer Dick
Peterson and organist Barry Curtis. That lineup sustained itself
through the remainder of the group's career.

But the Kingsmen had a problem. The vocal on "Louie
Louie," whatever else you could say about it, was quite distinctive and, whatever else Lynn Easton may have been, he was not
a good mimic of Jack Ely. As "Louie" exploded into the national
consciousness, the Kingsmen began getting concert dates all
over the country—the more so when they dumped Ken Chase in
order to work with the New York–based William Morris Agency.

Jack Ely might have been merely annoyed. The split didn't
irrevocably become a feud, at least for Jack, until the night the
Kingsmen taped their stage show at the Chase for the live Kingsmen LP. The bouncers at the door stopped him. "We've been
given instructions you are not to be allowed in tonight," he was
told.

But by the end of 1963 Jack Ely wasn't the band's only old
associate with a score to settle. Around that time he got a call
from Ken Chase, the Kingsmen's erstwhile manager and record
producer. Chase told him that after "Louie Louie" had popped
up to #41 in *Billboard*, he'd approached William Morris about
national bookings. A few days later Easton called Chase and
fired him, saying he'd signed with William Morris for all the
band's affairs. Now, Chase told Ely, the Kingsmen were doing
well out on the road—until it came time to do "Louie Louie," at
which point audiences tended to rise up and hoot, the most glo-

rious mysteries of *duh duh duh. duh duh* being absent from the Lynn-led rendition. Or so the story goes.

So Ely and Ken Chase reunited and the radio programmer gave Jack Ely and the Kingsmen—the unsurprising name Jack selected for his new band—gigs at the Chase, which was packed out for his return. Chase also arranged a record deal with RCA Records in Los Angeles. Soon Jack Ely and the Kingsmen were also on the road, billed as the band with the *original* singer of "Louie Louie." Their touring strategy was simple enough: They found out where Easton's Kingsmen were playing and booked themselves into the same town a night or two earlier. With the "original lead singer" moniker, they effectively cut the Kingsmen's business just about everywhere they tried it.

This quite understandably did not sit well with Easton or William Morris, and they responded by various means, including shouting and screaming; filing a lawsuit seeking to prevent Ely from appearing as the Kingsmen (a name Easton owned, as Ely very well knew) or from billing himself as the original singer of the record (which Jack certainly was); and, according to Jack, even sheer thuggery one night in Boston, when a couple of heavies had to be chased by a German shepherd posted in his dressing room.

For two years this standoff continued, Ely poaching Easton's gigs, Lynn lipsynching Jack's vocal, and everybody getting more and more confused about who actually did what. With Lynn singing, the Kingsmen did have other hits, notably "Money," a remake of Barrett Strong's Motown barroom staple that's as clumsy as it is noisy, and "The Jolly Green Giant," an unholy wedding of the Olympics' L.A. R&B fable "Big Boy Pete" with the Green Giant vegetable commercials then saturating television. Ely's records—more rocking, less silly—dented no charts at all (a peril of having signed with the major-but-decrepit RCA), but live he was still a nuisance and the lawsuits continued. Finally, in 1965 some Solomon convinced the factions to cut the baby in half: Ely got about $6,000 in royalties, while Easton became sole proprietor of the Kingsmen name; Jack continued with a backup group known as the Courtmen. Ely was allowed to bill himself as "the original lead singer of 'Louie Louie' "; Lynn could no longer appear on TV to lipsynch the record on which he didn't sing, although he retained control of the band's name, the most valuable property (since neither party received any of the "Louie" songwriting or song publishing royalties).

Jack signed with Bang Records—the house label of Bert Berns, composer of "Twist and Shout" and other significant termite icons. Jack's first two Bang singles were "Louie Louie '66" and "Ride Ride Baby" backed with the Raiders' "Louie" sequel, "Louie, Go Home." By the time those flopped Ely had been drafted. Berns died while he did his Army stint and Jack found his career dead-ended when he returned to civvies in 1967.

Despite such efforts as their caustic remake of Donald Woods's "Death of an Angel" and "Annie Fanny," an ode to Harvey Kurtzman's *Playboy* cartoon character, the Kingsmen never cracked the Top 40 after "Jolly Green Giant." In fact, after "Louie Louie" made its brief chart reappearance at #97 in May 1966, they disappeared from the charts—although not the minor league concert and frat party circuit.

But why was their "Louie Louie" still around two years after it was first concocted?

The answer is what you've been waiting to hear: It had been discovered that "Louie Louie" was a dirty song.

10

Combating Merchants of Filth: The Role of "Louie Louie"

Detectives to the right of me,
Detectives to the left of me,
Detectives behind me,
Sleuthing and spying.
Theirs not to question why—
Theirs but to sleuth and lie—
Noble detectives!
—Clarence Darrow

ack in 1963, everybody who knew anything about rock'n'roll knew that the Kingsmen's "Louie Louie" concealed dirty words that could be unveiled only by playing the 45 rpm single at 33⅓. (In a later version, they were audible to anybody who *really paid attention*, a cultic/conspiratorial touch worthy of *Foucault's Pendulum*.) This preposterous fable bore no scrutiny even at the time, but kids used to pretend that it did, in order to panic parents, teachers, and other authority figures. Eventually those ultimate authoritarians, the FBI, got involved, conducting a thirty-month investigation that led to "Louie"'s undying—indeed, unkillable—reputation as a dirty song.

So "Louie Louie" leaped up the chart on the basis of a myth about its lyrics so contagious that it swept cross country quicker than bad weather. Nobody—not you, not me, not the G-men ultimately assigned to the case—knows where the story started. That's part of the proof that it *was* a myth, because no folk tales ever have a verifiable origin. Instead society creates them through cultural spontaneous combustion. The time and conditions become propitious and, suddenly, puppies are microwaved, innocent tourists return from Mexican vacations with a stray dog that's really a rat, hooks dangle from the door handles of cars parked on Lover's Lane late Friday night, Procter & Gamble suffers under the sign of Satan, and truck drivers pick up hitchhiking ghosts, some of them reincarnations of Jesus. The fable of "Louie Louie" 's dirty lyrics is akin to those, although J. Edgar Hoover never sent his legions of over-scrubbed cementheads to investigate the illegal importation of Mexican rats as household pets.

"Where do such urban legends come from?" asks folklorist Jan Harold Brunvand, the University of Utah scholar whose studies of them are collected in such engrossing volumes as *The Mexican Pet, The Choking Doberman,* and *The Vanishing Hitchhiker.* "Usually, I have found, they evolve from older legends as people tell them again and again. . . . These generally stem from even earlier stories. Beyond that? Often no one knows. . . . Legends beget legends, but where it all starts remains a mystery."

Not even the FBI can say more, although with the help of its reports (revealed in January 1985 through a Freedom of Information Act petition by Eric Predoehl, editor of *The Louie Report* and auteur of a forthcoming film on Louiemania), we can trace this specific legend's devolution more easily than most.

The Bureau's "Louie" investigation stemmed from a very particular and particularly sinister form of this self-propelled legendry—what the British sociologist Stanley Cohen calls "folk-devils and moral panics," in which vilifications of a newfangled cultural condition inspire moral outrage as a million Mrs. Grundys and Jimmy Swaggarts cry warnings and predict brimstone. Moral panics stretch across the public history of rock'n'roll and R&B, from the riots associated with the appearance of Bill Haley's "Rock Around the Clock" in *The Blackboard Jungle* in 1955

to the "wilding" fantasies about young black males and rap records purveyed by police reporters and moral crusaders in the
late eighties. "Louie Louie" simply takes the phenomenon to its
most fabulous heights and ridiculous depths.

The dirty "Louie Louie" scare had an additional point of
Genesis: It was the first case, though sadly not the last, where J.
Edgar and his merry minions tried and failed to fathom
rock'n'roll's source and power. It is a tribute not to the hermetic
secrets of Louiemania but to the Bureau's total lack of soulfulness that it took the G-men two years of beating around the bush
to come within a hundred yards of reality.

That the FBI investigation determined that "Louie Louie"
was "unintelligible at any speed" is now part of the *duh duh duh.
duh duh* legend but no police bureaucrat in history ever phrased
anything so eloquently. The closest Hoover's hapless squares
came to such poetry was in notes like the one that Washington
FBI lab audiologists sent to the Indianapolis Special Agent in
Charge (SAC) on April 17, 1964: "For your information, the record . . . was played at various speeds but none of the speeds
assisted in determining the words of the song on the record."
But that was a *preliminary* conclusion, and not an especially ac-
curate one; the lyrics are only impossible to learn if you're willfully trying to hear what's not there.

The FBI lab and agents in several American cities spent the
next two years in hot pursuit of rock'n'roll as pornography. They
came to similar conclusions several times: "For your information, the record . . . was played at various speeds but none of the
speeds assisted in determining the words of the song on the record"—a sentence so overwrought and passive it almost had to be
composed by a cop.

Through it all, the Bureau-crats never got the joke. Which
was 1) that the lyric was a sea chanty, and 2) that in the viperous
new generation arising in America's schools, no greater sport
could be had or imagined than making all repositories of respectability cringe and groan over the unprovable. Somebody,
somewhere, came up with the idea of dirty "Louie Louie" lyrics
not only as a way of putting on other kids and panicking authority, but as a way of creating something that rock'n'roll needed: a
secret as rich and ridiculous as the sounds themselves. The teen-

age rumor mill spread it far and wide and nobody who wanted to survive study hall could afford to be so unhip as to admit that there really wasn't anything at all risqué to be heard. And what was true for a generation of kids hip enough to immerse themselves in the codes of rock'n'roll had to be that much more resonant for grown-ups so paranoid that they'd joined America's secret police.

The FBI files on "Louie Louie" detail an investigation for a violation of what it dubs "ITOM," the Federal law against Interstate Transportation of Obscene Material. Because of ITOM, copies of "Louie Louie" sent from an FBI office travelled under special "obscene cover" (which probably means festooned with warning labels, like the ones identifying nuclear waste and rap records), lest the Bureau itself be criminalized.

Such strictures against violating the obscenity laws applied to stuff that today's *Hustler* reader happily brings home to the kiddies. America locked down tight against the porno fiends. Max Feirtag claimed in 1964 that he'd never seen a copy of the dirty words because no one would risk mailing him one. The FBI actually destroyed the first few "Louie" specimens it analyzed. Contact with pornography, even if the porno in question could not be discerned, represented a contagion that could infect the mental and moral hygiene of Bureau-crat and civilian alike.

The feds' two-and-a-half-year pursuit of "Louie Louie" consumed the energy and attentions of agents in six major cities. Yet the vaunted G-men, for all their moral hygiene and ideological integrity, couldn't figure out the joke—let alone the lyrics— even though they had access to the most modern criminological tools, state-of-the-art surveillance techniques, and a Limax music crib sheet. The agents sat befuddled, staring at poorly typed copies of the "real" (that is, the spurious) words passed along by eager snitches. And they did this for twenty-one months, until November 1965, before they even figured out that it might be helpful to talk to Paul Revere and Raiders.

The FBI *never* talked to Jack Ely, the actual singer on the Kingsmen's actual "Louie." In fact, given the Lynn Easton—led Kingsmen's vested interest in steering everybody away from the fact that Lynn hadn't been the lead singer (viz., the liner notes to their first album), Jack believes that the FBI may not know *to this day* that he was ever involved in the record.*

Even a competent FBI would have been hard-pressed to figure out who originated the scam. But at least the Bureau might have spent some time trying to locate him or her, rather than deciding at the outset that the absurd rumor must be true and setting out to investigate the song, instead of the story.

Through its bumbling of elementary investigative principle, the FBI blew whatever slim chance there was of ever identifying the source of the original dirty "Louie Louie" fable. And this person (or persons) unknown is one of the true geniuses of the "Louie" legend, for it is this cock-and-bull story that ensured the song's eternal perpetuation.

Since we'll never know for sure, we're reduced to theories. One says that the whole thing started as a collegiate prank, dreamed up and spread around either by a cabal in a Midwest frat house or by a lone-wolf, Pacific Northwest college student. Richard Berry tried explaining it to the Indianapolis *News* in 1986: "What happened is that a bunch of college kids back in Indiana got hold of a printing press and started printing up and distributing their own ideas of what they thought they heard. Over the years, some of the lyrics have been changed by various people, which adds to the mystique of the song." This doesn't sound much like Richard Berry speaking, but there's no reason to suppose that the interview was done by an imposter. Is there?

The tradition of the covertly risqué lyric forms the essence of some notable rhythm and blues careers, for instance, those of Hank Ballard and Rufus Thomas. Heavy sexual innuendo informed everything from the El-Chords' merely dirty "Peppermint Stick" to Little Richard's "Miss Molly, who sure like[d] to ball," to Ballard's notorious "Work with Me, Annie" series. Among the adult black people who were their intended listeners, such records represented a realistic ribaldry. This was true from the earliest classic blues records (you want to hear dirty records,

---

*I type these words with trepidation. Based on this revelation, will the whole pathetic carnival recommence? Will Jack hear a knock on his door? Or have I just added a few more sheets to my own file? Are those footsteps in my hallway, or it is just another chorus of *duh duh duh. duh duh?*

Richard Berry onstage in his prime (*Courtesy Richard Berry family &
Eric Predoehl*)

Richard Berry on a rare day of glory. Was this the *real* origin of the "Louie
Louie" parade? (*Courtesy Richard Berry family & Eric Predoehl*)

The Wailers all up in the air over their impending success (*Courtesy Art Chantry*)

Classic Wailers, from the session that produced one of their album covers. That's Kent Morrell about to lose his grip on a limb. (*Courtesy Art Chantry*)

The Wailers in a moment of rare repose. At far left, Buck Ormsby prepares to conquer the universe, while his band-mates find the perfect coifs for the period, covering one ear, to impress the girls, while leaving the other uncovered, in order to placate parents, teachers, and police. (*Courtesy Art Chantry*)

A rare late seventies arty-fact, the Louie Louie wine cooler never caught on, partly because it got pulled off the market for copyright reasons. Also because its taste was purely "open at your own risk." Note the saxophone on the carton: Obviously, whoever produced this gunk had been deeply influenced by the Paul Revere and the Raiders version. Contains sodium benzoate as a preservative. Richard Berry used stronger stuff.
(*John Wagner*)

The motherlode of Berry albums, this Swedish reissue of his Flair and Flip sides from the fifties contains the indisputable "Louie" original and much more.
(*Eric Predoehl*)

After recapturing the rights to his masterwork, Richard Berry slowly came to terms with modern musical technology, in part thanks to his son, Marcel, here, accompanying the old man on electric bass in 1988.
(*Eric Predoehl*)

$\mathcal{P}$erpetrators of assorted "Louie"'s, all of extraordinary quality. *Coup de Ville* is the soundtrack from Joe Roth's film; *Idiot Show Classics* emerged from the termite-fevered brain of San Francisco deejay M. Dung; Paul Shaffer and Johnny Thunders represent *Duh duh duh. duh duh* at opposite extremes: lounge rock versus punk rock, melody versus noise, camping it up versus taking it to heart. (*Courtesy Eric Predoehl*)

It took a quarter of a century but Richard Berry finally made it to TV, during the "Louie Louie" marathon at radio station KFJC, 1983. The following video stills are from Eric Predoehl's documentary, *The Meaning of "Louie."* (*Eric Predoehl*)

Richard Berry tries to remember his lyrics, at a Tower Records autograph session during the 1983 "Louie Louie" marathon. (*Eric Predoehl*)

Duh duh duh. duh duh instigator Berry conspires on the air with "Louie"thon originator Jeff "Stretch" Riedle. (*Eric Predoehl*)

Loumania lays low yet another KFJC staffer. (*Eric Predoehl*)

Richard Berry and Jack Ely (*right*), the surviving giants of the *Duh duh duh. duh duh* set finally meet, at the KFJC "Louie Louie" marathon, August 1983. (*Karen Howe*)

Richard Berry jams one of history's longest "Louie"'s, at the 1983 KFJC "Louie Louie" marathon. (*Karen Howe*)

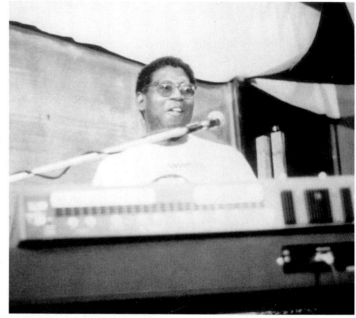

A "Louie Louie" summit meeting. *Left to right:* Filmmaker Eric Predoehl (chief conspirator behind *The Louie Report* newsletter); defrocked but still reigning Kingsmen vocalist Jack Ely; and Richard Berry, the almost-innocent who started it all. (*Karen Howe*)

That gleam in the eye is the dead giveaway that Rockin' Robin was no ordinary slide-rule specialist. The two photos of Robin reproduced here are the only two known shots of the seminal garage-punk singer. (*Courtesy Art Chantry*)

Rockin' Robin Roberts, in a shot that belies both the egghead academic and the hardass rocker sides of his personality (*Courtesy Art Chantry*)

The Wailers onstage; Buck Ormsby on bass at extreme left. (*Courtesy Art Chantry*)

4. APACHE .... Jorgen Ingman
5. GEE WHIZ (LOOK AT HIS EYES) ..... Carla Thomas
6. LOUIE LOUIE .... Rockin' Robin
7. I DON'T KNOW WHY .... Clarence "Fro

The Cash Box
Best Bets

AN
ETIQUETTE
RELEASE!
ET - 1

DISTRIBUTED
by
LIBERTY RECORDS
Los Angeles, Calif.

*1. BUT I DO - Clarence "Frog-
        man" Henry   28
  2. LOUIE LOUIE - Rockin' Robin Roberts
  3. ON THE RECORD - Floyd Cramer
  4. APACHE - Jorgen Ingman

Lou Laventhal,
one of the
discoverers of
Fleetwoods
says
"A Smash"

KJR Fo
THE BRIGHT EXCITI

ROCKIN ROBIN ROBERTS
(Etiquette 1)

(B+) "LOUIE LOUIE" (2:40) [Li-
mer BMI—Berry] Fine blues
vocal by the songster on a catchy ditty that was an oldie back aforetime
by clefer Richard Berry (his reading
is available again on the Flip label).
Roberts receives striking combo support. Date could move again in R&B-
pop circles. Liberty distributes the
label.

(B) "MARYANN" (1:55) [Pro-
gressive BMI—Charles] Infec-
tious work on a Ray Charles number.

NEED WE SAY MORE ?

LOUIE LOUIE
B/W MARYANN
BY
**ROCKIN' ROBIN
ROBERTS**

NO.	TITLE	ARTIST	No. Last Week	Week On Li
1.	Louie Louie	Rockin' Robin Roberts	2	4
2.	Runaway	Del Shannon	1	5
3.	But I Do.	Clarency Henry	8	4
4.	Blue Moon	Marcels	0	
5.	Bumble Boogie			

Promotional flyer for the Rockin' Robin Roberts (a/k/a the Wailers) "Louie Louie," including samples of its chart positions at Seattle radio stations, and the *Cashbox* review. (*Courtesy Art Chantry*)

Eric Predoehl, director of *The Meaning of "Louie"* and editor of *The Louie Report*, poses with the oft blacked-out F.B.I. files. (*Eric Predoehl*)

check out such blessed geniuses as Bessie Smith or Ma Rainey, on such items as "I'm Wild About That Thing" and the original "See See Rider," all of them made between 1920 and 1940 when Ronald Reagan's innocent America supposedly prevailed) right up through the "Annie" series. By the time Fats Domino added the leer to "I found my thrill on Blueberry Hill," though, teenage titillation rather than frank, adult sexual humor was at work. For R&B's new audience of young white outsiders, the early rock'n'rollers, unfamiliarity with the patterns of black speech coupled with poor recording fidelity spiced even innocent tunes. As R&B historian Peter Grendysa put it, "Getting there was half the fun, and sometimes what we thought we heard was much better than the real thing."

"Louie Louie," from Richard Berry's version to the Kingsmen's, had nothing to do with any of this. That poor half-in-the-bag Jamaican sailor can't even get into the same *country* as his girl. But the rumor that "Louie Louie" was a dirty record captured the American imagination, not just because teenagers need to know, right now and for sure, things that adults will never figure out in a decade, but because the Dirty "Louie" fable fundamentally reflected the country's infantile sexuality. An adolescent fixation would have run its course far more quickly. The idea that "Louie Louie" might be "dirty" sustains itself to this day because it hit adults as hard as it does kids—and if you take a cold, hard look at the real America, no wonder. We're dealing with the concept of someone actually (well, possibly) singing about *sex* (sort of) in a nation that still goes into a giggling spasm when someone makes a fart joke, a society that tried to put a TV star in jail for jacking off at an adult film. American needs to foster panics like the ones over "Louie" and Pee Wee from time to time in order to have a way of releasing the tensions caused by so many self-consciously tightened sphincters, artificially dehydrated vulvas, and willfully suppressed erections. In a culture that interprets puberty as a tragedy of lost innocence rather than as a triumphal entry into adulthood, the possibility of someone actually giving vent to sexual feeling remains deliciously scandalous. Sex is bad, and somebody singing about it would be *really* bad.

So the story circulated that if you listened to "Louie Louie"

with a knowing ear, you'd hear the Kingsmen describe debauch-
ery and bliss. And if you couldn't hear those dirty words even
after all that toil, you might be handed—as I was sometime in
1964 or 1965—a copy of the *real* lyrics at the back of the school
bus. A copy that you then went home and tried to hide from your
mother's prying eyes and then proceeded to lose, so that years
later you couldn't remember more than a fragment or two: "She
had a rag on, I moved above," "I stuck my boner in her hair."

Indeed, it may be fairly said that the only genuinely useful
purpose to which the FBI put America's tax dollars in the "Louie
Louie" investigation was in accumulating variant versions of
these supposed dirty words. The most common set, collected by
the FBI in Tampa, Florida, in 1964, went like this:

CHORUS: Oh, Louie, Louie, oh, no
               Get her way down low
               Oh, Louie, Louie, oh, baby
               Get her down low
               A fine little girl a-waiting for me
               She's just a girl across the way
               Well I'll take her and park all alone
               She's never a girl I'd lay at home.

(CHORUS REPEAT)

               At night at ten I lay her again
               Fuck you, girl, Oh, all the way
               Oh, my bed and I lay her there
               I meet a rose in her hair

(CHORUS REPEAT)

               Okay, let's give it to them, right now!

               She's got a rag on I'll move above
               It won't be long she'll slip it off
               I'll take her in my arms again
               I'll tell her I'll never leave again

(CHORUS REPEAT)

               Get that broad out of here!

Like the folk song collectors who prided themselves on compiling variant texts of the ancient Appalachian ballads, the Bu-

reau also dug up a couple of variant Dirty "Louie"s. The crudest wasn't even set out in the style of verse, just slammed down, word-after-word with all the dispassion of the most perfunctory porn. Or maybe it had been scribbled furtively in some junior high hallway, with the thought that the authorities were hot on its trail:

> Fine little girl waits for me get your thrills across the way
> girl I dream about is all alone she never could get away from home
> Every night and day I play with my thing I fuck your girl all kinds of ways. In all night now meet me there I feel her low I give her hell
> Hey youth bitch. Hey lovemaker now hold my bone, it won't take long so leave it alone. Hey Señorita I'm hot as hell I told her I'd never lay her again.

Then there's the one the circulated in Detroit during the song's 1965–66 revival there (the one I got on the bus, I think):

CHORUS: Lou-ii Lou-ii Oh, no. Grab her way down low.

(REPEAT)

> There is a fine little girl waiting for me
> She is just a girl across the way
> When I take her all alone
> She's never the girl I lay at home.

(CHORUS)

> Tonight at ten I'll lay her again
> We'll fuck your girl and by the way
> And . . . on that chair I'll lay her there.
> I felt my bone . . . ah . . . in her hair.

(CHORUS)

> She had a rag on, I moved above.
> It won't be long she'll slip it off.
> I held her in my arms and then
> And I told her I'd rather lay her again.

(CHORUS)

"Louie Louie" survived despite as much as because of the spell cast by the "dirty lyrics" legend. Exactly why either song or rumor persisted remains indecipherable. Surely no one—not Richard Berry nor Rene Touzet, not Max Feirtag nor Lynn Easton, not Buck Ormsby nor Ron Holden nor Mark Lindsay nor Rockin' Robin Roberts (God rest his rockin' soul), nor any man whose lips have ever shaped a "Let's give it to 'em, right now!" or fingers pounded out a *duh duh duh. duh duh,* and *certainly* not poor Jack Ely—could resolve any of "Louie" 's central mysteries, even if chained to a radiator and grilled for bread-and-water weeks with rubber truncheons and 300-watt bulbs angled square in the eyes, while a tape loop of Amy Grant singing the best of 2 Live Crew played ceaselessly in the background.

What *can* be deciphered are some facts: For instance, the approximate date when all this furor started. That would be about November 1963, when the Kingsmen's record began treating the *Billboard* charts the way King Kong dealt with the Empire State Building. The G-men learned of it belatedly. The earliest reference to "Louie" in the FBI file is contained in a March 27, 1964, memo from Indianapolis. This memo reports an unnamed local woman saying that "about November, 1963, she purchased a record under Wand label at Blanchard's, a record shop in Crown Point, Indiana. . . . Record was publicly displayed, was routinely priced, and was not suspected of being obscene when purchased.

"Sometime after buying the record, [blacked out] heard from various acquaintances the record had obscene lyrics if the 'Louie Louie' side were played at a speed of 33⅓ instead of the normal 45 rpm. About 1/29/64, a co-worker gave [blacked out] a typed sheet of lyrics, which were allegedly transcribed from the record when played in this manner, and which appear obscene.

"She said the record was widely played in the area and was once ranked first on the WLS Radio (Chicago) record survey.

"She said she played the record in the manner described above and the lyrics seem to follow very closely to the words on the typewritten sheet. She said the typed page was a transcription by some unknown person in Crown Point area and was not furnished with the record." The SAC also sent along her transcript of the dirty lyrics (the first set above) and asked the FBI lab to determine their authenticity by comparing them with the disc. The memo further reported that on March 25, Assistant U.S. Attorney (AUSA) Lester R. Irvin of Hammond, Indiana, asked the FBI to see if the record violated U.S. Code Section 1465, Title 18, the ITOM law. Irvin said that if Hoover's boys found the obscenity, he'd jail the perpetrators.

So the FBI lab made its initial "unintelligible" analysis. What did not follow, at least as far as can be determined from the released files, was what you'd expect: an interrogation of the woman who made the complaint, the co-worker who gave her the dirty lyrics, whoever gave them to the co-worker and on back to the source of the story. Instead of investigating the *story*, the Bureau took the tale at face value and set about investigating the *music*, with the object of making it criminal.

The Kingsmen's "Louie" held in the *Billboard* Top 10 from December 7 (when it made its virtually unprecedented jump from #23 to #4) into January, when it peaked at #2. (Although the record did make #1 in the industry's other trade paper, *Cash Box*, it's the *Billboard* ranking that's definitive.) Along the way, "Louie" outstripped such enduring wonders of the recording arts as Rufus Thomas's "Walking the Dog," "I'm Leaving It Up to You" by Dale and Grace, and the Beach Boys' so-jive-it's-cool "Be True to Your School." But our boy "Louie" was kept out of *Billboard's* top spot by—ring in another offbeat chorus of *duh duh duh. duh duh* 'cause there ain't a writer in the world with the guts to make this up—"Dominique" by the Singing Nun (Soeur Sourire a/k/a/ Sister Luc-Gabrielle), singing, in French, the praises of her Dominican order.

Now, nobody operating in their right mind, the record business or even *Billboard's* employ, ever believed that "Dominique" was more popular than "Louie Louie." In both the short and long run, "Louie" far outsold "Dominique" or any other record on the chart at the end of 1963. But "Dominique," quintessential elephant trash, was a #1 record, and "Louie Louie," archetype of termite trash, wasn't—because *Billboard's* Hot 100 chart measured not popularity or record sales but a combination of sales, airplay and proper decorum (and perhaps the amount of any given record label's advertising budget devoted to *Billboard*) as determined by a mystical formula comprehended by fewer mortals than grasp the essence of "Do wah diddy." So "Louie" and such Top 10 cohorts as the Murmaids' "Popsicles and Icicles" were cast into outer darkness while Soeur Sourire reigned.

Even if "Louie" was cheated without a glimmer of Christian conscience out of its rightful rank at the top of a chart that everybody outside the music business believed reflected record sales and not mumbo-jumbo, the Kingsmen enjoyed a good long run in the Top 10. Whether that run was stimulated or deterred by the dirty lyrics rumors is hard to figure out. Although "Louie Louie" fell to #3 on the year-end chart, by January 4 it was back to #2, probably because the rumors began to pick up speed. But such innuendo impedes radio airplay and demolishes decorum, the most intangible elements in the Hot 100 formula (ad lineage can be counted). Anyway, when "Dominique" finally faded on January 11, the record that cashed in the chips for the top was Bobby Vinton's cornball "There, I've Said It Again."

Vinton remained at #1 through January 25, with the Kingsmen breathing down his Mr. B collar, but slamming into third place was another foreign disc: the Beatles' "I Want to Hold Your Hand." (At #4, curiously enough, was the venerated termite classic, "Surfing Bird" by the Trashmen, a record that makes "I Want to Hold Your Hand" sound like "Dominique.") By February 1, 1964, the Beatles had conquered *Billboard*'s top slot and that was it for your basic American termite for a good, long spell.

"Louie" remained in the Top 30 through the end of February, but it dropped off the chart the first week in March, stifled by more than just John, Paul, George, and Ringo.

"Indiana Gov. Puts Down 'Pornographic' Wand Tune," yowled a page-three headline in the February 1 *Billboard*. "Say Kids Blew the Whistle." " 'Louie Louie' has been fingered by Indiana's first citizen, Gov. Matthew Welsh, as being 'pornographic,' " wrote Gil Faggen. After Welsh heard the record, he "told people his 'ears tingled.' " Welsh then promptly fired off a request to Reid Chapman, president of the Indiana Broadcasters Association, requesting that the record be banned from all radio stations in the state, and Chapman, vice-president of WANE

AM-TV, Fort Wayne, dutifully passed Welsh's request on to his membership."

"My position with respect to the whole matter was never that the record should be banned. At no time did I ever pressure anybody to take the song off the air," Welsh, a Democrat, told me in 1991. "I suggested to him [Chapman] that it might be simpler all around if it wasn't played." He contacted Chapman, Welsh says, because he "was a friend of mind. I knew him; we weren't close." Chapman listened and began investigating.

Welsh clearly feels frustrated that "Louie Louie" is all he's remembered for: "I thought the whole thing was a tempest in a teapot, and not worth any extended pursuit. I have no interest in it either way." He says he never banned the record, just suggested it not be played. But it doesn't take a First Amendment scholar to see the contradiction. If a record isn't played at the suggestion of the state's chief executive, it has been banned.

Welsh no longer recalls how he first learned about the purported rock'n'roll filth. Faggen wrote that "a high school student from Frankfort, Indiana, was first to send the Governor a copy of the allegedly pornographic recording. College students from Miami University in Athens, Ohio, followed suit by providing Welsh with copies of printed 'obscene lyrics.' " There's no telling if these words were the same or different from the ones in the FBI's files, or why students in Ohio decided to rat out "Louie" in Indiana. Although Welsh's action soon became notorious among rock fans, he says that the FBI never contacted him.

It wouldn't have helped. *Billboard* reported that, despite Welsh's tingle, "attempts by WOWO [Indianapolis] and other stations to capture the lyrics from the Wand waxing was neigh impossible because of the allegedly unintelligible rendition. . . ."

Scepter/Wand Records told Faggen, "Not in anyone's wildest imagination are the lyrics as presented on the Wand recording in any way suggestive, let alone obscene." "The feeling at the diskery," the story added, "is that a bootleg version may be the culprit. It also seems likely that some shrewd press agentry may also be playing an important role in this teapot tempest. Exactly whose press agent is hard to pin down at this point."

Probably not Scepter/Wand's, since the label was too small and unsophisticated to do much more than run to keep up with sales demand. Though Schlachter gleefully confesses to cashing in "when this whole thing started to mushroom," in a thirty-five-year music industry career, Marv Schlachter's specialty has never been orchestrating such exploitation, and if it was a put-up job, the "Louie" scam wasn't conducted by an amateur.

If not Scepter/Wand, certainly not Limax, which would probably have loved to have sold additional copies of "Louie Louie" sheet music except that none of the words that tingled the governor and the kid in Frankfort and the frat boys at Miami of Ohio appeared in the sheet music, so nobody bought it. Instead of rubbing his hands with glee at the prospect of windfall profit, Max Feirtag reacted like a man whose integrity had been impugned.

" 'Louie' Publishers Say Tune Not Dirty at All," read the page-four headline in the February 8 *Billboard*. "Publishers of 'Louie Louie' have fired off a letter to Reid Chapman, president of the Indiana Broadcasters Association, claiming that the lyrics on the record are not 'pornographic' as claimed last week by Indiana Gov. Matthew Welsh." The letter asked that Chapman inform Indiana stations "of the true situation so that they may feel free to continue spinning the disk."

"Publisher Max Feirtag told Billboard he would award a check for $1,000 to anyone finding anything suggestive in the lyrics as recorded by the Kingsmen on Wand Records," said the unbylined article. "Feirtag's attorneys state that another set of lyrics is in circulation, which they think is being used to interpret the unintelligible renditions on all the disks covering the tune. Feirtag said he had been informed copies of the lyrics have been found around Louisiana State University."

Feirtag knew about LSU because of Vern Stierman, of KEEL in Shreveport, Louisiana. In defense of "Louie," KEEL aired an editorial, read by Stierman, on February 5 and 6 that said, in part: "We can censor the material we put on the air, but we cannot censor the minds of people. Little minds think little thoughts and, unfortunately, dirty minds think dirty thoughts. Which leads me to the currently popular record, 'Louie Louie.'

"Someone, somewhere, with an obscene imagination decided to write lyrics that in his opinion sounded like the sounds on the recording by the Kingsmen. Then he took it upon himself to object to the lyrics, which didn't exist until he wrote them. He sent these lyrics with the record to the Governor of Indiana. This story was relayed across the country by the news services, and little minds all over began to write their own lyrics to the song . . . lyrics which do not exist on the recording of 'Louie Louie' by the Kingsmen. These are the actual lyrics. Not Shakespeare, admittedly, but not obscene by any stretch of the imagination." The station manager then read them.

Obviously, the guy just didn't get it.

Several bureaucracies now ground into action. The Marion County, Indiana, prosecutor's chief trial deputy, Leroy K. New, looked into "Louie" and said, "The record is an abomination of out-of-tune guitars, an overbearing jungle rhythm and clanging cymbals." But even Leroy New didn't think that the *words* were obscene, and the ITOM law just didn't reckon with dirty *sounds*.

On January 28, Wand received a semi-threatening letter from the National Association of Broadcasters (NAB). "NAB's Code Authority has received a number of inquiries and complaints from member stations on the recording 'Louie, Louie' being circulated with a Wand label," it read. *"Here are the facts* as we understand them:

"The Code staff has listened to the record on all standard RPMs and has found nothing objectionable in it. In the Code staff's opinion, the lines, delivered in rock and roll and calypso style, would be unintelligible to the average listener.

"NAB has received from the music publishers copies of the lyrics and has found nothing objectionable in them. However, it also has received from another source a purported set of lyrics which are unfit for broadcast.

"The phonetic qualities of this recording are such that a listener possessing the 'phony' lyrics could imagine them to be genuine."

On February 12, United Press International reported: "The Government has dropped investigations it had been conducting into complaints that a popular rock-and-roll record has obscene lyrics. . . . Investigations of the record were started by the Federal Communications Commission (FCC), the Post Office, and Justice Department after complaints were received from about a half-dozen persons, including Indiana Governor Matthew K. Welsh.

"All three governmental agencies dropped their investigations because they were unable to determine what the lyrics of the song were, even after listening to the records at speeds ranging from 16 rpm to 78 rpm." But this story, perhaps another source of the "unintelligible at any speed" factoid, was far off base. If the Post Office conducted an investigation, it left no paper trail. The FBI, which is a branch of the Justice Department, would still be looking into "Louie" two and a half years later. And the FCC continued its inquiry the very next day.

The FCC had no jurisdiction over the record business, and the Commission is forbidden to practice censorship by the law that created it. Nevertheless: "The Commission has received complaints to the effect that certain radio stations have, by playing one of your records titled 'Louie Louie,' featuring The Kingsmen, violated the federal statute which prohibits the broadcast of obscene, indecent, or profane language," wrote the FCC's Ben F. Waple to Wand on February 13.

"The staff has conducted an inquiry into these complaints. Before terminating its inquiry the Commission would appreciate receiving, as promptly as possible, your comments on this matter, including any information in your possession which might throw light upon either the source or the validity of allegations that the lyrics as sung by the Kingsmen were in any way obscene. We also should appreciate your comment whether, even though unobjectionable lyrics were used in recording the song, there was improper motivation on the part of the singers or anyone associated with the production of the record in making the recorded lyrics so unintelligible as to give rise to reports that they were obscene."

On Valentine's Day, the record company also heard by phone from a Mr. Raye of the FCC by phone. Wand wrote him back the next day, sending along two copies of the record and two copies of the official "Louie" lyrics, and giving the record company's side of the story. Wand vowed that "all the people connected with the making and the sales of this record . . . wish to bring to justice anyone connected with the dissemination of libelous information," even offering to play the basic track from which the record had been made for any agents the Commission wanted to send by. Wand's letter also states that "our sales figures do not indicate any infringement by any outside source," meaning that, despite what *Billboard* was told, the company had no evidence of any bootlegging.

But the FBI stayed on the case like hound dogs snoopin' round a door.

> File #145-2961 (Tampa)
> SAC Tampa to FBI lab 2/17/64
> Subject: UNKNOWN SUBJECT
> PHONOGRAPH RECORD
> "LOUIE LOUIE" DISTRIBUTED
> BY LIMAX MUSIC, N.Y.C., N.Y.
> ITOM
>
> Transmitted herewith are the following items for examination by the FBI Laboratory:
>
> Lyrics of "Louie Louie" as published by Limax Music
> Record "Louie Louie" (under obscene cover)
> Reported obscene lyrics for "Louie Louie." (Under obscene cover)
>
> On 2/10/64 [long black out] advised SA [blacked out] his department received complaint from [long black out] advising that captioned record is very popular with the high school students, and he has been furnished lyrics for the song which are very obscene.
>
> [blacked out] he determined that this record is very popular, is a best seller in the area, and is played by the local radio stations. He said the record is a calypso-type song, and the words are hard to recognize. However, with a copy of the obscene words to refer to, it sounds like the lyrics are identical with the enclosed obscene lyrics.
>
> [longest black out of all] furnished what Limax Music Company claims to be the actual lyrics of the song, which is Enclosure #1. However, [blacked out] said the lyrics of the song do not seem to be the same.
>
> Laboratory is requested to determine if enclosed record, "Louie Louie," can be considered obscene for purposes of prosecution under ITOM statute.

Over the next thirty months, such subliterate internal mem-
oranda foamed within the FBI's internal pipelines, eventually
generating close to 250 pages of released material.

What the FBI tried to do is not necessarily so outrageous,
presuming that you're willing to live in a country where the biggest nerd in the eleventh grade is encouraged to seek his revenge
by becoming a government snitch, and where witch-hunts are
conducted against the singers of songs. As performers from Pete
Seeger to Public Enemy can aver, this has been the case in
America for fifty years, though perhaps a patriot would deny it.

The FBI's hunt for the source and substance of the dirty
"Louie" plays out such McCarthyite tragedy as farce. For example, on March 2, 1964, Tampa's Special Agent found his
course blocked because "the 'Louie Louie' record is no longer
popular in the Sarasota area and apparently . . . the obscene
lyrics . . . are no longer being distributed or even discussed."

But the Special Agent can't drop the case just because it's
now irrelevant to ninth-graders. He can't even recognize the evidence that these kids have survived their knowledge of the filthy
excesses contained in the lewd "Louie." Not even if he wants to.
Because two days later, a faculty snitch from another school "obtained a handwritten copy of the obscene lyrics from one of his
students who came to him voluntarily, saying he had found the
lyrics on school property. [Mr. Faculty Quisling] said his inquiry
then determined that the obscene lyrics were 'all over the
school.' " The educator/fink reported that his students believed
the dirty lyrics came from "a college somewhere." But even he
admitted interest in them was dying out. Then in April, yet another Sarasota teacher/rat surfaced. This new snitch told the
G-man, "The obscene portions of the written lyrics corre-
sponded to the slurred portion of the record," a pretty wild eval-
uation, since you'd have to be stone deaf not to notice that there
is no part of Jack Ely's "Louie" vocal that *isn't* slurred.

Preoccupied as it must have been with purifying America by
trying to foil the civil rights movement, the Bureau continued its
stumbling pursuit of rock'n'roll smut. Before the end of March,
as San Diego joined the list of FBI offices investigating the subversive platter, an agent contacted Richard Berry.

Berry went to the FBI office in downtown L.A., where he was

told the Bureau was handling the case because the lyrics had crossed state lines. "They said, 'Well, you know, you could go to jail,' " Richard told me. "I said, 'For *what?*' 'Cause we went down with the sheet music that the Kingsmen had. When the Kingsmen came out with the record, that's when the first sheet music came out, and everything was on the sheet. I always knew that nobody could take your song and turn it around. You know, you just can't do that." Berry had little else to tell, since his only current association with the song was his semiannual BMI check.

The FBI files don't include detailed transcripts of interrogations, so there's no telling who else was threatened in this noble pursuit of justice. But after a letter to Hammond, Indiana, AUSA Irvin in May, the Bureau's "Louie" file lapses, without any record (up to this point) of discussions with, for instance, Feirtag, Dennon, Chase, the Kingsmen, or Wand, let alone Rockin' Robin Roberts or any other significant auxiliaries. Maybe the G-men were sloppy, maybe the Bureau's still suppressing a couple tons of documents, but as it stands, the G-men's "Louie" research would barely merit a C on a ninth-grade term paper.

A year later, when cries of dirty *duh duh duh. duh duh* again registered, this time from the vicinity of Detroit, the Bureau was somewhat more alert to the record biz end of the story, perhaps because the United States had by then been well and truly infested with Beatles and other foreign and domestic long-haired insurrectionaries making what the memos call "rockin' roll."

At the end of March 1965, just as sap began its annual rise in all creatures, AUSA Robert J. Grace of Detroit set up a meeting in his office with the FBI, the FCC, and two complaining parents from suburban Farmington, Michigan. Mom and Pop brought along the Kingsmen's "Louie Louie." "They stated that this record has become very popular over the radio stations which cater to the teenage 'rockin' roll' fans in the greater Detroit area," the Detroit SAC wrote to his D.C. bosses (the Kingsmen's "Louie" enjoyed an annual springtime revival in several cities throughout the mid-Sixties). The couple also brought along the dirty words, the Bureau's "Detroit version."

The very next day, as the pull of the sap grew stronger, another educator cried out from an unnamed Michigan school.

This time, the offending lyrics had been confiscated from a student. (So established was the investigation becoming that the Detroit SAC now referred, with politesse acquired by drawing up sealed indictments, to "Louis Louis.")

AUSA Grace went ahead on his own and contacted radio station WKNR in suburban Dearborn. Wand wired WKNR the real lyrics, and WKNR passed them to Grace. The Detroit FBI's report concluded by reproducing that innocuous barroom saga, followed by a single comment: "It is noted that when this record was played in the Assistant United States Attorney's Office on 3/30/65, it was difficult to get all the words in this song."

Putting its portion of tax revenues to work most scrupulously and effectively, FBI headquarters a fortnight later sent its Motor City representative the whole file—everything that had been generated in the Florida, Indiana, and California investigations—with the note: "For your information, the Department of Justice has previously received a copy of the record 'Louie Louie.' . . . The Department advised that they were unable to interpret any of the wording in the record and, therefore, could not make a decision concerning the matter."

Here is the FBI at its most brilliant: We don't know what we're dealing with and it seems to be gibberish, but that gibberish must be presumed guilty until all rampantly paranoid parents and teachers stop believing the fantasies of teenagers suffering from hormonal overload.

As late as May 25, 1965, the Detroit FBI office was trying to get its N.Y. brethren to sweat a confession out of Scepter/Wand. On June 18, Motown's criminological geniuses sent the FBI lab yet *another* copy of the Kingsmen's "Louie," as if intelligibility might vary from specimen to specimen, with the notation: "The lyrics contain obscene language." They did?

Well, maybe the virus of *duh duh duh. duh duh* had infested the FBI all the way up the chain of command, because no supervisor ever told the obsessive Detroit troops: "This is a gigantic waste of time. Knock it off immediately. Bring me a commie." So by the laws of Instant Karma, within two years the Detroit SAC had to contend with an actual Communist rock band, the infamous MC5 and its notorious teenage White Panther fans, a legion devoted to the political platform succinctly summarized as "Rock'n'roll, dope, and fucking in the streets." Needless to say, the MC5's repertoire featured "Louie Louie."

Meantime, the "Louie" folk-devil persevered, Motor City radio stations kept spinning the disc, each year's new ranks of high schoolers circulated the "real" words, and parents who'd seen too many episodes of "I Led Three Lives" kept calling the cops. The June 1965 complaint came from Warren, a tank-manufacturing suburb. The Warren source may have been subject to auditory hallucinations, since, according to the FBI memo, he told AUSA Finn that "the language in the record is clear and undoubtedly obscene." *Me see Jamaica, moon above?*

It was only now that FBI agents finally visited Wand Records, a call they paid on May 19, 1965. Marv Schlachter remembered the visit only vaguely. "There's no question that there was contact," he told me. "But I don't think any of us ever had any feeling that we were part of any conspiracy or anything that would put us out of business." Certainly, he seemed more bemused, amused, and amazed than frightened or worried about the course his little Worst Record of the Week had taken. "There were a number of times when, in effect, the record was banned. Every time that happened, we would re-release the record and sell another million," he told me. (Actually, even though estimates range as high as twelve million copies sold, Schlachter told me that "Louie Louie" initially sold between two and three million copies, which is more consistent with the mid-sixties record market.)

Beginning in June, 1965, J. Edgar Hoover personally received a letter from a "concerned citizen" in Flint, Michigan.

"As a member of the [blacked out] dedicated in the fight against pornography," it read in part, "this is how we . . . became involved in a war of legal semantics. It all began this winter when a group of vocalists called the 'Kingsmen' appeared at a local hall. They played their million-dollar record, 'Louie Louie.' In a matter of weeks the record was selling like hot cakes and rising on the 'Top 40 Show.' We became aware of the dual set of lyrics and that, without a doubt, someone had masterminded an 'auditory illusion.' Our prosecuting attorney with whom we consulted said, in his opinion, there was nothing legally that can be done, since he believed you cannot prove which set of lyrics they are singing. This seemed rather irrelevant since they were capitalizing on its obscenity, and when every teenager in the country 'heard' the obscene not the copywritten lyric.

"Our attempts to have something done about the record were met with frustration. But that is all prologue. We realize the damage is done and the 'Louie Louie' purveyors are getting away with setting a new precedence [sic]. That along with the movies, the magazines, the paperbacks—our kids will now be hit with a fourth front: records.

"We have also been in contact with Mr. Lawrence Gubow, U.S. Attorney in Detroit, and he informed us that your bureau was investigating the record in question. He wasn't too explicit, however. *Can you tell us what is being done? What can we do to help?* Mr. Hoover, do you think more of these type records are inevitable? Is there perhaps a subliminal type of perversion involved?

"In Mr. Gubow's answer to us, he stated that in order for matter to be declared obscene, it must be 'objectively obscene.' I am confused. How can anything be objectively obscene? Obscenity is not indifferent, but has definite goals. It is not impersonal and unemotional. How can it possibly be? By its very nature, obscenity is *subjective*."

There was more, but the nub of it concerned the means whereby the Flint patriots could do their bit for The Greatest Country on Earth, and an inquiry as to whether that goal might be aided by distributing an "obscenity questionnaire" to highschoolers.

More efficient or simply better staffed than his underlings, Hoover wrote back just a week later. "I strongly believe that the easy accessibility of such material cannot help but divert the minds of young people into unhealthy channels and negate the wholesome training they have already been afforded by their parents," declaimed Clyde Tolson's roommate. "With reference to the record you described, I am unable to make any comment concerning current investigations being conducted by the FBI. You may be assured, however, that this Bureau is continuing to make every effort to discharge its responsibilities with the highest degree of thoroughness and dispatch."

A "Backnote," not mailed, on the next page, exhibits Hoover's paranoia in its pure form: "Correspondent is not identifiable in Bufiles. The record 'Louie Louie' is subject of investigation under character of Interstate Transportation of Obscene Matter. Bufiles 145-2961 and 145-2972 contain complaints from numerous individuals, including [blacked out (maybe Lady Bird Johnson had overheard a dangerous *duh duh duh* . . . coming out of Lynda Bird's room at the White House?)] regarding this record recorded on the Wand label by the Kingsmen. It has copyrighted lyrics but off-color lyrics are being circulated. . . ."

Hoover did send the Flint flake copies of the Bureau's pamphlets "Poison for Our Youth" and "Combating Merchants of Filth: The Role of the FBI."

Still, *duh duh duh. duh duh* throbbed throughout the land. So, on July 12, the Detroit FBI asked its brethren in New York to stop by Wand Records and listen to the Kingsmen master, with special attention to its vocal track. Brother agents in Seattle were asked to track down Jerry Dennon at the Craig Corporation in Seattle regarding the circumstances of the misbegetting of "Louie," while the Bureau brethren congregated within the perdition of Los Angeles were sent to track down Richard Berry and Limax Music.

The Detroit office operated at the request of AUSA Grace, who proceeded at the behest of Assistant Attorney General Fred M. Vinson, Jr., who headed the Criminal Division of the Justice Department. Perhaps Vinson had finally come to the limit of his patience, but he was also responding to "congressional inquiries" (although no congressional contacts are specified—maybe the intensified investigation was sparked by blasting "Me gotta go!" from the family hi-fi?). Grace told the Detroit agents that Vinson wanted "to bring the case to a logical conclusion," which shows that even Vinson didn't quite get it, since nothing about "Louie Louie" had ever been colored with the faintest tinge of logic and the story certainly never had the slightest chance of being wrapped up on such a note. So off they went, in ones and twos, each agent bravely pursuing the facts and nothing but.

The importance of accomplishing this task was emphasized when his fan from Flint once more wrote Hoover on July 14, partly to report that she'd done some homework, comparing a tape of Wand 143 played at "somewhere between 45 and 33⅓" with the Kingsmen's June 22 appearance on *Shindig* in which "by no stretch of the imagination is the obscene lyric audible," but mainly to inquire what J. Edgar thought about the high school obscenity questionnaire, a question evaded in his reply to her first letter, and to ask for fifty copies each of the Bureau's anti-porn pamphlets to distribute to Flint's porn-endangered young persons.

Notwithstanding the fact that his Flint follower had now exhibited more prosecutive zeal and sounder investigatory method than any of his field staff (or maybe because she seemed a little *too* good at this, which may have suggested to his ever-ripe fear mechanism that she could be a KGB plant), Hoover's response was to generate a Bureau report on her subversive potential. This investigation netting nothing indictable, Hoover wrote back on July 27, dismissing the idea of the FBI getting involved in the questionnaire and sending twenty-five copies each of "Poison for Our Youth" and "Combating Merchants of Filth: The Role of the FBI," because the Bureau *could not afford* the bundles of fifty requested.

It took the New York agents until August 23 to reach Wand, where, without a court order, Florence Greenberg handed over a copy of the Kingsmen's master tape. (She refused to give up the more valuable original tape without a subpoena, perhaps fearing an FBI bootlegging scam.) To their disappointment, the agents learned that Wand had only a one-track master, so there was no separate vocal track to listen to. (If there had been, the agents wouldn't have been there because Ely's giraffe-neck gabble could have been mixed clearly.)

The FBI lab got the copy of Wand's master on September 16 and compared it to the sample disc sent from Detroit. "[N]o audible differences were noted." On September 22, the Bureau generated a lengthy memo summarizing the entire history of "Louie" from Berry's composition (without any mention of Rene Touzet) to the Kingsmen's recording (without any mention of Jack Ely).

The Bureau inched onward, talking with Berry again (he sounded aggrieved mainly that his friends were teasing him about having written a porno tune), and around September 12, someone who seems, from his familiarity with details about the copyright number (E Eu 471125), Flip, Limax, various cover versions, and the situation in Shreveport, to be Max Feirtag (although Feirtag told me in 1991 that he'd never been interviewed by the FBI). Feirtag, if it was he, also helped Hoover's blockheads understand what should have been obvious from the start: "Playing a record at a slower speed would slow the music and speaking pattern down to such an extent that it would be very difficult to understand."

The Kingsmen got the third degree, one after another, on September 7, 1965. With only the most minor variations, they all told the same story: "There was no deliberate attempt to include any obscenity in the recording and . . . only those who want to hear such things can read it into the vocal."

A more detailed account was obtained from one band member; a good guess would be Lynn Easton or Mike Mitchell. This interview confirms that the Kingsmen "Louie" "was quickly recorded with one or two run-throughs and no change in the standard lyrics." It also recounted how the Kingsmen learned of their dirty lyrics:

"Around January 15, 1964, the 'Kingsmen' received an inquiry from one of the wire services concerning the suggested obscene wording and were told that the Governor of Indiana had banned the playing of the record on the air or in any public performance. A month or so before an individual unknown to them put through a call to a hotel where they were staying and said he had detected obscenity when the record was played at a rate of 33⅓ rpm rather than the 45 rpm for which it was intended.

"He said they considered this caller had a dirty mind, particularly since anything spoken at the lesser rpm could not have been recorded for that speed and would be accidental. . . .

"He said there are unintelligible words or sounds in their vocal where those who want to apparently find the obscenity, but these were honest vocal effects without thought of intended obscenity and that neither [blacked out] can hear the suggested obscenity today. He said the result of the action taken by the Governor of Indiana, and similar publicity, has been to spur sales of the record but [long black out—two-and-a-half lines]. The record sold well initially and then fell off until the obscene wording rumor spread when sales again soared. The record to date has sold about 2,000,000 copies."

This Kingsman also pointed out an interesting quirk of the "Louie Louie" myth: the belief that the dirty lyrics could be heard only on the 45 version, but not on the LP. In fact, the two versions were made from the very same master recording.

On November 30, 1965, the Raiders finally talked to the cops, saying, "With this type of rock'n'roll music, a listener might think he heard anything being said that he imagined."

After that, the whole mess got tossed into the lap of AUSA Grace in Detroit, who "advised that in his opinion the investigation of instant matter disclosed no evidence of a ITOM violation and that he was, therefore, recommending that no further investigation be conducted."

Only then, two years and uncounted tax dollars after it began, did the Bureau's pursuit of the filthy "Louie Louie" cease. The file sounds a final, almost mournful note in an October 10, 1966, memo from the FBI lab to the NY SAC, returning the tape and lyrics sheet obtained from Wand: "You should be guided by the opinion of the United States Attorney in determining whether this material should be returned to [blacked out] Wand Management Corporation, 254 W. 54th Street, New York City."

No one recalls whether the Bureau's New York agents gave it to them right then or not.

11

The "Louie" Generation

Now it came to pass in the fullness of time that "Louie Louie" begat all that was Mod within British beat. "You Really Got Me," "I Can't Explain," "All Day and All of the Night," "My Generation," all these "Louie Louie" begat. And "My Generation" in unwed union with frat rock begat "Wild Thing," "Gloria," "She's About a Mover," "Wooly Bully," "Double Shot (of My Baby's Love)"—yea, even unto "Purple Haze" did it beget the unholy ructions of rock'n'roll.

And "Purple Haze" begat many deformed spawn, even "Kick Out the Jams." And "Kick Out the Jams" begat "I Wanna Be Your Dog." And "Kick Out the Jams" and "I Wanna Be Your Dog" begat the New York Dolls. And the New York Dolls begat the Ramones, and the Ramones and the New York Dolls begat the Sex Pistols of "Anarchy in the U.K." and the Clash of "Clash City Rockers." And in those days punks walked in the earth.

Verily, I tell you truly, amidst a legion of termites gnawing away at expectations, the Noise raved on.

— The Gospel of Alan Freed, Ch. VI V. 9–11

To the extent that the innocent, teenage American-malt-shop rock'n'roll portrayed on "Ozzie and Harriet" and "Happy Days" ever existed, "Louie Louie" was both its purest product and the engine of its demolition. It was inconceivable that its good-bad-but-not-evil legend could have erupted at any other time in the still-fresh history of rock'n'roll except at the instant when the scene was about to be exploded by British torpedos. But without "Louie," as music and as folk-devil, the arrival of the Beatles and the crashing realization that rock'n'roll really *was* here to stay would not have seemed so fraught with danger. Although the role is usually assigned to the assassination of John Kennedy, it was really "Louie Louie" that prepared the way for the disruptive brilliance of "She Loves You" and "I Want to Hold Your Hand."

Yet "Louie Louie" in all its undeniable raucousness and dubious raunchiness was also the way itself. With "Louie Louie" rock'n'roll history began a cycle that would repeat itself, only with the farce preceding the tragedy.

So the Kingsmen's "Louie Louie" is both the end of an era — an era defined by Richard Berry and the Rillera brothers and Rockin' Robin Roberts and Buck Ormsby and their brethren — and the beginning of an era — an era characterized by both Lynn Easton's unceremonious dumping of his fellow band members and by any teenager's delight in getting the joke the G-men and vice-principals missed.

The wreckage of that innocence is on frozen display in a video of a Kingsmen appearance on the old ABC TV series, "Shindig." Programmed purely according to network standards and practices, without the faintest taint of *intentional* scandal or rebellion, "Shindig" was nevertheless the most subversive show on TV for the two seasons (1964–1965 and 1965–1966) that it lasted, simply because it so often presented so much music with so much anarchic energy.

"Shindig" began with its audience at full shriek and continued that way for a whole half hour, even if the guest host was an old-time show biz has-been like Hedy Lamarr (who hosted the show the Kingsmen did in October 1965). To see a band like the Sir Douglas Quintet, with Doug Sahm and Augie Meyer already trailing hair down past their shoulders when the Rolling Stones still thought twice about concealing their ears; to see Doug Sahm himself bouncing around like the personification of the startle reflex; to watch Jackie Wilson assault the TV audience as if he were in the throes of godly possession; to see all this not in some

Music-TV ghetto but in the heart of network prime time, was to glimpse a hint of the kind of culture that TV ordinarily erases.

The Kingsmen came to "Shindig" with the one song that best bespoke such inchoate insurrection and nevertheless flopped. A great band might have taken the success of "Louie Louie" as a commandment to continue to Bring the Noise. But the Kingsmen were not a great band, and they pursued only the song's puerile notoriety, its cachet as a junior high rumor, and it made them no more dangerous than Smurfs. Dressed in black slacks and waist-length white jackets lacking both collars and lapels, they looked and sounded like they'd become a house band on a cruise ship—for that matter, as if they were grateful to have the job. Big-boned Lynn Easton held his mike straight up as if it were a drumstick that he was unsure whether to bang or gobble; wearing a newsboy cap that suggested a yacht and not Bob Dylan, he looked like a Dutch boy in search of a dike to plug, and he couldn't have moved less gracefully if he'd been wearing Hans Brinker's silver skates. In the close-ups, Eddie Haskell also comes to mind; Lynn Easton gives us the first "Louie" with a smirk.

On "Shindig," the Kingsmen exposed themselves as a novelty act, smarty-pants frat boys with no more imagination than Doug Clark and His Hot Nuts and less brazen courage than 2 Live Crew. They seem much more in their element in the advertisement in *Billboard*'s 1966 college special, or on the cover of their album *The Kingsmen on Campus*, where they appear as the Lettermen reprogrammed with a quick wink and a lewd, protuberant tongue. The Kingsmen had become an irrelevancy, ready to pass into memory, if not history.

"Louie Louie" refused to go along for the ride. Popping up the charts over the next few years came a stream of songs based on one way or another upon Richard Berry's lost masterpiece. Often, as in "Mony Mony" and "Sugar Sugar," such sons of "Louie" used sexual innuendo better than their model. But "Louie" was now most important as a piece of music—Zappa's "stock module"—that dozens of songwriters and musicians called upon in the flash heat of inspiration, a vehicle for gestures with a particular meaning—in "Louie" 's case, most often a joke, though the gag was more often garage-rock subcompetence, or R&B "simplicity" than sniggering sexual innuendo.

The first rewrite of what Zappa calls "the 'Louie' texture" was Richard Berry's own "Have Love, Will Travel," which the Buck Ormsby–produced Sonics did to a brilliant, scorched-throat crisp on 1965's *Here Are the Sonics*. The next "Louie" progeny was sired by the Raiders, with "Louie, Go Home." This putative extension of the "Louie" saga is a pure stage piece, a la the Isley Brothers' "Shout" or Ray Charles's "What'd I Say," although without gospel feeling—Paul Revere and company being worshippers solely of the transcendence that emerges from carnal, comic punch lines. In "Louie, Go Home," Louie does not go to Jamaica or, at least, if he does, we're left with no real reason to infer it because it's really just a chant, albeit with a great last line: "Louie, where have you gone?"

England, obviously.

Because the English delight in the belief that they inhabit the world's most sexually repressive society, their national folk myth about "Louie Louie" inevitably took the form of denial and banishment. More than one British rocker will tell you that the Kingsmen's record was never allowed to be a hit in their fair land, that "Let's give it to 'em, right now!" was too licentious for the early sixties mores of pre-swinging London, let alone the priggish provinces. In the land of its nativity, the governor of Indiana may have expelled "Louie" from his state's airwaves after it was already a hit but, the Brits will smugly assure you, the BBC sanitized the whole nation's airwaves.

Nevertheless, the Kingsmen's "Louie Louie" *was* a U.K. hit. In 1963, *Billboard* tracked British hits by reporting the Top 30 hits in the English music weekly, *New Musical Express (N.M.E.)*. There, "Louie" entered at #29 on February 8, 1964, and bounced around it for more than a month, rising as high as #17, before dropping off the list of March 21. (In the chart published by *Record Mirror*, *N.M.E.*'s competitor, "Louie" reached only #27 in its seven-week stay.)

In a country then besieged by a series of new pop bands (often great ones), this was an excellent showing. There was no hint of a "Louie"-inspired moral panic, the British folk-devil of the moment being the mods, a teen cargo cult, whose members Frank Roddam's film of the Who's *Quadrophenia* quite accurately shows dancing their amphetamined arses off to *duh duh duh. duh duh*

The impact of "Louie Louie" on British musicians was a true termite infestation, far more indelible than chart rankings could have signified, even if the Kingsmen had scored a #1 there. The Kinks and the Who, two of the most important British Invasion bands, blatantly based their best early hits on the *duh duh duh. duh duh* schematic.

The two groups had several things in common, including the arch-artistic pretensions of their respective songwriters and (not undisputed) leaders, Peter Townshend of the Who and Ray Davies of the Kinks. But their most important link was producer Shel Talmy, an expatriate American from Los Angeles. Talmy made records that are among the British Invasion's greatest glories, great trash heaps of barely restrained chaos that sounded hotter, raunchier, and noisier than any other UK-made discs of the time.

Greil Marcus describes the Kinks' version of *duh duh duh. duh duh* as "chopped and channeled," and the hot-rod lingo makes sense, because the tempo was also souped up. "You Really Got Me" isn't necessarily a "Louie" that Richard Berry or Rene Touzet would recognize. Indeed, Ray Davies claims that he came up with the riff after seeing *Jazz on a Summer's Day,* the film about the Monterey Jazz Festival. Yeah, sure—no sixties jazzman this side of Sun Ra would have had the guts to tinker with "Louie Louie" and allow it to be permanently encoded in a film.

What connects "You Really Got Me" to *duh duh duh. duh duh* is its use of gaps and silences, its grouped bursts of the I-IV-V chord sequence, and most of all, the groaning ecstasy and agony with which Ray Davies recounts the hold love has on him while his brother, Dave, bashes his guitar.

The idea that the Kinks borrowed, to put it kindly, from Richard Berry's greatest hit is reinforced by their second stop-time cluster-chord hit of late 1964, "All Day and All of the Night," especially Ray's gabbled "Aw-oh, come *on*" just before Dave's scrambled-Dangel solo, both grifted straight outta the Wailers via the Kingsmen. The Kinks went on to commit "Louie Louie" itself on both their 1965 albums, *Kink-Size* and *Kinkdom*, a year in which they also scored a minor hit with "I Need You," a third slice off Richard Berry's inspiration.

By the following spring their "Louie" revamp had been pinched by the Who, who built around it their first single, "I Can't Explain," albeit with the novel fillip of showcasing Keith Moon's drums as the lead instrument.

Peter Townshend wrote "I Can't Explain" as much like the Kinks as he could, in an effort to capture producer Talmy's attention. But he got a bonus from the ripoff, because "Louie" as riff and rhythm was so extraordinarily flexible. British beat groups could no longer just colonize American R&B. In the wake of the Beatles, rock bands were expected to actually come up with "new" songs, although those songs were still required to stay within the formal bounds of R&B-based rock'n'roll. "Louie Louie," or at least *duh duh duh. duh duh,* became a mighty template for constructing such material.

Just how far you could take the basic "Louie" structure was shown in the Who's third single, which Shel Talmy also produced. "My Generation" sped up *duh duh duh. duh duh* almost beyond recognition (you can hear the theme clearly stated in John Entwistle's bass solo), surrounding it with clattering drums and a stuttered Roger Daltrey vocal that defined varieties of frustration including but not limited to the sexual, the socioeconomic, and the existential. At the end of the record, these pent-up emotions boil over and *duh duh duh. duh duh* literally explodes, then rains back down in Townshend's infamous concluding feedback extravaganza.

Such antics left "Louie" dazed and battered and with no recourse other than to return to the United States, where it was being manhandled more gently, if less creatively.

"Louie Louie" wasn't only a song to rewrite. It had become a song to remake, as near or as far from the Kingsmen or the Wailers or Richard Berry as you dared. In 1964 and 1965 alone, versions of "Louie" were committed by the Beach Boys (in a rendition so faithful to Berry's Angeleno-revered original that out-of-towners are still shocked by its decorum); the Angels of "My

Boyfriend's Back" fame; the Bobby Fuller Four's Anglofied rockabillies, in a medley with those other frat-rock masterworks, "Farmer John" and "Jenny Lee"; Jan and Dean on *Command Performance* from the all-time rock-concert movie, *The T.A.M.I. Show* (despite the enduring mystery of the song's unaccountable absence from the film); and the pot-bellied pioneers of Northwest rock, the Ventures.

The best of the era's "Louie"s was created by soul king Otis Redding, on an album appropriately titled *Pain in My Heart*. Redding buttressed the basic beat of "Louie" with a full horn section. Otis garbles the lyrics so completely that it seems likely he made up his verses on the spot. He relocates the song to Saturday night in the small-town South, makes it the story of a hot pickup on date night, and converts the chorus to a cry amounting to "Mission accomplished!" Redding may have been the only singer in history who imagined "Louie" as a woman's name. (Tina Turner, on the other hand, later sang *her* "Louie Louie" from his avaricious girlfriend's point of view; Ike and Tina Turner's version is certainly the only "Louie" in which the forlorn sailor owns a yacht.)

Otis had it both ways: He kept "Louie" structurally intact, but he rearranged it to suit his style and sang a story that made sense in his life, words that must have been especially fitting for weekend gigs at Southern fraternity parties. This was the typical gestation of all forms of "frat rock," the raucous, rough-edged, good-time party music of which festive fifties rockers like "La Bamba" and "Louie Louie" are the sourcepoint, the Swingin' Medallions' "Double Shot (of My Baby's Love)," with its rhetorically perfect equation of sex and falling-down drunkenness, the epiphany, and *Animal House*, the enduring spectacle.

Frat rock, less a sound than a sensibility and thus more easily circumscribed than defined, was sometimes made by what Lester Bangs called "garage bands," after the places where such amateur groups typically practiced their yowls. In the hands and mouths of most such aspirants, rock music was less than simple. Coming from bands like the Music Machine (whose "Talk Talk" used explicit "Louie" elements) and the Blues Magoos (whose big hit was the protopsychedelic fumble "We Ain't Got Nothin' Yet"), the stuff was outright crude. But similar yawp also spewed from more professional groups like the anything-but-inept Righteous Brothers (whose "Little Latin Lupe Lu" marked the second time that their backup musicians, the Rillera brothers, were on hand for the creation of a protopunk anthem), Mitch Ryder and the Detroit Wheels, and the Sir Douglas Quintet.

Frat rock was based in a variety of Southern, ethnic, and subcultural genres: mainly rhythm and blues, but also Mexican *norteño*, surf music, Chicago blues, dirty mouth party jokes a la Doug Clark and the Hotnuts, Redd Foxx and Rusty Warren, even honky-tonk country. Los Angeles and the Pacific Northwest, Texas and the industrial upper Midwest (especially Detroit and Chicago) were among frat rock's most important sourcepoints, although the South's fraternity-party circuit gave it a name and generated such stellar examples of the form as the Swingin' Medallions, the Gants ("Roadrunner"), the Gentrys ("Keep On Dancing"), and John Fred and His Playboy Band ("Judy in Disguise"). But even Boston (the Remains, the Barbarians) produced a couple.

Whether you called what they did "frat rock" or "garage rock" or "blue-eyed soul," such ragtag rockers were the principal American alternative to the British Invasion. Their successes included ? and the Mysterians' "96 Tears," Sam the Sham and the Pharoahs' "Wooly Bully," the Sir Douglas Quintet's leering "Shindig" vehicle "She's About a Mover," Cannibal and the Headhunters' revved up "Land of 1,000 Dances," Mitch Ryder's various Little Richard–based medleys and his edge-of-coherent "Sock It to Me" ("every time you kiss me it feels like a . . ."), the Premiers' "Farmer John," the Barbarians' "Are You a Boy or Are You a Girl," the Shadows of Knight's (but not Them's) "Gloria," the Standells' "Dirty Water," and Count Five's wacked-out Bo Diddley renovation, "Psychotic Reaction," even soul records like Wilson Pickett's "In the Midnight Hour" and "Mustang Sally," Tommy Tucker's "Hi-Heel Sneakers," and Parliament's "I Wanna Testify." Frat rock even had its English analogues in the Animals' "We Gotta Get Out of This Place," the Yardbirds' "I'm a Man," the Nashville Teens' scabrous "Tobacco Road," and the Rolling Stones' "19th Nervous Breakdown" and "Have You Seen Your Mother, Baby, Standing in the Shadows."

Buck Ormsby created some of the greatest examples of frat-rock sensibility with the crazed nonhit masterpieces he produced with a young Tacoma-grown group called the Sonics, whose fuzzbuster guitar and screaming vocals provided the truest and most perfect link between the deep mysteries of "Let's give it to 'em, right now" and psychedelia rampant.

All these owed a debt—usually a conscious one—to "Louie Louie." Those of them that didn't borrow the chords or rhythm of "Louie" drew upon its tough little termite heart, reaching out for (and at best, actually grasping) its ability to create from something so utterly simple as that I-IV-V progression and the stupid story of a lonesome, lovesick sailor a work of towering, mind-boggling fascination. In the wake of "Louie" trailed bands who sang "Doo wah diddy diddy," chanted loopy slogans like "Aw-uh, Baw-ston, yahr mah home," and challenged listeners to fathom a thing with "two big horns and a woolly jaw." If you had half a mind, you could trace all of them back to "El Loco Cha Cha," and if you had more mind than that, you were overen-dowed for the project anyhow.

Even if "Louie Louie" didn't sell seven to twelve million copies, the two to three million it actually sold were supplemented in the late Sixties by versions made by bands such as the Beau Brummels (who recorded it twice) and the Challengers, soulsters like the Checkmates, Ltd., and the Tams, Latin bandleaders in-cluding Mongo Santamaria, middle-of-the-roaders David McCallum and Julie London, and pure instrumentalists like drummer Sandy Nelson, pianists Floyd Cramer and Willie Mitchell, fuzz guitarist Travis Wammack and clarinetist Pete Fountain.

By 1970 "Louie Louie" had been a hit for the easy-listening group the Sandpipers, whose 1966 rearrangement made it sound like their earlier hit, "Guantanamera"; it had been re-corded by Wilbert Harrison, the king of "Kansas City," in a beautiful New Orleans arrangement by Allen Toussaint, and by the Messengers, a group on Motown's Rare Earth subsidiary, as brassy bar-band scraggle; there were records by Sweden's The Flippers, Australian Crawl, a down-under surf band (overoptimistically titled "The Last 'Louie Louie' "); and by Los Apson, a fine Mexican garage-rock combo. The primo psychedelicists, Jefferson Airplane, even played "Louie" live at Fillmore East in the ballroom daze.

"Louie Louie" inevitably had an effect on reggae; although that music's roots in other Caribbean music forms are more important, the lyric's Jamaican milieu provided an obvious entry point for young musicians from that island who wanted to get it on in the broader world rock and soul promised.

Toots and the Maytals, the first group to reshape Jamaican ska and bluebeat into reggae, performed a masterful chatterbox "Louie" in which the verses are abandoned for free association ("fine little girl" and "me got to" and "me gonna sail the sea" pop out of the sax-led stew) on their album *Funky Kingston.* Island Records took Toots Hibberts's improvisation as reason enough to give him song publishing credit on the album sleeve — or maybe they just thought "Louie" was some decrepit folk tune its Kingston-based eccentrics had adapted. (They compensated by crediting one "R. Berry" with writing Toots's "Funky Kingston.")

The Kingsmen may have "destroyed" Richard Berry's greatest song, in the opinion of his South-central L.A. friends, most of whom had heard it before its composer finally did, but Richard could never bring himself to feel insulted. "They never looked at it in a musician's type thing," he told me. "Even if somebody destroys your song, it was a type of flattery, if somebody picked up your tune. Let's face it, a lotta artists, especially a lotta black artists, would not have the recognition today if it wouldn't have been for an Elvis or even a Pat Boone, you know. If nothing else, it gave your song prominence . . . I couldn't feel that the Kingsmen had did any disservice to me, because my record was in 1956 and they came back in 1963 and did it."

Even though he was scuffling around playing after-hours gigs for hustlers and poker players in cocktail lounges, Berry wasn't really mad at anybody, not even the Feirtags, who were cashing big checks based on his need to get hitched. (The marriage to Dorothy Berry lasted about ten years; Richard would go through a couple more weddings and divorces.)

Actually, Richard, who listened only to black-oriented soul and R&B radio stations, had little idea of how widely disseminated his 1956 B side had become, even after he finally heard the Kingsmen's record several weeks after it leaped up the charts. During the post-Kingsmen Sixties, he heard only four "Louies."

"Julie London was one," he said. "I heard the Kingsmen, then I heard the Sandpipers and Rod McKuen, I heard all those three together. I heard Rod McKuen one time." He didn't hear Rockin' Robin Roberts do the original "Let's give it to 'em, right now" until the Eighties.

Of all the "Louie" rewrites, only one caught Berry's ear: "Wild Thing," the *duh duh duh. duh duh* extension by New York songmill craftsman Chip Taylor (who also wrote "Angel of the Morning," a hit for Merrilee Rush and the Turnabouts, another Spanish Castle crew). "Wild Thing" became a huge hit for an inept English combo called the Troggs in midsummer 1967. Philosophical as Richard Berry tried to remain about his estrangement from the fruits of his genius, that one burned him. "I mean, 'Willld thing, *duh duh duh*,' that's 'Louie Louie' all over the place."

The Kingsmen are the Cro-Magnons of *duh duh duh. duh duh*, but the Troggs (short for "troglodyte," which means a kind of "prehistoric" cave dweller) are its Neanderthals, men who play like they're trying to bust solid granite with fingers still stiff from the Ice Age. If the analogy seems inappropriate because the Neanderthals didn't have the ability to create art, you've obviously never heard "Wild Thing."

Taylor, a staff writer for April-Blackwood, a large song publishing company, pieced it together on a summer's afternoon in New York in 1966. He'd just gotten a call from producer Gerry Granahan, who pleaded for a song to record with Jordan Christopher and the Wild Ones. Christopher was the boyfriend of Sybil Burton (the woman whom actor Richard Burton dumped for Elizabeth Taylor); they ran the chic Manhattan discotheque Arthur. Granahan's session was scheduled for the following day.

"That afternoon I had a demo session planned for a country song. I'd scheduled it at five o'clock in the afternoon and it was, I guess, around one o'clock when I spoke to Gerry Granahan,"

Taylor told Bob Shannon and John Javna for their book, *Behind the Hits.* "I didn't have anything until around four o'clock, and then I started to get this little riff going on the guitar, and between my office at April-Blackwood and the studio, which was about four blocks, I was humming this crazy little thing, 'Wild thing, you make my heart sing,' and just had this groove going."

At the studio, Taylor told the engineer to keep the tape rolling while he charged through his new tune. He kept a steady beat on his guitar: *duh duh duh. duh duh* distorted to the brink of psychedelia. Over this Chip improvised the verses, using the "Wild thing" line as a chorus. His demo lasted six minutes, including a solo played by engineer Ron Johnson on his hands. Taylor and Johnson spent a few minutes editing the tape before moving on to the country tune.

The next morning Taylor sent over the tape. But when Granahan cut the song, he added a horn section and messed with the beat. The Jordan Christopher project died, and Taylor gave instructions that no one else was to hear the demo.

Despite those orders, a copy fell into the hands of Dick James Music, April-Blackwood's aggressive English associate. The Troggs picked it out of a pile of about fifty other demos. The next thing Chip Taylor knew, his monstrosity was topping the charts from coast to coast and across the seas.

The Troggs' "Wild Thing" opens with an extended guitar glissando and then explodes into a bass-heavy stomp: "duh duh, duh duh, duh duh," like "Louie" on Quaaludes. "Wild thing! You make my heart sing," chants leader Reg Presley. "You make every–thing . . . groov–y. Wild thing." It's the sound of a man with a rocket in his pocket, a guy so horny he's gotta be careful how he moves, lest he set himself off. And after a couple of choruses it resolves into an impression of Ron Johnson's handclap solo, played on something called an ocarina, which results in a sound like what you'd get from gargling stagnant spittle, a solo so insipid that even the unforgettably weeny way Reg's voice returns ("Wild thing, I think you move me," he tries to croon, sounding like a first-rate nerd) cannot begin to reduce its memory.

Art it may not possess, but in its own way "Wild Thing" is a rock'n'roll classic. The way it descends to lower depths with each bar is so astonishing, its unending thud so remorseless (the Troggs aren't playing this way because it's effective, even though it is—they're doing it *because they can't think of anything else*), that it just about takes your breath away, clouds your vision, brings unbidden moistness to the corners of your eyes. Of course, these symptoms might be nothing more than a neurological reaction to the axe murder of Western musical civilization, but let's cut the clowns *some* kind of break.

The Troggs didn't even get to do the greatest version of "Wild Thing." Jimi Hendrix did. Hendrix featured "Wild Thing" at the 1967 Monterey Pop Festival, his band's American debut, and he literally burned it up.

Jimi played "Wild Thing" the way he often played pop songs, with a mixture of malice and glee. He knew exactly what he was doing, too, for as a true son of Seattle, he had long studied the sacred art of "Let's give it to 'em, right now."

Once you know the legend of the Wailers at Castle and the facts of Jimi's attendance there, the lyrics of his "Spanish Castle Magic" seem haunted by homesick nostalgia. "It's very far away, it takes about half a day / To get there, if we travel by my ah . . . dragonfly," he sings, in the voice of a kid stranded a couple of continents from home. (It's tempting to wonder if Hendrix didn't write his later song "Castles Made of Sand"—which, he declares, "slip into the sea, eventually"—after learning of the Castle's demolition.)

Hendrix recorded "Wild Thing," and he recorded "Louie" 's distaff soulmate, the Van Morrison-penned "Gloria," but he never committed his own version of "Louie Louie" to wax. Or maybe it's best to say that he hid his most direct relationship to the rock'n'roll anthem of his native region.

On the hipster rock scene, the reputation of "Louie" crashed. It wasn't sophisticated. It was intoxicating, but definitely not psychedelic. Torn between the need to explode on the scene as a total original and the desire to "give it to 'em, right now," Jimi pulled one of his favorite tricks: He turned "Louie" into an allusion quoted so abstractly that nobody guessed it.

But it's right there at the top of his first American hit. The way you probably remember it, "Purple Haze" opens with an explosion of crazed guitar, the likes of which had never been heard before. But not quite—Hendrix doesn't just burst in. Jimi staged a drama. *"DUH. duh. DUH. duh. DUH. duh. DUH. duh,"* the record begins. Then: *"duh duh duh. duh duh duh."* By adding so many stops, then suddenly removing them, Hendrix contrasts "Louie" with his own vision, rupturing the link just before his voice "gives it to 'em, right now!"

"Purple Haze" took the idea of reconstructing "Louie Louie" and put it on a rocket to the stars, light years beyond the wildest dreams of Richard Berry, Rockin' Robin Roberts, or anybody else who'd ever frequented the Harmony Ballroom, the Castle, or, for that matter, any of the swinging London joints where "My Generation" was common currency. But the means of propulsion was still *duh duh duh. duh duh.*

The next few muscial trends left "Louie" in the lurch. *Duh duh duh. duh duh* was the antithesis of the folkish singer/songwriter movement. The era of heavy-metal groups fantasizing orgies eclipsed the now-seemingly-innocent fable of the song's dirty lyrics. The FBI's most prominent rock'n'roll investigation of the Seventies was its role in the attempt to deport John Lennon, not as a merchant of porn-with-a-beat, but as a left-wing political conspirator.

Yet "Louie Louie" could never be exterminated from the heart of rock'n'roll. To prove it, in 1973 "Brother Louie" leaked out of England.

"Brother Louie" originated with Hot Chocolate, a London-based mixed-race pop combo. Hot Chocolate initially appeared on the Beatles' Apple label with a version of "Give Peace a Chance," before moving on to RAK Records, run by U.K. power-pop entrepreneur Mickie Most, who'd made hits with both the schlocky and the inspired: Herman's Hermits and the Animals, Donovan and Jeff Beck, Lulu and Suzi Quatro.

In Hot Chocolate's Errol Brown and Tony Wilson, Most found a writer of distinctive melodies and strongly sentimental lyric dramas ("Emma," "You Sexy Thing," "Every 1's a Winner") to couple with an extravagantly dramatic singer with a built-in melismatic tremble. The pairing turned Hot Chocolate into one of the BBC's staple commodities; several of the group's series of U.K. hits also climbed the Yank charts.

When "Brother Louie" appeared in 1972, listeners found its "Louie" connection less noteworthy than its subject matter: interracial sex. Brown's Louie was a brown boy in love with a white girl; she reciprocated his affections, but her parents forcibly disapproved. "Brother Louie" eschewed the platitudinous liberalism of Janis Ian's 1967 "Society's Child." It made the British Top 10 in the spring of 1973.

But Britain only pioneered the trade in chattel slaves; America lives with its legacy. When "Brother Louie" fell into the hands of Stories, a New York–based art-pop group, a few months after its British success, they reversed the lyric's roles: A white guy fell in love with a black girl: "*She* was black as the night / *Louie* was whiter than white." Since the guy still sang it, the listener was now asked to identify with the pain of the *white* kid, robbing the punch line, "Ain't no difference if you're black or white / Brothers, you know what I mean" of its bitter irony. For that very reason, the lyric alteration proved essential to the success of "Brother Louie" in America. Few American taboos outrank the prohibition of sex between white women and black men.

Michael Brown formed Stories after having the Left Banke, where he'd composed the wimp-rock monument "Walk Away, Renee." Stories also featured singer Ian Lloyd. The group picked up a drummer and guitarist and signed to Kama Sutra Records, but the temperamental Brown left during the recording of the second album. In part, he rebelled against producers Kenny Kerner and Richie Wise, who wanted to bring in outside material that might have a chance of getting on the radio and selling, like "Brother Louie."

Kama Sutra released the Stories version of "Brother Louie" in June 1973—almost exactly a decade after the Kingsmen's intoxicated *duh duh duh. duh duh.* It hit the chart on June 23, and for two weeks in August, it resided at #1, an extraordinary feat for a record that had trouble being heard in the South.

Its new arrangement couldn't be denied even in Dixie. Kerner and Wise's production gave the tune a Carole King-style singer/songwriter piano-bass-drums groove. There was no hint of stop-time, let alone *duh duh duh. duh duh.* But the spirit of "Louie Louie" *had* returned. In its root emotion, the yearning for a lover to whom the singer is denied access, "Brother Louie" is one of the truest heirs *Richard Berry's* "Louie Louie" ever had. The soft but intense chorus—"Loo-ee, loo-ee, loo-ee, loo-eee-ee / Loo-ee loo-ee loo-ee loo-ay / Loo-ee loo-ee loo-ee / Loo-ee loo-ee, you're gonna cry"—was shadowed by an irony hardly less bitter than the one Errol Brown intended.

Stories proved no more able to sustain itself at this level than the Kingsmen. "All of a sudden we had a big hit with a song that did not represent *our* music and the direction we were trying to go in," Lloyd later whined to Russell Weiner of *Triad*. "I didn't think it would affect me that much, but it did." After one more album, and no more hits, Stories split.

On Top 40 radio, "Brother Louie" represented the last overt episode of the "Louie Louie" saga. But that reflected the renewed isolation of termite rock'n'roll from mainstream pop more than it did any waning of the power of *duh duh duh. duh duh.* Indeed, "Louie Louie" can be found at the core of one of pomp rock's most majestic monuments.

In the early Seventies, Tom Scholz, a senior product manager at Polaroid Corporation in suburban Boston, began to devote all his excess income to equipping a very elaborate home studio. Scholz, a guitar player with a degree in mechanical engineering from MIT, by all accounts reincarnated the techno-nerd side of Rockin' Robin Roberts. For the better part of six years, Scholz worked and reworked at taping a set of songs he'd written. It was true solo work, done by one man and an increasingly elaborate array of machines.

Although *The Rolling Stone Illustrated History of Rock & Roll* lumps Boston into a one-line "art rock" dismissal, Scholz's taste wasn't nearly so arty as other high-tech one-man rock bands like Frank Zappa and Pete Townshend, or even Stevie Wonder. True, his music reflected an obsessive delight in texture, but those textures were for the most part, quite consciously coarse, not smooth and harmonically overdeveloped like the art rock of Kansas or Yes. Like a true termite, Tom Scholz devoted all those slack hours from Polaroid trying to perfect a one man band concept whose roots were in the nasty grunge grind of heavy metal: thunderous chords from multiple guitars, often supplemented with and distorted through synthesizers and other pieces of electronic gimcrackery, set against uplifting melodies and huge, bashing beats. Or, to follow the outline Scholz once gave, "power guitars, harmony vocals, and double guitar leads."

Around those tapes, Scholz built a nominal group, highlighted by the extraordinary singer Brad Delp. With technocratic bonhomie, they called themselves Boston. Signed to Epic Records, they produced an album that primarily consisted of the demo tapes. Out of its polished melodic maelstrom leaped a single tune, the anthemic "More Than a Feeling." It opened with Led Zeppelin-like acoustic guitar banging into drum thunder, then unfolded a Who-style melodic passage before exploding into its gorgeous chorus, on which both guitar and voices soar. Underpinning that chorus was a beat so familiar it plain took your breath away: *"duh duh duh. duh duh."* it proclaimed. *"Duh duh duh. duh duh."*

Scholz encoded "Louie" into "More Than a Feeling" so organically that perhaps only fellow guitarists realized what he'd done. But those mighty strains of *duh duh duh. duh duh.* inhabit its grooves unto this very day as "More Than a Feeling" is recycled every 12 hours on album-rock radio stations across America. Now, *that's* termite culture.

12

In Search of the Ultimate "Louie"

"Why is language, Ignatz?"
"Language is that we may understand one another."
"Is that so?"
"Yes, that's so."
"Can you unda-stend a Finn or a Leplender or a Oshkosher? Huh?"
"No."
"Can a Finn or a Leplender or a Oshkosher unda-stend you?"
"No."
"Then I would say language is that we may mis-unda-stend each udda."
—George Herriman, Krazy Kat, January 16, 1918

If you ask a lot of termites, the early Seventies was the greatest sinkhole rock'n'roll ever fell into. "Underground rock" splintered the rock scene into a dozen fragments: Europhile art-rockers, laid-back singer/songwriters, head-banging metal-heads, hirsute Southern boogiers, unctuous post-soul crooners, weeny dance-pop fashion slaves, post-melodic noise worshippers, fearsome funkateers and snarling punks. It was rock'n'roll hell: All nicknamed it; none could claim it. At the top of the heap, music became corporatized, mechanical, heartless. But even so-called "corporate rock" consolidated nothing of importance except profit and airtime. One result was the restoration of the color line against contemporary black pop.

Down the economic, if not artistic, scale a few steps rock became peripheral, formless, exclusionary. All that such anarchic elitism accomplished was the alienation of any consensus that might have overturned the hegemony of the commercial. This "alternative" roomful of synthetic blends also bleached itself lily-white.

At the bottom, grubbing for elbow room and airspace, lay an audience all but stunned into silence. Rock fans went from being active participants capable of raising forbidden faces into the spotlight to a puling wad not forced but *willing* to choose among slim pickings without a peep of protest. Even rebellion had been codified and, within the codes, circumscribed.

You can feel the new pop order in all its frustrating malignancy in singer/songwriter Tim Buckley's 1974 "Wanda Lu," a track from his final studio album, *Look at the Fool*. Its beat summoned *duh duh duh. duh duh.* But Buckley replaced the "Let's give it to 'em, right now!" spirit with bitter cynicism. Both the vocal ("Wanda Lu, could you ever be true" goes the chorus) and the guitar playing sound forced. It's a love song without a trace of love, a sex song without a hint of affection. Yet, it's still "Louie" at its core and somewhere in the background, a shout or two suggests somebody remembers how much lift it could provide.

Whatever else you can say about it, "Wanda Lu" is certainly no fun. It sounds like a record made from pure spite—maybe Buckley's handlers told him his mystic-visionary repertoire needed a song that had a prayer of being played on the radio. Maybe Buckley was just in the mood to tell the world to fuck off. Whatever caused it, "Wanda Lu" waves "Louie" in the face of gloom and, unlike any previous "Louie," it never comes close to shaking off those bad vibes. Which makes it the pure product of its time.

But the true depths of alienation, the dark caverns of despair into which the soul of *duh duh duh. duh duh* now descended could be fully encompassed only in the tongue of a singer whose most shining moments incarnate nihilism. Through that singer, Iggy Pop, and his band, the (once Psychedelic) Stooges, "Louie Louie" entered its darkest hour.

Not only squares missed the point. "You know, I heard one by Ziggy and the Stooges or something," said Richard Berry. "Oh man, it's somethin' else. He's talkin' 'bout the whole 'fuck you in your black ass,' you know. This was a live recording. And I heard him say, well, if you want to throw some rotten eggs up here, we're ready. Jee-sus, man!"

Iggy and the Stooges shaped their sound and sensibility in Ann Arbor, Michigan, a college town on the fringes of Detroit, just as the postwar prosperity of Autoworld disintegrated, first in the anarchy of the Detroit riots during 1967's "summer of love," then in the aftermath of OPEC. The Motor City's working class went from being the richest in the world to double-digit unemployment with a barely discernable transition. The three albums Iggy and the Stooges made between 1969 and 1973—*The Stooges, Funhouse*, and *Raw Power*—comprise a sonic account of their home territory's all-front (economic, social, political, spiritual) collapse. Since that collapse ultimately took on national and worldwide dimensions, these albums, for all their crudity, now rank among the most profound and powerful records ever created.

The Stooges began as the little brother band of the revolution rockers, the MC5, but Iggy and his gang flipped the coin: They didn't advocate revolt; they acted revolting. The Five's essential message boiled down to agit-prop optimism, but the Stooges were having none of it. The Stooge perspective was summed up in their anthem: "No Fun." Spanish Castle Magic turned black in their hands.

The Five's emcee, Brother J. C. Crawford, ranted: "Brothers and sisters, it's time for each and every one of you to decide whether you are gonna part of the *problem* or whether you are gonna be part of the *solution*."

"Problem," the Stooges replied without dropping a beat (for the first and only time in their careers). They proceeded to slash long, droning scars across the musical landscape with chordless, feedback-clouded credos like "I Wanna Be Your Dog" and "Search and Destroy."

Thus the Stooges in all their infamy marched across America and on into several seasons of expatriatism in England and Europe, earning the derision of everybody who knew anything about *music*, but inspiring deep devotion from the few who heard within this silly, sassy alienation the throbbing pulse of the all-but-lost *duh duh duh. duh duh.* In 1969 they received the most gruesome reviews of any band in the history of rock criticism; by 1975, they were darlings of the music press. By 1976, they were falling apart, several members having dug deep holes in the crooks of their arms as they dealt with the actuarial tables like an escalator that knew only one direction—straight down. As his band imploded, Iggy took to playing straightman for audiences that avidly missed the point: A bottle would break near the stage, he'd slash his chest with the shards and receive the greatest applause of his career.

The Stooges played their final show at the Michigan Palace, a Detroit theatre, on the cold night of October 6, 1976 (frigid indoors, no matter what it was like outside), with Iggy on vocals, accompanied by guitarist James Williamson, electric pianist Scott Thurston, Ron Asheton (their original guitarist) on bass, and his brother Scott (a/k/a Rock Action) on drums, before an audience of bikers and other denim and leather louts. That show ranks among rock's all-time debacles—it is an Altamont of the heart, the Devil's own amateur night, without the mercy of a hook waiting in the wings. The songs—which included such gems as "Rich Bitch" and "Cock in My Pocket"—disappeared in livid anti-Stooges tumult, met with barrages of over-ripe fruit, vegetable, egg, and beer. The full battle wound up encoded upon the quasi-bootleg album *Metallic KO*—and never has a recording been more aptly titled.

Even decades later the completeness with which this audience and this artist fail to comprehend one another remains awesome. Iggy manages to complete "Cock in My Pocket," but the song goes nowhere. It would, in the mind of anyone who respected his own life, be risky to continue antagonizing this audience. The tape reveals his courage and stupidity.

"Aww, it'll all be over soon," he yells, then moans like a

schoolkid playing war—the artillery's coming in. "I won't fuck you when I'm workin'," he notes to someone in the crowd who has proposed something along those lines.

"Anybody with any more ice cubes, jelly beans, grenades, eggs they wanna throw at the stage, c'mon. You paid your money, so you takes your choice, y'know."

The pianist plays random notes, no chords. The bass and guitar futz around with pick noise and feedback. Iggy is silent. Suddenly, he speaks again, perhaps to the band: "But when they throw eggs, you always say they throw 'em at me." Then, once more addressing these very active spectators:

"Ladies and gentlemen, let's have a big hand for Mr. James Williamson on guitar, right here." The Ig pauses, as if anticipating gasps of recognition. "Rock Action on drums . . . Ronald Frank Asheton on bass . . . A big hand for Mr. Scott Thurston on piano, vocals, and harmonica. And let's not forget your favorite well-mannered boy, the singer. Let's hear it for the singer."

Silence at the mike.

"I am the greatest." Another silence.

"Thanks for the eggs. Thank you for the eggs—do we have any more eggs? More eggs! What am I bid for a dozen eggs?" At least that many come flying at him. "Aw, y'missed! C'mon, try it again! C'mon . . . Listen, I been egged by better'n you. C'mon now.

"Is it time for a riot, girls? RIOT!" A pause. Guitar tuning. Another air strike, perhaps. Direct hit, apparently: "Let's get a towel for the egg yolk. I don't want to get caught with yolk in my face." He smacks his lips, then in strangled falsetto: "Awh, baby, c'mon. Mommma, Mommmma, Mommmma.

"Light bulbs, too! Paper cups?" Something hits a guitar. "Oh my, we're getting violent.

"Well, there's two guys left the stage. Well, we'll all have to leave, we'll see ya later." Another silent moment, then Iggy's back at the mike, speaking in an accent that crosses your basic Sylvester Stallone and a retarded version of the New York Dolls.

"Uh, thank you, ladies and gentlemen." A pause. "Whaddya wanna hear?" A slightly longer pause. Then he switches back to his normal voice; inspiration has arrived.

"I think a good song for you would be a fifty-five-minute

'Louie Louie.' " To the band: "Let's give 'em an extra and do 'Louie.' . . ." To the crowd, like a beleaguered parent: "Would you rather we ran through our programmed set that looked real slick[!], or would you rather we just did 'Louie Louie?' "

The crowd responds as before; more of that seemingly endless supply of projectiles smash into the stage and the band.

" 'LOUIE LOUIE!' " Iggy screams, and the band throws itself into a punkish *duh duh duh. duh duh.* "I never thought it'd come to this, baby!" he mutters, and then simply rides the piano chords and fuzzy guitar for a moment until, with a shrill "Owwwww!" he begins his climactic "Louie," singing the words as he remembered them from junior high:

> Louie, Louie, away I go now
> Louie, Louie, said away I go
>
> Fine little bitch, she waits for me
> Just a whore across the way
> Every night I take her, park all alone
> She ain't the kind I lay at home
>
> Louie, Louie, away I go now
> Louie, Louie, said away I go
> Let's give it to 'em, right now

Williamson plays a deranged, fuzzy guitar solo; it sounds skillful at first, then falls apart. In the Stooges' first audible act of wisdom all night, he retreats to the basic chords.

"Take it down!" Iggy cries. "Take it way down! Ah, take it down," he shrieks. "Now listen to me."

> She got a rag on so I move above
> It won't be long before she'll take it all
> I feel the rose down in her hair
> Her ass is black and her tits are bare
>
> Louie, Louie, away I go now
> Louie, Louie, said away I go
> Away I go now!
> Away I go now!

Away I go now!
Let's go!

The music crashes to its conclusion as Iggy shouts, "They threw a Stroh's!"

After the last drone dies out, he returns and stands at the mike amidst the rubble to offer a few final thoughts:

"Ladies and gentlemen, 'Louie Louie' . . . Thank you very much to the person who threw this glass bottle. You nearly killed me, but you missed again. But keep tryin' next week."

The last sound heard on the record is broken glass being kicked by a boot leaving the stage.

The Stooges broke up a few days later. Improbably, "Louie" survived.

> The song "Louie Louie" was in the film *Animal House* because in 1962 it would be the song the Deltas would sing. The screenplay always indicated that "Louie Louie" be playing long before John Belushi was involved with the project. John's version of "Louie Louie" is the one heard in the film and is available on the soundtrack album.
>
> Your story that the song was the accompaniment to John's first sexual experience I'm afraid I cannot verify, as I wasn't there. However, I can state unequivocally that almost everything printed about John since his death is bullshit.
> —Letter from film director John Landis to Eric Predoehl,
> editor, *The Louie Report*, September 4, 1984

But unless Belushi's Bluto Blutarsky and his companions at the Delta Tau "Animal House" attended school in the Pacific Northwest (and Faber College is specifically identified as being in the Northeast), "Louie Louie" would certainly *not* have been what they were singing in 1962, since the Kingsmen didn't hit until 1963. Yet when Bluto teaches "Louie" to the Delts' incoming pledge class, *he already knows the dirty words.*

There's only one way that could have happened, and that's if the Delta "Animal House" of Faber College wasn't fictional—if it was the 1962 Delts of Dartmouth (the school on which Faber is based) who secretly originated the "Louie" lyrics legend. Is it possible Bluto and Otter and their classless pals dreamed up such a scam and just waited for the right pack of hapless rock'n'roll suckers to appear on the airwaves? Could it be that in 1978 their successors dreamed up *Animal House* to see how much more they could get away with?

Okay, that's too good to be true even in this tale. But what was there about *Animal House* that wasn't farfetched—including its role in reviving the sacred secrets of *duh duh duh. duh duh?*

Animal House originated with the *National Lampoon*, the post-hippie humor magazine. It reflects the *Lampoon* style before it became not merely insensitive, but belligerently revealing of its true subject matter, the mainly petty angers of the white male hipster-supremacists who wrote and edited it.

In *Animal House* the portrayals of women, Italians, and blacks reflect a new species of resentment that matured into Lee Atwater's Willie Horton commercial. Since Landis's directorial signature is using excess as compensation for lack of comedic timing and narrative coherence, the movie hasn't held up well— as an early Sixties nostalgia piece, it's just *too* Seventies.

The project succeeded for one reason: comedian John Belushi, who made his national reputation even before joining "Saturday Night Live"'s "Not Ready for Prime Time Players," as a cast member of the troupe that toured with the *Lampoon*'s rock'n'roll farce, *Lemmings*.

Cruelty and rage also provided the basis for Belushi's humor—in *Lemmings* his star turn consisted of an impression of Joe Cocker as a helpless spastic—but when he became engulfed in a characterization (most often, in one touching on music), he mesmerized audiences like a hurricane concoction of charisma and recklessness. Rather than compelling the suspension of disbelief, Belushi shoved his audience's face in it; his best bits always inspired the reaction, "I don't *believe* this shit!"

In *Animal House* Belushi plays Bluto Blutarsky as an all-but-insensate slob whose primitive impulsiveness incarnates the anarchic energy that every "sane" force at Faber College fears, despises, and tries to stamp out. He's the guy who starts the food fight in the cafeteria, then ducks out when it erupts; he's the consummate goldbrick, still in college, after seven years of not studying, because it's a way out of the draft (which proves he's not dumb); Bluto's response to a threat of expulsion is "Toga!

Toga! Toga!''—a demented demand that the frat hold an orgi-
astic party. Bluto's destiny is to come up with one tremendous
scam after another; his doom is to have each of them backfire;
his solution is to drink himself blind. Given Belushi's early
checkout at the end of a smack needle, it's impossible not to read
Bluto Blutarsky as autobiographical.

Is he funny? If a man with a mouthful of mashed potatoes
imitating a zit is your idea of a good joke, he's hilarious.

Inevitably, Bluto's—and thus the movie's—theme song is
"Louie Louie." As the two dweeb pledges walk up to Animal
House for the first time, a headless mannequin flies through a
second-story window and lands at their feet in a hail of shattered
glass, and *duh duh duh. duh duh* fills the soundtrack. A second
later Bluto makes his entrance, unlocking the door and ushering
the dweebs into the chaotic party inside. "Louie Louie" plays
twice more during the ensuing 10-minute party scene. Later, on
pledge night, it's Blutarsky the pledgemaster who seals the ini-
tiation ceremony by leading everyone in a "Louie" complete
with dirty lyrics (of which the most distinguishable line is "Each
night at ten, I lay her again . . .").

A Belushi "Louie" even got released as a single from the
soundtrack album: a rinky-dink romp sung in the hoarse,
squeaky voice Belushi later made famous with the Blues Brothers. But Belushi didn't record the Bluto version—he sang the
original lyrics. The record's high point thus became the concluding bellow, *"Right now!"* But it doesn't sound like Bluto; it
doesn't even sound much like Belushi.

Wretched as Belushi's record was, the new "Louie" at least
brought "Let's give it to 'em, right now!" back to the charts—or,
at least, it would have if Belushi hadn't replaced that line with
an unintelligible scream. The disc hit #89 on the *Billboard*
chart, where it rested for the entire month of October 1978.

Part of the hype, as the Landis letter to Predoehl indicates,
was that Belushi insisted on singing "Louie Louie" in his mo-
tion picture debut, ostensibly because he revered the number as
the soundtrack to the moment when he lost his virginity in the
backseat. Maybe he did or maybe he didn't (it would be impossible to set the story straight if Belushi had lived and the humor-
less Robert Woodward hadn't become his posthumous biogra-

pher). Anyway, Belushi didn't have anything to do with putting the song in the picture. That honor fell to soundtrack producer Kenny Vance, a veteran New York studio rat, who took charge of all the movie's rock'n'roll elements.

Iggy and Belushi, *Metallic KO,* and *Animal House* were mere sideshows amid the glittering fragments of mid-Seventies superstardom. The broader picture of the period comes clear in the contrast between punk and disco: raging, ragged, anti-social, amateur-hour rhythmic chaos pitted against cool, machine-glossed, fashionable, ultra-pro metric discipline. True, in less than a decade, punk wiped off the sweat and cleaned up its act, while disco denizens toned down a peg and picked up on the aesthetic of rage; then dance-rock and hip-hop ruled the Eighties. But in their heyday, only a fool or a music critic (pardon the redundancy) would have tried to keep an ear in both camps. But the legacy of *duh duh duh. duh duh* penetrated both.

In style and attitude, punk's "Louie" lineage couldn't have been clearer. The path from the Wailers, the Kingsmen, and the Sonics to the MC5 and the Stooges to the New York Dolls and the Patti Smith Group (all of whom executed various live versions of "Louie") to the Ramones, the Clash, and the Sex Pistols—and from that trio to a whole universe of unheralded groups and clusters of do-it-yourself anti-musicians—is a beeline. The crazy happenstance of *duh duh duh. duh duh* shaped the backbone of punk spirit and the FBI's blinkered goose chase through the "Louie" archives epitomized the genre's ambition: to create a spectacle revealing the imaginative bankruptcy of society, particularly as expressed in conventional concepts of "culture" and "morality."

To the entrepreneurs and paragons of punk, "Louie" offered a trove of possibility, yet "Louie Louie" as a trope made virtually no appearance during the punk rock heyday and the couple of efforts that found their way to wax (the Bloodclots' 1977 affray, for instance) don't amount to much. "Louie" served punk as the hounds of the Baskervilles served Sherlock Holmes: It was the dog that didn't bark, a blank spot that ought to have been filled.

"Louie" 's virtual absence in punk resulted first and foremost from simple musical practicality. The essence of "Louie

Louie" is that stop-time rhythm: *duh duh duh. duh duh.* But punk's sonic purpose was to obliterate all the stops. Punk's greatest groups, the Clash and the Sex Pistols, built themselves around rhythmic slashes and smears respectively, and they had no time for anything requiring so much tinkering with bar lines. The Kingsmen changed "Louie" profoundly just by omitting a rest; the Pistols and the Clash took it the rest of the way and wiped out all the spaces between the beats—the rhythmic basis of punk amounted to *duh duh duh duh duh duh duh duh duh duh duh duh duh duh duh duh duh duh duh duh duh duh* until either the performer or the audience dropped from exhaustion or rebelled at the stasis.

Echoes of "Louie" crop up nevertheless: On the first Clash album, in the distressed reggae—*"Duh-duh-duh duh-duh-duh"*—of "Remote Control" and as a ghost behind the forcebeat of "Garageland" (an ode to all the bands the Kingsmen's subcompetence inspired: "25 players! 1 guitar!") and on *Never Mind the Bollocks, Here's the Sex Pistols* as a faint glimmer behind the jackboot beats of "Problems," "Submission," "17," and "Bodies," a quartet of songs whose anti-physical bile might be construed as a series of attempts to write a song that's genuinely as obscene as the rumors made "Louie Louie." These songs catch a glimpse of what "Louie Louie" used to stand for back in the days when a battle of the bands amounted to an invitation to rumble.

When punk iconoclasts finally constructed a "Louie," they naturally declined to conform to tradition. Chrissie Hynde and the Pretenders' 1981 "Louie Louie"—from *Pretenders II*—connects with the original *only* through her concluding bark, "Right now!" Otherwise, it's a wholly different song.

The same year, the California-based "hard-core" punk band Black Flag slowed down long enough to assay an actual "Louie." "Louie Louie" is, in fact, as close to a rock'n'roll classic as the bitter, muscular Black Flag ever came. Led by the extremely rowdy and obnoxious Henry Rollins, an artiste whose self-destructiveness let to a mutual admiration pact with John Belushi, Black Flag are the first and only band ever to scare the producers of "Saturday Night Live" into using censorious tape delay, to preserve NBC's federal license. On "Louie Louie" Rollins sang with a blistered voice against hot-coal chords, replacing the verse with a confession that owed its soul to the spirit of Rockin' Robin Roberts and "Let's give it to 'em, right now!":

> You know the pain that's in my heart
> It just shows I'm not very smart
> Who needs love, when you got a gun?
> Who needs love, to have any fun?

But the most audacious punk-derived "Louie" came from punk's first high priest, Sex Pistols impresario Malcolm Mc-Laren, an anarchist poseur and dance-beat colonialist. McLaren did it with a group led by a 14-year-old Anglo-Asian girl, Annabella. Bow Wow Wow's 1982 single "Louis Quatorze" climaxed a short but spectacularly hyped career that supposedly incarnated the fixation of post-modern adolescents on "tribalism," by which McLaren might have meant the awareness of the global village induced by satellite and electronics technology, if he hadn't abandoned each of his theories on the verge of coherence. In any event, using McLaren's ideas, Bow Wow Wow successfully fell short of stardom.

Still, "Louis Quatorze" is not only the most interesting "Louie" uttered by a punk fixture, but the most fascinating outrage of McLaren's post-Pistols career. His post-punk-pop expropriations of hip-hop, old-timey Kentucky fiddling, South African dance music, and opera themes were all superseded by better efforts in the same genres, but in "Louis Quatorze" McLaren crafted a mini-scandal—the record's lyric portrayed bold English Louie raping underage Annabella, while the single's sleeve depicted her topless in a seriocomic ripoff of Manet—and a memorable extension of "Louie," since what Annabella shouts during the portion of the record when she is purportedly being rogered by the swain Quatorze is "Louie-Louie-Louie."

Bow Wow Wow thereafter reached a total dead end, although McLaren did assay the group's rescue by implanting a new lead singer—the gorgeous semi-transvestite Boy George, well before the advent of Culture Club. Unfortunately, even this merger did not sound so much ahead of its time as confounding of the precise period in which one heard it.

*   *   *

Disco also produced no significant "Louie"s and the reasons
were also rhythmic. But the disco scene did produce Richard
Berry's all-time favorite "Louie": The version by Barry White,
who took the song from pure rock'n'roll to pure moan'n'groan.
White, then a couple years past the peak of his popularity (which
stemmed from such Top 10 orgasmic orchestral grunts as "I'm
Gonna Love You Just a Little More, Baby," "Never Never Gonna
Give You Up," "Can't Get Enough of Your Love, Baby," "You're
the First, the Last, My Everything" and "It's Ecstasy When You
Lay Down Next to Me"—and you wonder why some folks hated
disco!) even cut his "Louie" in half (the length! the length!) and
put it out as a single. He even performed it on "Soul Train."

Richard Berry loved it because White's version finally
brought to life his original vision of "all the timbales and the
congas going, and me singing 'Louie Louie,' " which Max Feirtag had nixed in favor of "a good, R&B-sounding record."

"Barry White did it exactly the way I wanted to do it," Berry
enthused. "I mean, he had [sings] *dah–dah, d-d-d–dah*. It was
13 minutes, too. I loved it. It was on his last good album—the
Beware album. 'Cause he did Jesse Belvin's 'Beware' and he did
'Louie Louie.' He almost had a hit going with it, 'cause I think
it was on *Billboard*, #77 with a bullet. They stopped promoting
it, said, 'Well, "Louie Louie" will make it on its own' and, of
course, they lost the record."

Berry got the details wrong—White's "Louie" workout
wasn't thirteen minutes long, just 7:14, with the single edited
down to 3:35. And it didn't chart. But Richard got the spirit right:
In White's arrangement "Louie Louie" emerges as an up-tempo
Latin groove, driven by timbales and congas and punctuated by
brilliant trumpet riffs, while White supplements the chorus with
the plaintive interpolation, "Comin' home, Jamaaaica!"

White's "Louie" reveals an intimate familiarity with every
bit of the phrasing from the original version—it's an extension
and White keeps a respectful distance. Anybody familiar with
Berry's vocal style will notice what should already have been apparent, if history was fair: White's vocal style owed a huge debt
to Richard Berry's. Indeed, White succeeded Richard as the bass

voice of choice among early sixties L.A. studio rats. His hom-age—no matter late, it came,—was intentional and sincere.

After White's "Louie Louie" came out he tracked Berry down. "When I sat down and talked with him he said, 'Man, I used to see you ridin' down the street and I said, 'One of these days I'm gonna sing just like Richard Berry,' " Richard remem-bered. "And he said he used to stop me and I used to say, 'Yeah, man, just keep goin'.' But I don't remember none of this." Berry chuckled. "Even when he was on 'Soul Train' he said, "I'm gonna do this song that this black guy wrote. Everybody thinks that these white guys recorded it, but a black guy did this.' I mean he went through the whole thing on 'Soul Train,' which is great. Even on the liner notes on the album he did it.

"So when he did 'Louie Louie' he was lookin' for me, 'cause he wanted me to hear it. And he sent all kinda people out lookin' for me. He had a pretty nice taste of bread, he had more money than I ever had when I was comin' up. I guess he was paying homage or whatever you call it. Later on I called it bullshit. He started saying, well, come out to the house and I'm gonna get all the old artists and I'm gonna record 'em and bama bam." But when Berry finally arrived, White only suggested they write songs together, to which Richard—who right about then was busted flat—replied, "Man, get outta here."

Mainly, "Louie Louie" survived in white rock as a goof. Bruce Springsteen did his onstage at Notre Dame as a genuflection to frat rock, former New York Doll Johnny Thunders bumbled through his somewhere in the wilds of Europe. Politicians from Thurston County, Washington–Commissioner George Barnes and the Original Trendsetters to disgraced former-San-Diego-Mayor-turned-radio-host Roger Hedgecock of the Arnold-Hedgecock Experience fluffed their way through vanity label renditions, while Paul Shaffer, David Letterman's answer to Doc Severinson, actually received a major label release for a treat-ment that belonged in a Holiday Inn lounge. Former Velvet Un-derground drummer Maureen Tucker cut hers with Texas hip-sters (on an album called *Playing Possum* on the termitous Trash Records). Members of such "progressive rock" groups as Hat-field and the North, Pavlov's Dog, and even the punko-metalloid

Stranglers also committed "Louie"s, though all of them used pseudonyms.

Few eighties versions of "Louie" received the imaginative adaptation provided by jazz-rock fusioneers Stanley Clarke and George Duke in 1981. Clarke and Duke gave it to their audience right then as a fable. "Come on over here, little brother, and sit down on your daddy's knee," Duke begins, "and let me tell you a story about your Uncle Stanley and me. Once a long time ago, we was lost at sea, sailors of love in distress—I tell this tale to thee." They proceeded to do a straightforward exposition of your basic *duh duh duh. duh duh.* "So the moral of this story is," Duke concluded a little over five minutes later, "if you sail the seven seas / Take your women with you and set your mind at ease."

A good joke, but nowhere near the best. That came in 1988 from a rap group called the Fat Boys. The trio (Mark "Prince Markie Dee" Morales, Damon "The Human Beat Box" Wimbley, and Damon "Kool Rock-ski" Robinson) were so plump they made Barry White look as pipestem as Whitney Houston.

They'd been making records since "Jailhouse Rap," an hysterical 1984 account of getting sent up the river for busting into a pizza joint with a bad dose of the hungries. By the fall of 1988, they'd exhausted the most obvious fat-boy jokes and began recycling rock'n'roll standards, first taking a shot with a weenie remake of "The Twist," accompanied by the Beach Boys, a group by then on or over the borderline of pop senility, but nevertheless white enough to help them garner some pop airplay. Then they made their move to "Give it to 'em, right now."

The Fat Boys were the most elephantine termites ever put on public display, but they performed "Louie Louie" like men born for the task. Their producers, the Latin Rascals, retooled the music with scratching, shrieks, and raw guitar counterpointed with chiming synth, reinforcing and extending the basic *duh duh duh. duh duh* with drumming so powerfully electronic it feels real. Because hip-hop (the name for the sound and culture that developed around rappers) provided a home to all manner of gangstas, reformed and unreformed, converting "Louie" to that style brought the tune up to date as rebel rock.

The Fat Boys (together with Jim "Jimbo" Glenn) did an even

better job of updating the "Louie" lyric with an eye toward current events, which included the late Eighties' witch-hunt for dirty lyrics in rap. Their rap chronicles a pursuit of the song's real words that's sparked by Mark's mother's reminiscence of her youth, when "Louie" caused "A big ass rumble / They thought it was filthy because the words were mumbled." Moms lets the boys in on how it was with "Louie" back in the day:

> Down at my mom's school, it was all they talked about
> It was about gettin' busy and they had no doubt
> It was un-precedent-ed, what they said on that platter

At this point Moms turns on an oldies station, and for the first time the rappers experience the wonders of "Louie"—but they can't understand the words. So off they quest, determined to discover their new favorite's deep Secret. Eventually, they run into The Great Bunfy (whoever he may be) and "he knew every word." Indeed, he tells them, it's the rap of his dreams, even though his interpretation boils down to "Say what?"

The greatest exposition of the Fat Boys' updated "Louie Louie" comes in the music video directed by Scott Kalvert. Essentially, Kalvert plays the song as a parody of *Animal House*: It opens with a nerdy dean declaring, "I want that fat-ternity closed down" and follows through with a party scene (at the FAT frat) that makes the one in *Animal House* look like a Junior League prom. This video is literally one long food fight, complete with dancing girls, water balloons, exploding plumbing, and refrigerators that whirlwind chow into the Fat Boys' mouths.

In terms of sheer anarchic energy, Belushi and company didn't even come close. But still—sometimes you make history; sometimes history makes you. The Fat Boys entered pop-chart annals for that wimpy remake of "The Twist," which got lots of airplay thanks to their bondage to the Beach Boys. "Louie Louie" got very little exposure, even on MTV. Yet to true believers in the science of "givin' it to 'em, right now," the Fat Boys' "Louie" remains the last great "Louie Louie" to date.

13

"Louie" Marches On

In my hungry fatigue and shopping for images, I went into the neon
fruit supermarket, dreaming of your enumerations!
—Allen Ginsberg, "A Supermarket in California"

The Carolina Lanes Lounge, Inglewood, California, Summer 1964

Richard Berry had been playing in this dreary lounge since 9 PM,
but even at midnight his night's sentence had another six or
eight hours to run.

Dives like this were the prime venues for Berry's music, now
that the old Los Angeles studio R&B scene had died out, its vin-
tage harmonizers replaced by Anglofied rockers and Motown-
happy soulsters. After Richard split Flip he spent years bouncing
from label to label—tiny outfits like Paxley, Hasil, K&G, AMC,
Bold Soul, PAM, and Smash. The closest he came to a hit was
writing "Moments to Remember" by Jennell Hawkins, his old
duet partner, in 1961—her record nudged up to #50 on the pop
chart.

Dorothy Berry now had the family's more successful career;

she made "The Girl Who Stopped the Duke of Earl" and "Ain't That Love," both produced by H. B. Barnum, and from the mid-sixties through the end of the decade, she toured with Ray Charles as a Raelette. Ten years after Richard sold his song to buy a ring, the couple (who'd had two children—a boy and a girl) split up. Berry later had three daughters with a woman he never married, although he always financially supported their off-spring, and then remarried for four years, which brought him a fifth daughter, Christie.

With so many mouths to feed and his studio work dried up, Richard retreated to the half-lit world of after-hours sessions. A subterranean circuit of them existed, and he worked it, still playing off that old Jesse Belvin principle: grab the cash, fast.

Berry called the shows he did after midnight until the wee, wee hours and on into midmorning "jam sessions," but he didn't mean the kind of free-blowing gig where any kind of song or approach could be attempted. The club owners made certain of that. They wanted Top 40 material, convinced that anything newfangled would send the clientele elsewhere. Whether they were right or wrong, Richard was stuck playing the hits of the day. Richard squeezed in a few of his own tunes, but at the price of cutting into his tips from playing requests.

About the only song of his own these clubs regularly permitted Richard was the one that went *duh duh duh. duh duh.* Berry could have been excused for being sick of *that* one.

In the late autumn of 1963, "somebody told me, 'Some white guys, man, they *destroyed* your song.' And when I heard it . . . it was strange. Because I had heard so much about it, I didn't know what to expect when I heard it. I wasn't *insulted.* It was just strange . . ."

Berry did feel embarrassed and angry. "I was flattered when it became a hit, but then I got bitter about it. Here I was, the writer, but all those millions of dollars went into somebody else's pockets," he told Steve Propes. "If I had thought very much about it, I probably would have gone crazy or killed somebody."

It wasn't that the Feirtags had cheated him—he knew that the deal was just business as usual. "But then people started askin', 'Well, man, you gonna start gettin' money, now, ain't cha? Where's your hog?' That's what they called a Cadillac in those days. How am I gonna tell these people, 'Well, I done sold the song for seven hundred dollars'? But before this, seven hundred and fifty bucks was a *lotta money.*"

That's how things stood on that midweek midnight at the Carolina Lanes when three white guys, fresh off the Strip and far too slick for *this* room, walked in and took a table near the stage. At the next break the oldest of them introduced himself as Roger Hart, manager of Paul Revere and the Raiders. The other two, he explained, were the Raiders' lead singer, Mark Lindsay, and its lead guitarist, Drake Levin. "They'd like to see if you have any more original material that we could do," he said.

Richard just did the regular Top 40 set he was being paid to do, which was, as Levin recalled it, worth the trip by itself: "It was so funky and so soulful, I thought this guy was like another Ray Charles." But Berry didn't—because he couldn't—play original songs.

Hart remembered that, afterward, Berry "got into either the piano bench or a briefcase," and dug out 'Have Love, Will Travel.' " But Levin remembers Richard as being very "unappreciative" of the inquiry. So Levin says, "Mark went home and wrote his own follow-up, 'Louie, Go Home.' " From which Richard Berry earned precisely nothing, though he did get a small slice of the B side, which was "Have Love, Will Travel."

Richard Berry played the afterhours circuit for 20 years, from 1960 to 1980. And even there he became a kind of legend, starting at the Casino Club in Gardena: "They catered to the little Vegas acts, the lounge acts that came out of Vegas."

"When I started working in that club [the Casino], I was making like twelve bucks a morning, and when I left there, he was paying me like four thousand a week," Richard remembered. "I made him go union and everything. But I stayed there for four and a half years, until my price started rising so high and he said, 'Well, I can't give you any more money.' "

About that time H. D. Hover, one-time manager of Sammy Davis, Jr., and a former owner of Ciro's, a comparatively swank club up on Sunset Strip, ("They called him The Last of the Big-Time Spenders," said Richard) came into the Casino to make Richard an offer.

"Man, I like your band," said Hover in his muted rasp. "It wouldn't go over in my place, because I've got a younger clientele. But I tell you what—you come out and play Monday night and I'll pay you for the audition, and we'll see what happens."

"Shit, I went out to that place on Monday night," Berry remembered in 1990, "and there was standing room only. 'Cause of the word-of-mouth thing. I got all the youngsters in there. By the time I finished that night, he had a contract ready for me to sign."

Richard regretted only one thing about the move: "I found out that my older clientele wouldn't come to the Century with the youngsters. They just didn't like 'em, you know," he said. "But every time I gained it was better for me. 'Cause from 1960 up until 1980, I did nothing but night clubs. All around the Southern California area—from San Fernando Valley to Orange County to San Gabriel—I mean, I just had the circuit sewed up."

Though Richard Berry's name was lost to the big-league record business, he at least managed to document his typical live show on LP: *Wild Berry! Live From H. D. Hover's Century Restaurant* by Richard Berry and the Soul Serchers [*sic*], cut for PAM Records during a 1969 stint.

"When I first recorded that, we were makin' so much money we had a bank account. No musicians have bank accounts! We had about six grand in the bank from the tips that we'd get. I'd make anywhere from three to four hundred bucks a week in tips—just from doing requests."

Out of that savings account, Berry hired portable recording equipment. *Wild Berry!* featured three original songs ("Wild Berry," "Down Here on the Ground," "Spread Your Love") and Jimmy Ruffin's Motown hit, "Give Her All the Love I've Got." The Soul Serchers consisted of saxophonists Billy Collins and Carson Oliver, Willie Briggs on bass, drummer Gary Hensen, two conga players and backup vocalists Dorothy Durr, Julia Tillman, Maxine Willard, plus Richard himself on lead vocals and electric piano.

The album's new songs aren't much more than variations on the soul styles of more famous singers ("Down Here on the Ground," the best of them, *is* Chuck Jackson in both phrasing and dramaturgy). Berry's voice remains distinctive, but he's clearly a singer caught between eras, too late for R&B, too soon for Barry White–style lugubrious love moans. The band reeks funk on the breaks, but it's mainly trapped in lounge arrangements whose prime purpose is not to offend. Richard performs in the guise of a man with a past, calling off the names of old haunts ("One time for Long Beach! One time for the El Rey Club! One time for the Raintree"), but it's hard to discern a palpable present.

Wild Berry couldn't jump-start Richard's career, but the album undeniably served its more Belvinesque purpose; Berry sold every one of the 7,000 albums he pressed, at ten bucks apiece.

In the mid-seventies it got a lot more complicated. Richard and his second wife split up and he kept custody of his youngest child, Christie. "It was an interracial marriage and she [the mother] said, 'Well, she's not gonna be able to survive in my world.' I think she did it because she thought maybe I'd be a complete asshole and put the kid in a foster home.

"My whole lifestyle had to change because I had to get up in the morning, take her to school, pick her up at 12 noon. And I'm singin' at night, and tryin' to have a girlfriend, and stay over at my girlfriend's house, then I had to get up at 6:30 in the morning—cause I didn't want my mom to do it—come across town, take my daughter to school, come back and get in bed and sleep, and then get up at noon and pick her up.

"But I think that was the most sufficient, meaning[ful] time. Because I was in what you call a [quandary], you know. Like I said, 'What am I gonna do with this kid?' I had to be responsible. I didn't want my mom to have to raise her, while I'm out diddlin' around, hangin' out, layin' up with some broad or somethin'.

"Most days, you know, the kid had to get up and go to school. And I was always the type that didn't want my kid to walk to school until I figured that she was old enough. 'Cause you know, you gotta watch kids.

"But I mean I was determined. I walked her until she said, "Well, I don't want you to walk to school with me no more. I want to walk to school by myself.' I said, 'Okay, man, you know.' And even when she started out, I followed her. It took me a while to let go. Then I says, 'Okay, the broad can make it on her own.' "

* * *

As Richard Berry found his life engulfed by his daughter, he lost track of his other great creation. Estranged from pop radio and from the rock scene that grew up in the wake of the Beatles, and with a relatively minute stake in the issue, he missed the sixties' "Louie Louie" boom, failed to notice as his greatest hit became one of the most recorded songs of all time.

The original Richard Berry and the Pharoahs' "Louie" disappeared into the maw of bargain bins and collectors' obsessions. Flip licensed its masters to Era, which specialized in reissuing old 45s, and briefly put it out with "Rock, Rock, Rock" on the flip side. Richard wasn't even aware of that single's existence.

Also, unbeknownst to Richard Berry, the Kingsmen enjoyed an entire Top 40 career, spinning off from their "dirty" "Louie." According to Dick Peterson (the Kingsmen's third and longest-tenured drummer) the band learned from a reporter that "Louie Louie" had been banned in Indiana while recording a follow-up in a Seattle studio in the spring of 1964. Perhaps. Peterson also claimed in a 1986 interview in the San Jose *Mercury News* that the band "went to federal court over it, and the judge wanted to hear the record. He listened and all he could do was laugh. He said he couldn't understand one word of it; he didn't know how they got dirty or even clean lyrics out of it." This conflates the FBI and FCC investigations with the results of the Ely lawsuit; no such courtroom adjudication of the record's quality or obscenity ever took place, or it would be written large in the annals of the First Amendment such a case would violate six ways to Sunday.

The Kingsmen's later interviews are checkered with such apocrypha. Most of it can be written off to the entertainer's instinct to make a good story better. Sift enough old interviews, though, and suspension of disbelief grows ever more unwilling.

Certainly, one would like to believe that "when we would do our concerts people would be watching us and getting into the music, but when it came time for 'Louie Louie,' we lost their eyes to a piece of paper they had wadded up in their wallet. They would open it up and try to read along with the lyrics. So all we would see were tops of heads looking down at their lyrics. After these shows you would see some of these versions. These sweet-looking little, young girls would come up and say, 'Are these the real words of "Louie Louie"?' There would be some pretty dirty stuff on these papers."* But who knows how close it conforms to reality?

Closer, perhaps, than some other yarns. According to Mike Mitchell,** the group's fourth single recycled Flip's other R&B hit, Donald Wood's "Death of an Angel," and it was also banned in some places "because kids were jumping off bridges and blaming us." *Low* bridges, presumably.

The Kingsmen ran into real trouble in 1965, when another Top 10 record, "The Jolly Green Giant," knocked off the Green Giant TV commercials for canned and frozen vegetables ("In the val-ley of the Jolly / Ho! ho! ho! / Green Giant"). The Kingsmen weren't the first to base a hit on a commercial jingle—the Monotones' noble "Book of Love" took its melody from Pepsodent's "You'll wonder where the yellow went . . ." in 1958, and an Alka-Seltzer ad became the T-Bones' "No Matter What Shape Your Stomach's In," also in 1965—but they definitely set the record for getting in the biggest jam over it.

"In those days we had no control over recording. Not over the quality . . . nothing," an unidentified Kingsman told Shannon and Javna. "We were just high schoolers that had a band . . . and they'd say, 'Go into the studio and record whatever you know.' And we'd record everything that we played live, and then pretty soon it would show up on records.

"We knew this song, 'Big Boy Pete,' which we did live all the time." [It originated as a badman ballad by one of the great L.A. doo-wop groups, the Olympics.] "So as a joke, because we always recorded everything we played, we wrote these lyrics up for the Jolly Green Giant version. Then we went into the studio on one of our jaunts, recording 800 songs . . . thinking that the record company was going to say, 'What in the hell is this bull-crap?' 'The Jolly Green Giant' was like our revenge."

But before the Kingsmen knew anything about it, Wand released the song. Because the parody was so strong and the "Big Boy Pete" melody so compelling, the song hit fast and big. But

*From Allan Vorda's interview in the April, 1990 *DISCoveries* magazine.
**In the same Vorda interview.

they'd neglected to obtain rights to the Green Giant from Libby, the corporate monolith that had the big guy trademarked.

"The West Coast office realized they had this [great promotion]," according to the Kingsman. "They used to send us boxes of peas and carrots, tomatoes and stuff to give away at our concerts. At one point they sent this Jolly Green Giant that must've been about ten feet tall to stand on the stage next to us."

But the corporate headquarters–types back East didn't find the record (which depicted the Giant as a guy in dire need of a woman who could accommodate him) amusing at all. The next thing the Kingsmen knew, their second-biggest hit was also in danger of being banned. Twenty years later corporations often used rock performers—including the Kingsmen—as commercial pitchmen. But in 1965, rock'n'roll was disreputable. Libby accused the Kingsmen of "defamation of their company image." Although the record wasn't pulled, the controversy made an embarrassing splash in the press. Which helped sales—of records, if not broccoli.

By 1967 Lynn Easton decided to ditch the rock'n'roll one-nighter circuit for a Vegas-style club act. But the other band members resisted, and this time it was Lynn who left the fold. He returned to Portland and took a job in the advertising business. (In the eighties Easton developed a lecture presentation on the saga of "Louie Louie.")

The Kingsmen continued for about six more months before folding for the duration of the decade. A Seventies comeback attempt by a group that included Peterson, Barry Curtis, and one original member, Mike Mitchell, went nowhere; the same band also played the oldies circuit in the Eighties.

Of the other Kingsmen, only keyboardist Don Gallucci and latter-day bassist Norm Sundholm stayed in the music world. Gallucci formed Don and the Goodtimes, who appeared regularly on TV's "Where the Action Is" alongside the show's house band, Paul Revere and the Raiders, then put together a group called Touch and when that folded, became an Elektra Records A&R man, where he produced Iggy and the Stooges several years before *Metallic KO*.

Sundholm stayed in the Northwest and, with the assistance

of his brother, formed the Sunn Instrument Company, one of the first firms to market large, loud rock'n'roll–oriented amplifiers.

Jack Ely never regained his momentum after his return from the military and the death of Bert Berns; he did re-enter music, scoring industrial training movies ("Now this is how we work the drill press") for a Portland firm. By the early Nineties, though, Jack had licked chemical dependency, started a new family, and begun playing on the oldies circuit and demoing new music.

In 1980 Richard Berry burned out on the after-hours life. The night clubs killed his enthusiasm by demanding no original material at all, which Richard considered "a prostitution-type thing." Besides, he'd become too old for such dives. "I kept visualizing myself falling dead playing a B-flat chord and telling my horn player, 'Don't let me die in this dirty place. Drag me outside where the moon or the sun can shine on me. Just don't let me die in here.' We're doing drugs to go to bed, we're doing drugs to get up, I'm doing five nights a week of two jam sessions.

"And something started happening to me spiritually, too. 'Cause you know, I wasn't going to church, I had been out of church. But something started happening, like something was saying to me, 'You need more than this.' You know, it just kept happening to me. And in 1980 I went back to church [his neighborhood Cornerstone Baptist, where he'd been baptized in 1943]. You know, I don't go around saying, 'I'm a born-again. Glory hallelujah, look what the Lord's done for me.' But that was the time when everything started to change for the positive for me."

Quitting the after-hours circuit may have been a necessity, but alternative job opportunities didn't quickly present themselves. Berry's only remaining music income came biannually from BMI. That's what saved me between starvation and a foot in the grave sometime." But the BMI income didn't amount to much—a few hundred bucks one period, a few thousand if something extraordinary took place.

In 1987 Berry found himself on the welfare line, receiving $240 a month in state aid. "When I got a couple little gigs on the side, it would just supplement the money that I was getting offa welfare. 'Cause if I hadda been totally dependent on welfare—nobody can live off that. And the thing is, what they say about it is true. It's really fucking degrading, man. They give you just enough but not enough. I mean, the check you get from the first to the fifteenth is great, but waiting for that check from the fifteenth to the first is a long ass time, you know.

"And you get in that position where you says, well, I should go out here and get a job. But I don't know how to do nothin' else, I'm a musician, and I got a handicap—you start making excuses. And then you start sittin' up there, lookin' at soap operas all day. And then pretty soon you become a hermit. I was like a hermit in this bedroom, you know."

Idle and bored, Richard responded to a radio ad offering job training. "I figured that somebody would hire me and pay me to learn on the job. But when I got down here, this was a *school*, you know. I didn't want to go to no fuckin' school. So I come home with the papers they gave me and everything, and talked to my daughter. I said, 'Well, they want me to go to school, it's not really a job. You know, I'm the oldest dude in the school.' "

With Christie's encouragement, Berry accepted the deal; the school arranged a loan and in the summer of 1982 Richard went back to school "to learn to program. Now I had to learn how to type. I always wondered how come the typewriter didn't say 'ABCD, EFG.' So I went through this course and I learned how to type, I think, about 45 words a minute. But I got a job. Not computer programming, but I got a job working the keypunch machine, and I was doin' payrolls at this place and everything. I had a job. My first check, I said, 'Hey man! I made a hundred and fifty dollars!' "

But in the spring of 1984, Berry's luck failed again. His neighbor's pit bulls, one of the great media monsters of the Eighties—but, in this case, all too real in their viciousness—got loose from behind a fence and attacked him. As Berry tried to shove the gate closed, one dog jumped up to bite at his hand. Richard fell back against his car. The fall pinched the discs in his lower spine.

"I was laid up close to 45 days. And I lost the job. I was just gettin' off of welfare at that time. So I went to this doctor who's the head spine specialist at the orthopedic hospital."

"I can't afford to be laid up," Berry told the doctor. "I got a job, working computers."

"Well, you won't be able to do that anymore," the doctor replied. "You won't be able to sit that long."

"Oh man," groaned the Columbus of *duh duh duh. duh duh.* "I took this course and you mean to tell me I can't do the work anymore?"

"What were you doing before you got into computers?" the doctor asked. "You don't look like an old guy but you're pretty up there. C'mon, you must have done *something.*"

"Well, I was an entertainer."

"You were an entertainer, you could *entertain.* You gave that up? To do computer work? What kind of entertainer?"

"Well, I was a songwriter and I wrote songs and I recorded."

"Have I heard any of your songs?" asked the doc.

"Well, I wrote this song, 'Louie Louie.' "

"Well, he was one of those baby-boomers," Berry remembered. "He said, [in a growing growl of excitement] 'You wrote *"Louie Louie"?* And you quit *performing?* And went to *computers?*' He made me feel good; he made me feel good enough to feel like, well, maybe I do have a career in this business after all. He told me, 'Well, Mr. Berry, I would advise you to go back to entertaining.'

"And that's when I did. My daughter was takin' me to the job. I was walking up on stage with a cane and I'd sit on the amplifier and sing, 'til my back got better. And after that, like I said, things started to move."

Richard Berry picked the most ironic time to leave music. The early eighties witnessed a steady revival of "Louie"mania. The key year proved to be 1981, when a college deejay's gaze became fixated upon "Louie" in the middle of a very long night.

Jeff Riedle—"Stretch" as the six-foot-five-inch student deejay was known—worked the graveyard shift at KFJC (89.7 FM), the station licensed to Foothill Community College, a two-year school in Los Altos Hills in the midst of California's Silicon Valley, just north of San Jose. Students ran KFJC under the nominal guidance of "station supervisor" "Doc" Pelzell, a man possessed by a vision of radio as an artistic communications medium, a vision perpetually frustrated by the dictates of advertising-driven broadcasting. Pelzell trained radio guerillas and Stretch took his credentials *cum laude.*

One night in the summer of 1981, when he figured his audience amounted to hardly anyone, Stretch began musing about the most recorded rock'n'roll song of all time. The way things were going in commercial radio, he figured the industry would narrow everything down to one song soon, and he might as well get the jump. So he went through the station's massive LP collection and located every "Louie Louie" he could find. There were thirty-three. On his next shift he proceeded to air them, one after the other: If you don't count Woo Woo Ginsburg's double-play on his "Worst Record of the Week," this was the first broadcast "Louie Louie" marathon. It lasted about an hour and a half.

Why did Riedle select "Louie"? For the usual reasons. "When I was looking for songs, I found about 15 versions of 'Hey Joe' and 'Satisfaction' and 'Pipeline,' " he told the San Jose *Mercury News.* "I've heard that there are over 1,000 versions of 'Yesterday,' but I would think that a lot of those are schmaltzy Muzak versions. Besides, 'Yesterday' just wouldn't be the same."

Even while the special aired, listeners called up with tips on where to find more "Louie"s. And about the same time, KALX-FM—the University of California at Berkeley's campus station—surveyed its listeners to determine their favorite all time rock song. "Louie Louie" won. Mel Cheplowitz, a/k/a The Amazing Mystery Deejay, took up the challenge. He took KFJC's list, dug up an additional seventeen "Louie"s and aired fifty in a row in December 1981. In midsummer 1982 Riedle stretched the record to eighty-eight renditions, and the following December, Cheplowitz broadcast an awesome "Lou-A-Thon" of twelve hours, featuring two hundred consecutive variations on "Let's give it to 'em, right now!"

Cheplowitz said he was quitting. KFJC escalated anyway. "We started this thing and we intend to end it," Riedle told the San Francisco *Examiner.*

Riedle, Pelzell, and KFJC air personality Phil Dirt (Frank Luft) decided to assemble a full-scale, all-out assault: "Maximum 'Louie Louie.' " They would go on the air on Friday, Au-

gust 19, 1983, at six in the evening, and stay on the air with an
all–"Louie Louie" format until they had broadcast every version
of the song in existence—known, unknown, celebrated, disreputable, professional, amateur, long, short, reggae, classical (as
"Ludwig Ludwig"), heavy metal, jazz, country and western,
marching band, Spanish, French, Chinese, Italian. They would
air "Louie" in a 35-minute disco version (by the Disco Twits, a
group whose leader was one Jeffrey Riedle), reshaped by 40-plus
minutes of Hell's Angel grunts, and ramcharged in 55 seconds
by the Patti Smith Group. They'd feature "Louie" as played on
a home computer and with kitchen utensils, with door chimes,
and on a touchtone phone's keypad. KFJC would air "Louie"s
sent from Holland, France, Italy, El Salvador, Mexico, and Ja-
pan. Not only would the station broadcast special "Louie"s
made by established recording acts like the Chambers Brothers,
Jonathan Richman, David Peel, Randy Hansen, and the Beau
Brummels; rediscover versions rendered by such "pro" talent as
comedian Buddy Hackett and actor David McCallum (the latter
blessedly instrumental, the former torturously not) and by semi-
fictitious artists like the Bowl of Slugs, the Bloodclots, and Debbie and the Panty Lines, but every two hours it would take a
break from the recordings and broadcast "Louie" live as performed by local bands. KFJC would fly Jack Ely down from Oregon, drag Richard Berry up from L.A. by train, and air a
ninety-minute "Louie Louie" featuring the pair's first-ever personal or musical encounter. They'd even play the Kingsmen's
hit. But no "Louie," not even the Kingsmen's, would they repeat.

   With its 250-watt signal, KFJC could be heard all over the
Bay Area, a hotbed of professional, semi-professional, and upstart garage- and living room–bands. Because they'd be accepting—indeed, soliciting—submissions from the audience as the
marathon went on, the programmers had absolutely no idea how
many "Louie"s they'd air: The *Examiner* headline promised
four hundred.

   But as the weekend wore on, it was as if some sort of inverse
cargo cult had developed—or, to be precise, as if a modern potlatch ceremony had spontaneously begun. People who had no
plans to ever make a tape of anything, let alone a song with "two

notes and three chords" (as Pelzell described it), cooked up arrangements and drove—sometimes many miles—to KFJC to
hand their cassettes over, often without quite knowing why. One
woman showed up with a homemade rendition, the *Wall Street
Journal* reported, and when a staffer praised her courage
("Three chords and no talent is all you need" was the slogan
going over the air), explained that the tape had been made by
her mother, who stayed out in the car.

On Sunday morning Pelzell and Riedle aired a call for no
more new "Louie"'s, on the grounds—said Doc—that "we could
be playing 'Louie Louie' 'til next August if we're not careful."
KFJC staffers crashed on couches, posted messages of impending doom on the office bulletin boards ("All this Louie is making
me itch"), wandered hallways in search of respite or at least caf-
feine. They were drained; they'd given all their spirits possessed.
The potlatch was complete.

Yet the station had committed to airing everything submitted,
and it wasn't until Monday morning that "Maximum 'Louie
Louie' " reached its blessed conclusion. An astonishing *eight
hundred* variations on Richard Berry's cosmic termite trash
spilled out into the ether over Silicon Valley. Listeners to 89.7
FM had heard sixty-three consecutive hours of *duh duh duh. duh
duh.* And there were people who wondered why the "Maximum
'Louie Louie' " logo was the song title, encircled and with a red
slash across it, the universal symbol for "no more 'Louie
Louie.' " As Doc Pelzell said, "After you've listened to five to ten
hours of 'Louie Louie,' it's a very appropriate symbol." After
programming sixty-three hours' worth, it must have constituted
a prayer.

But when Pelzell was asked if his crew hadn't gotten sick of
it all, he said, "Not at all. It's just like the way you feel when you
get off one of the thrill rides at an amusement park. You want to
rest for a while."

As befit an educational institution with a community service
mandate, KFJC treated "Maximum 'Louie Louie' " as a lesson
in radio marketing. Thus, the program had been thoroughly
scheduled, rampantly promoted, and used not only as a satire of

the commercial radio process but as a projection of termite sub-version.

For a time Pelzell and company actually tried to market "Maximum 'Louie Louie' " to other broadcasters as a weekend-long stunt that could galvanize local listenership. But the idea couldn't be sold because it was too easily poached—an appropriate penalty, perhaps, for trying to merchandise potlatch. Well into the Nineties, stations around the United States (KROX, Dallas, Texas; WNOR, Norfolk, Virginia; WRQN, Toledo, Ohio) would institute all—"Louie Louie" formats. Usually these lasted briefly on an outlet about to change formats—say, from album-rock to country, or oldies to Top 40. The "Louie" marathon became a device by which programmers drove old fans away. Presumably, any new listeners attracted by the all—"Louie" broadcast would be swiftly alienated by whatever followed—or so programmers must have hoped, because who the hell could sell ads to an audience composed of beings who sat around going *"duh duh duh. duh duh"* all the time?

Yet there *was* a substantial "Louie" constituency. Stretch Riedle had reinitiated a national obsession, though by now a lot more people were in on the joke. In 1984, when Bill Taylor of WTMA, Charleston, South Carolina, offered to send listeners a list of all the four-letter words in "Louie Louie," WTMA was flooded with self-addressed envelopes. The list included "ship," "girl," and "fine." KFJC tapped into the all—"Louie Louie" market most successfully by convincing Rhino Records, a Los Angeles label that specialized in rock reissues, to put together its *Best of Louie, Louie* compilation to coincide with "Maximum 'Louie Louie'." Only ten tracks long, the anthology omitted many of the most interesting versions of "Louie"'s in favor of novelties. But it featured the Wailers, the Kingsmen, the Sonics, and the Berry remake, plus speed-punk and marching band renditions. Drum majorettes rocked, record collectors quaked, and at least one deejay rubbed his hands in glee.

On March 21, 1985, John DeBella—the top-rated morning-show host at Philadelphia's rock-oriented WMMR-FM—took a copy of *The Best of Louie Louie* out of the station library. DeBella regaled his audience with an account of the "Louie" marathon and the bizarre history of the song. Meantime, he was "needle-dropping the album"—that is, playing bits from various tracks, without letting them play all the way through.

"I started to imagine the other versions of the song we should have: The Mayor's version. Billy Graham's version. Making up an explanation of what Richard Berry had done. I was just winging it," DeBella said. "I started about 9:20 and about 9:40 I went to another record, and then I came back on and said, 'Wouldn't it be funny if we had a parade where the only song people played would be "Louie Louie"?' And I asked listeners to write letters about what they'd do in that kind of parade. That was Thursday and I was off Friday, Saturday, and Sunday. In the mail on my desk that following Monday, there were eighty responses. Eighty responses from one mention!"

"John walked into my office after his shift that Monday and out of the blue asked me, 'How do you put on a parade?' " WMMR general manager Michael Craven told *Billboard.* Craven had little idea either, but DeBella went on the air the next morning and announced that the following Monday—April Fool's Day—WMMR would stage the first "Louie Louie" parade, across Chestnut Street to Independence Mall.

Amazingly, four hundred participants showed up, played kazoos, wore funny hats, and marched to the *duh duh duh. duh duh* beat. Even more amazingly, five thousand spectators turned out to watch them make happy fools of themselves. At the end of the parade, everybody gathered 'round and sang "Louie Louie." At least, they sang the parts they could recall. The rest they hummed or played on kazoos.

"The time was right," explained the jovial, walrus-mustached deejay. Through the gentle outrages of his morning drive-time program, "I was sort of Philadelphia's unofficial entertainment director." But it never occurred to either DeBella or Craven that the "Louie" parade could be repeated.

The following January, though, people started phoning WMMR to ask, "Are you going to do the 'Louie Louie' parade again this year?" The second-most-frequent inquiry: "How can I be in it?" By the first of February, DeBella knew that the event would be repeated—this time on a slightly longer route—but even *he* didn't imagine that the turnout would be so much greater: 1,000 marchers and 60,000 spectators. Once again the day closed with a "Louie Louie" singalong. Once again DeBella said, "Everybody knew the chorus. *Nobody* knew the lyrics."

DeBella developed his own theory about the parade. For one thing, he pointed out, "Everybody can do a version of this song. It cracks me up. I remember, I had Lou Gramm of Foreigner on the show, live, and I asked him, 'Can you sing "Louie Louie"?' 'Of course I can.' So he sang it, backed my band, the Flaming Caucasians. And he even sang it with the mistakes in the right place."

Besides that, there was the whole idea behind the parade: Everybody was eligible to participate; everybody who'd never had a parade finally got one. "Men who can't tie shoes—they have a parade," DeBella proclaimed. "But this was a parade for no reason, a parade for people who could never be in a parade." There were only three reasons for marchers being excluded: If they were too similar to an earlier entry, excessively stupid, or doing something flat-out dangerous.

As a result the parade, like "Maximum 'Louie Louie,' " became a ceremony as close to potlatch as consumer society could come, a ritual in which those who ordinarily found themselves asked for nothing except rampant consumption and noncriminal (not even "good") behavior, found a place to pour out everything they had. All because they needed to fill the same gnawing gnostic cavity as Rockin' Robin Roberts, bringing forth what was within them to save their very souls, even if the destruction they faced was nothing more than silent strangulation amidst the mid-Eighties landscape of grasping greed and claustrophobic conformity.

WMMR sponsored the parade but it grew out of all proportion to the station's investment. "Logistics was our true function, really, and that didn't amount to much," said DeBella. "I don't think we ever spent more than six or eight weeks on it." The population of greater Philadelphia, in a rare moment that actually did manifest something like a brotherly spirit, made it a mass event. The third year, 1987, the parade drew 1,200 marchers, including a re-formed version of the Kingsmen. The total number of sidewalk supervisors reached 95,000.

"There were parents with kids in strollers," remembered

DeBella. "There were papier mache heads of me flying paper airplanes. There were the Steuben Newsmakers with their Grub Grub Machine; there was the Safe Sex Brigade, dressed in great white trash bags, handing out condoms; there was the Louis Louis XVI Brigade, with drums, wagons, and Marie Antoinette; and the Franklin Institute Science Museum put together a 'Louie Louie' science project and blew these huge bubbles." Marchers included a troupe mounted on Harley Davidsons; the Fill Yer Mug Up Orchestra, who played "Louie Louie" by clinking on beer bottles; and classical music themes represented by the locally famous "Louie Louie" String Band. The climax was a mass "Louie" in front of the 100,000-seat JFK stadium. "The Louie heard 'round the world. Or at least in Scranton," *People* called it.

"Louie Louie" had come so far from its termite beginnings that it would now garner an ultimate American accolade of respectability: It would become the official song of a disease.

The Leukemia Society of America (LSA) numbered among its fundraisers several Philadelphia natives residing in Rochester, New York. They persuaded Rochester's WCMF to hold a "Louie" parade as a Leukemia Society benefit. The event raised more than $3,000 and gained multi-media attention for the station and the Leukemia Society. A few months later the Leukemia Society approached WMMR about making the next year's Philadelphia parade a benefit. Funds would be raised through a variety of mechanisms, including corporate sponsorship (arranged by the radio station) from Taco Bell, which made a donation and sold charity kazoos at its outlets—junk food wedded to junk music.

The Leukemia Society and Taco Bell franchised the parade; that first year they sold 150,000 kazoos in Philadelphia, Baltimore, Cleveland, and Louisville, Kentucky. In its most sophisticated variation, the Leukemia Society made money from corporate donations, from ten-dollar registration fees for joining the parade, from kazoo sales, and from a Walkathon tactic, in which individual marchers solicited donations from friends and neighbors based on the number of miles they walked.

The fullest blowout came in 1988, when WMMR and 50 other stations tied "Louie Louie" and leukemia together with parades, "club nights" that sometimes developed into "Louie" marathons, and even kazoo sales at big-league baseball stadiums. On August 7, during the LSA's annual telethon, national grand marshal John DeBella presented the LSA with a $120,000 check representing the combined donations from all the parades.

But by 1989 "Louie Louie" and the Leukemia Society began to become untethered. John DeBella had found that he was "doing more interviews than radio shows," and the Philadelphia city administration—unprepared or unwilling to cope with the security and clean-up—began making permit difficulties. WMMR sued the city for its obstructionism and in 1991 there was no parade—and wouldn't be, DeBella said, until the city changed its attitude.

Meantime, the Leukemia Society ran into copyright trouble. Nobody had ever bothered to acquire permission to use "Louie Louie." Probably, nobody thought of the song as anything but a piece of American folk culture. But "Louie Louie" *was* copyrighted material, and if the copyright proprietors allowed the LSA and Taco Bell to continuing using it without permission, they'd jeopardize their ability to collect from other users. The matter was worked out behind the scenes but having to cough up for the rights made the parades less lucrative to the Leukemia Society. Anyway, even though the "Louie" association remained a terrific fundraiser, it didn't exactly add to the gravity of leukemia's image. So the LSA backed off.

These difficulties couldn't entirely stamp out the *duh duh duh. duh duh* virus, however. On into the early nineties, DeBella said, "People are still doing them all across the country. Some for leukemia, some for the hell of it." Termites rule.

14

The Return of "Louie Louie"

Is there no balm in Gilead? Is there no physician there?
—Jeremiah Ch. 8, V. 22

The Leukemia Society of America dropped "Louie Louie" because it smacked into a miracle: In January 1986 Richard Berry reacquired his song. Henceforth, Richard would receive not only his BMI money, but three-quarters of publishing proceeds from record sales and use of "Louie" in movies, TV shows, and commercials, for instance.

Richard's interest in "Louie" revived just as mid-eighties interest in the song peaked. Besides "Maximum 'Louie Louie,'" the "Louie Louie" parades, and two volumes of Rhino's *Best of Louie Louie* (the second appeared in 1987), "Louie" maniacs began a campaign to make "Louie" the Washington state song. April 12, 1984, was proclaimed "Louie Louie" day at the state capitol in Olympia. Hundreds of "Louie"ites turned up wearing as a symbol of their abiding commitment, grey buttons stamped with a pink outline of the state and "Louie Louie" printed over it. Buck Ormsby, fellow surviving Wailers, and other Seattle music notables turned up to pledge their support and, on the floor of the Senate, Senator Al Williams of Seattle, the resolution's

primary sponsor, debated Senator Arlie Dejarnatt of Longview,
in whose district lived Helen Davis, the composer of the current
state song. (Senate majority leader Ted Bottiger, a Tacoma kill-
joy, informed the Senate press desk that the debate took up only
what would have been lunch hour.)

Richard Berry came, too, in the state of suspended disbelief
he'd maintained ever since a network television reporter first
called him about the story. "Gimme a break" was his initial response. But he agreed to train back to the Northwest and even to
a rewrite: "Me ride the train, goin' with the Wailers, the Kingsmen, they all gon' be there," a version that Buck Ormsby actually recorded with Junior Cadillac, a local Seattle band.

"And then it started really getting political," Richard said
with his characteristically rueful attitude about all the crazy shit
important people have done with his tune. "Like the governor of
Washington had never heard 'Louie Louie,' and the other Sen-
ators were saying, 'Well, you know, what kind of governor is this,
he's never heard the song?' And so the governor sent out to get
all the versions of 'Louie.' "

Finally, in March 1985 a resolution was introduced in the
Washington state Senate to make "Louie Louie," with the new
words, the state song. Sponsored by Williams with the support
of nine others, it included among its various clauses, "Whereas
'Rock and roll' musicians have provided some of our citizens the
ability to express their pride, energy, and creativity through the
art of dance," from a legislature that would, less than a decade
later, attempt to prevent minors from listening to the stuff;
"Whereas Rockin' Robin Roberts, singer for the 'Wailers,' a
Washington musical group, was the original vocalist for the song
'Louie Louie' " (a story retailed with the politician's usual re-
gard for fact); and best of all, "Whereas some of our legislators,
citizens, and even the governor are not familiar with the song
'Louie Louie,' " which you had to love, since this was undoubtedly the first time a career politician had ever been chided for
not being an aficionado of something the FBI considered a
moral threat. The resolution passed the Senate the easy way, by
voice vote.

For better or worse, the governor and the Washington House
did not agree, so "Louie" 's status remains unofficial. Which

was okay with Richard: "I said, 'I'm really flattered, but can you imagine someone going to meet a dignitary at an airport and playin' *duh duh duh. duh duh?*"

Anyway, unofficial status is appropriate, since Richard Berry's recovery of "Louie" had nothing to do with the letter of the law. American copyright law allows nothing like the so-called moral right recognized by France and other nations, under which a creator retains an inalienable smidgen of control over the way in which his or her work is presented, displayed, and performed, no matter who owns the *commodity*. There's not a breath of U.S. legal precedent akin to the judgment of British courts that if a record company or music publisher has obtained excessive economic leverage over an artist, the contract is void and the author gets his material back. In America the principle is "let the seller beware." If a composer dies, his estate can recapture rights 28 years after the initial copyright was granted. But if the writer lives, he's stuck with the deal.

Richard Berry accepted these terms as the down side of the Jesse Belvin "grab the cash and split" principle. He'd never made an effort to recover the "Louie" publishing rights. He preferred to write the deal off as bad luck.

Max Feirtag's wisdom consisted of two things: risking the $750 for the rights to the song and holding onto those rights, rather than selling them off himself for less than they were worth. Make no mistake: Feirtag acquired the song entirely within the bounds of record industry practice. In fact, he was fairer than the Bihari brothers, since he never denied or muscled in on Richard Berry's creative credit. The deal *was* unfair but the unfairness was built into the system. "The Feirtags have read some things that were taken out of [context]," Berry told me. "I've never ever accused them of stealing the song from me. I went to them. I said I need some money to get married. And I knew the only way I was gonna get this money was I had to offer them something. And I had these songs that I had written." Such deals were the rule, and not only for black artists: According to Jack Ely, the contract eventually signed between the Kingsmen and Jerry Dennon gave the band a 3 percent royalty, while the one between Dennon and Wand Records gave him 10 percent.

Richard's harshest criticism of Feirtag reflects his disappointment in a lack of paternalism. "Even after the record became a big record, I think if they hadda came to me and says, 'Look, Richard, we know that at the time you signed this song [over] your condition wasn't what it could have been or what it should have been. So we feel that maybe there was a little unfair advantage that we had, because you wanted to get married and you needed it, so we're gonna give you another $100,000, and we really want you to sign a paper saying 'Adios.' . . ."

For many years, Richard just avoided the whole "Louie Louie" issue. But in 1983 his old friend, schoolmate, and sometime backup singer, Darlene Love, got in touch with Richard. Love perhaps the most talented female vocalist rock has ever known, served as both the true queen of the Phil Spector Wall of Sound (though she got no royalties at all for her work on such great hits as the Crystals' "He's a Rebel") and, as the lead of the Blossoms, the premiere vocal backing group on L.A.'s sixties studio scene. Love told Richard that a man named Chuck Rubin wanted to talk to him about regaining the rights to "Louie Louie."

Rubin, a reformed booking agent, started looking into recapturing publishing and record royalty monies for R&B singers in the late seventies. By 1983 his company, Artists Rights, had made some impressive settlements. Artists Rights was deeply entangled in a long (and ultimately successful) lawsuit with the notorious mobster/mogul Morris Levy and Roulette Records over the copyright renewal for Frankie Lymon and the Teenagers' "Why Do Fools Fall in Love?" It had also begun a long-term battle to badger Atlantic Records into giving more honest royalty accountings to the Coasters, Drifters, and Sam and Dave, among others.

Rubin didn't lack respect for the music, but he went into the business of R&B equity because he realized that recapturing song copyrights and adjusting royalty accounts could be highly lucrative, especially since his fee was 50 percent of the recovered proceeds, in perpetuity. A steep commission, but it seemed like a bargain to writers and performers who'd gotten nothing but a shaft for two or three decades.

"When I told Chuck about 'Louie Louie' and how I sold the

rights, he said, 'Well, let me look into it. I'll tell you right off the bat if there's anything that can be done,' " said Richard.

Rubin asked Berry for a copy of the copyright assignment to Limax. Richard sent it along with all due skepticism. "I still felt that it was a no-win situation," Richard told me. "I knew that legally there wasn't anything that the Feirtags had did. I mean, like they didn't coerce me into signing. I tried to make myself believe that at times, when I started feeling guilty about [selling the song]. But they didn't."

Maybe not, but Rubin hadn't become a successful entrepreneur in the rhythm and blues field without learning the tricks of the old school. For one thing, the nuisance value of any lawsuit couldn't be underestimated. Anyway, Richard had operated under an unfair disadvantage—you could argue that case for *any* black man in America from the first slave who stumbled off the boat up to Michael Jackson—and though it was hardly likely to stand up in court, there was no rule against trying. Did Feirtag really want to go to the expense of proving the case? There may have been other elements that Rubin brought to bear, though he's cagey about what they were. Or maybe Richard just got lucky for once.

In any event, when Rubin called back, Richard recalled, he said, "I think that there's something that might be done."

Rubin got nowhere on the matter for the first two years; in fact, his entreaties served only to alienate Max Feirtag further. That's why Feirtag refused to allow Rhino to use the original Richard Berry and the Pharoahs' recording on the *Best of Louie Louie* compilation. (Berry's re-recording sounded so close to the original that Feirtag threatened to sue producer Richard Foos. It took an expert opinion to persuade him that the Rhino track was a new version. Copyright does not [yet] impede a performer from imitating himself.)

In 1985, Rubin and Berry caught their break. Limax didn't want the song tied up in litigation because a big deal was in the offing. Chiat-Day, a Los Angeles–based advertising agency, wanted to feature the song in a commercial for California Cooler, a brand of "wine coolers" (the fizzy, fermented soda pop enjoying a mid-eighties buzz). "Louie Louie" would be the theme song for a campaign featuring California Coolers as "the

Real Stuff," the original surfer's choice cooler. "The beach-party theme . . . shows frat rats and party animals downing the stuff from the original wide-mouth jars," wrote the San Francisco *Examiner* when the California Cooler ads hit the air the following autumn. "It stresses surfers, the outdoors, revelry, and good times—in essence, everything that's wonderful about the Golden State."

Chiat-Day wound up using such frat-flavored party songs as the Spencer Davis Group's "Gimme Some Lovin'," Little Richard's "Tutti Frutti," and Booker T. and the MGs' "Green Onions" in other aspects of the campaign. "Louie Louie" was the ideal centerpiece—but if there was an ongoing legal squabble, "Wild Thing" might serve the purpose.

That wasn't quite all there was to it, but it was enough to put the deal over the top and, effective January 1, 1986, Limax gave in and reassigned half the copyright of "Louie Louie" to Richard Berry's American Berry Music, which gave him 75 percent of the song (half the publisher's share plus the entirety of the writer's share). Of the twenty grand Chiat-Day paid for "Louie," American Berry and Artists Rights split $13,500. Richard Berry was off the welfare line for good.

He lost only one important point. "When Chuck made the deal, he says, 'Now we can get the song, the publishing, the copyright, but no back money.' And I was hoping that I could get maybe thirty or forty grand in back money. But I knew that we had the wine cooler commercial and that was seventy-five hundred right there for me. Which looked a hell of a lot better than two hundred and forty a month on welfare."

The California Cooler ads kept the mid-Eighties "Louie" revival alive for another season, and it had a substantial payoff for Richard. The commercial was one of the most brilliant uses of rock music ever made in an advertisement. The Kingsmen barging into the soundtrack brought it to life, and there followed a glimpse of what the song had become: A jazz group, an opera singer, and a mariachi combo fell under "Louie" 's spell.

This time, Richard got paid not only a BMI smidgen when his song hit the airwaves, but also every time California Cooler gave away a copy of *The Best of Louie Louie* as a promotion; every time the Kingsmen, who got back together to do a promotional tour sponsored by California Cooler, did a gig. "When we got that wine cooler commercial, I knew. Hey, that made me feel so good. Because for one time when they were singin' 'Louie Louie,' I said, 'Yeah, I'm gettin' *paid. I'm gettin' paid.*' "

Richard even settled with the taxman on the BMI income he'd previously been unable to pay. From the first year onward he said, "I made more money in one year than I think I've ever made in this whole business." In 1989 he made almost $160,000 from the song.

Still, "Louie" seems destined to be dogged by controversy. Chuck Rubin and his attorney in the matter, Richard Bennett, had a falling out and Bennett tried to claim that Berry should be paying him a commission, in addition to or rather than what he paid Artists Rights. The Leukemia Society made sparing use of the song after Rubin reminded them that there was a price to pay. Nevertheless, "Louie Louie" is ubiquitous, a staple of oldies radio stations, frat-party weekends, punk bands in search of a third chord, balding baby-boomers looking for a tune that signifies glory days. The marching band version has become a staple of the Los Angeles Lakers, and the Los Angeles Dodgers, the University of Southern California Trojans, and Notre Dame, and every high school half-time band that hopes to finally get the grandstand to give it some attention. "Louie" pops up in movies like *Naked Gun* and *Fright Night 2.* Listen closely on your next elevator ride and you just might catch Muzak's *duh duh duh. duh duh,* though, of course, "Let's give it to 'em, right now" gets lost in the translation.

The complications could be personal, too. "The accountant told me this year, 'Well, you know you're in the 39 percent tax bracket,' " Berry recalled a couple years back. "I said, 'What is that?' He says, 'Well, you know, you gotta figure that you owe 39 percent of whatever you made to the government.' I said, 'You're kidding—39 per cent? You're talking about forty thousand dollars.' He said, 'Yeah, I can get it down to about twenty-five but you gotta give me five.' I said, 'Take it.' "

But Richard has a ready resolution for such difficulties. "You know, it's like a friend of mine says, 'Four years ago you would have given anything to make what you payin' in taxes, wouldn't you?' I said, 'I would've given anything to have made *twenty* thousand dollars.' So it is a difference. And Artist Rights have really worked with the song. I mean, you know, because sometimes if you get the rights back to the song, all you've got is a piece of paper, because generally there's no money. I just happened to be lucky."

That's one way to look at it.

In this sense the story of "Louie Louie" boils down to long green. But if there's one thing to be learned here, it's that a song like "Louie" exists and persists for reasons more cosmic than commercial. Getting paid doesn't even head Richard Berry's list of satisfactions—he talks with more relish about his son, Marcel, whose music fills Richard's answering machine tape, and about his daughter, Christy, and her striving for a criminology degree: "She wants to be an FBI agent."

Richard himself has lost the desire to record. Today the process is too cold. There are no more hits made on foggy holiday nights—although the practice of running in a ringer when a group's lead singer proves inadequate remains common.

Now the Jesse Belvin principle has evaporated because there's mainly only memory to grab hold of. Yet the music made on those L.A. nights retains its power and magic. On CD, "Pass the dynamite!" and "Roll with me, Henry!" and "A fine little girl, she waits for me," continue to capture imaginations. It's history.

And history has changed "Louie Louie." "History has changed it because the majority of people who are familiar with 'Louie Louie' now are familiar with 'Lou-ay, lou-ay,' " said Richard. "You know, mine is 'Lou-ee, Lou-ee.' I'm doin' it 'Lou-ay, Lou-ay.' I'm doin' it their way. That's the way people wanna hear it.

"I mean, I mix it. Some nights I'm not up to the Kingsmen; sometimes I just wanna say, [sweetly] 'Lou-ee, Lou-ee.' But then I know to get that *party* thing, it's gotta be 1963."

Was that all it was, that party feeling? Was that what Hunter Hancock and Rockin' Robin Roberts and the Kingsmen and you and me and all our termite brethren had (yes, Jack Ely's mother *was* correct) fallen in love with? Richard thought it over.

"Well, you know what it was. I think it was—at that period of time, if anybody would have asked me . . . I think just because it was 'Louie Louie.' " He almost whispered the words.

It was the rhythm? The sound?

"And not only that, it was just 'Louie Louie.' You know, when I really think about it, it was," he crooned the words softly, to himself, the way he might have done back in the Harmony Park Ballroom: " 'Louie Louie, me gotta go.' It wasn't like if you said, 'Joey Joey' or 'Billy Billy'; it was *'Louie Louie,'* you know. And for me it was still the identification. I think that's the greatest idea I could have ever had."

15

"Louie" Reaches Nirvana

There are certain queer times and occasions in this strange mixed affair we call life when a man takes this whole universe for a vast practical joke, though the wit thereof he but dimly discerns, and more than suspects that the joke is at nobody's expense but his own. However, nothing dispirits, and nothing seems worth while disputing. He bolts down all events, all creeds, and beliefs, and persuasions, all hard things visible and invisible, never mind how knobby, as an ostrich of potent digestion gobbles down bullets and gun flints. And as for small difficulties and worryings, prospects of sudden disaster, peril of life and limb; all these, and death itself, seem to him only sly, good-natured hits, and jolly punches in the side bestowed by the unseen and unaccountable old joker.
—Herman Melville, Moby Dick

"Louie Louie" remains the best of songs and the worst of songs. It has been a rock'n'roll song, a calypso, a sea chanty, filthy and obscene, and certainly, it tells the story of rock'n'roll all by itself, just as promised. No one, having come this far, can deny that it remains a ridiculous, damnable piece of trash, though, of course, it's equally undeniable that the culture that breathed life into "Louie" wages eternal war over the nature and value of trash. That "Louie" casts a spell and ought to have been forgotten, that it has served R&B and punk equally well, that its text is both as sacred as anything in urban folklore and the very locus of barbarism in the legendry of our time—none of this can be denied. It persists as an old story, though perhaps the legend is marred, for it's surely no longer an untold story.

Does "Louie Louie" answer our questions? It answers the answerable ones and spits in the eye of anybody who demands a solution to the ones that aren't. What Richard Berry, Rockin' Robin Roberts, Jack Ely, and the paraders and marathoners who are their brethren and heirs have to teach us is this: Embrace "Louie Louie" tightly enough and you may come to know more about yourself than it's easy to contemplate, let alone tolerate. But you'd better watch out: Squeeze it in the wrong place, or for a millisecond too long, or with one erg too much energy, and it'll squirt all over you like a plastic bottle of ketchup—and "Louie" 's even more likely to leave a stain. 'Tis not only the floor of heaven that's littered with banana peels. If it's worth anything, so is the floor of the Rock & Roll Hall of Fame. (To which "Louie Louie" remains shockingly unadmitted—unadmissible, even, which makes some sort of statement about *that* fine institution.)

Which is to say that even the answerable questions only lead to further imponderables. Those who know, know; and those who don't, can go right ahead and ask because there is not, in this medium, any way to spell it out any clearer than by continuing to inquire. Does that make all the foregoing just a shaggy dog story about the ontogeny—not to say ontology—of Frank Zappa's musical stock module? Is it a parable about what happened to rock'n'roll on its journey from being a despicable species of throwaway R&B to something so utterly respectable its Hall of Fame merits an $80 million mausoleum in Cleveland? Can you figure it out from understanding what made Richard Berry croon a secret into Rockin' Robin Roberts' ear that Jack Ely overheard and yawped at the world, which slightly misunderstood him? Does the intro to "Purple Haze" really make reference to "Louie Louie"? Did J. Edgar Hoover really miss the point or was he the only one who truly grasped its true danger to the moral and cultural health of our Nation? And for that matter, if our world were conquered by the potlatch mentality, would an undercurrent of *duh duh duh. duh duh* replace the voice of the turtle in the land? Each of us, perhaps, has our own answer. We sing about that homesick sailor to discover how close our personal version comes to the others.

I say "Louie Louie" shaped the modern rock'n'roller's entire world. Go ahead and dismiss the very possibility, the way your ancestors laughed at the idea that all mammals are ultimately the offspring of beings the size and shape of shrew. You'd rather descend from a monkey like John Lennon—I know you would and so would I (and so would he)—but you're descended from "Louie" anyhow and there ain't a damn thing you can do about it except either claim it or nickname it.

Oh, you dwellers in this time of absurdity and despair! Need I convince you that it was "Louie Louie" that prophesied it all, beginning with the deterioration of "musical quality"— and I mean "quality" as defined by players of rock'n'roll, let alone more high-falutin' types. Remember, when the dimwits claimed he'd dissed Jesus, Lennon, under pressure from his comrades and manager, *backed down.* "Louie Louie" did not back down; it wallowed in its spurious obscenity forevermore and without apology, no matter what the achy breaky feelings of its proprietors.

Today (Right Now! as that idiot Sammy Hagar might bellow) the cutting edges of popular music provide the Rosetta Stone for understanding the legacy of "Louie." Not that decoding the portents found in the fable of *duh duh duh. duh duh* requires the expertise of a cipherer or semiotician. Fuck theory. All you really need to do is *pay attention,* though our age of Ten-Minute Wonders eschews that task in favor of semiotic filibusters.

In the first place, "Louie Louie" connects to Right Now! back at the main stem; Richard Berry's South-central L.A. bad-ass persona, exemplified in "Riot in Cell Block #9" *et seq.,* not only grandfathered the nineties generation of gangsta rappers, but the trouble "Louie" had with the cement-headed minions of J. Edgar Hoover foreshadowed the ways in which rappers like N.W.A., Ice Cube and, most famously, Ice-T have been battered and beleaguered.

Clearly, termites have been at work here, for the chain of descent that links "Louie Louie" to "Cop Killer" reverses Marx's pseudo-Hegelian dictum that, when history repeats itself, tragedy precedes farce. What happened to "Louie" represents a species of low comedy, a bungling bureaucratic nightmare in which their own preconceptions prevented the Bureau's geniuses of criminology from reaching a perfectly obvious conclusion. But in 1989, when the FBI wrote to Priority Records, condemning N.W.A.'s album *Straight Outta Compton*, because it contained the song, "F--- Tha Police," and suggesting that the company place cops beyond criticism; and when it turned out that the cement-head in question, who reported directly to Hoover's successor, had written his missive without ever hearing the song in question; and when that led to the banishment of the song from the group's repertoire on a nationwide tour; and when that led to a police riot and the illegal detention of N.W.A. in Detroit, the only place where so much as a verse of their best-known song got performed, farce had, for the first time in human history, for all I know, come about *before* the manifestation of tragedy.

The direct consequence of that FBI letter (an epistle in fact spawned by an anti-N.W.A. campaign conducted by a far-right church group with big league connections in the Reagan/Bush White House) was the banishment of dozens of rap albums by America's largest record retailers; the spectacle of teens lining up to find an of-age "buyer" for their favorite music, the way we used to try to find one at the liquor store; a national "debate" over whether rappers threatened the lives of cops, which marshalled all manner of anecdotes without the hint of a policeman actually so much as stubbing his toe while carrying a case of Ice Cube cassettes to the pyre; and ultimately, the banishment and public excoriation of Ice-T for daring to conceive a song in which a fed-up ghetto dweller decides to end the cycle of police abusing citizens by any means necessary. You can't avoid the fact that this FBI probe had its (conceptual, if not procedural) roots in the one surrounding "Louie Louie" but it's no farce—you can tell by the bruises on Rodney King's face.

Don't, for God's sake, take that as an indication that farce has gone missing from "Louie" 's story. In an age when the residue of elephant trash piles up way higher than knee-deep from here to the White House, the very idea of farce's absence qualifies as an absurdity. Indeed, the trendiest musical development of the early nineties steeped itself in farce (partly as a means of coping with assorted tragedies). As it happens—or maybe not so coincidentally—that trend sprang up out of Seattle.

This was grunge, the postpunk response to the undying potlatch impulse, a brand of music—or let's say, given its cultivated amateurishness and doting on dissonance, a distinctive assortment of noises—determined to explode pomposity once and for all, preferably by dancing on its face. Loud, fast, nasty; careening, furious, as influenced by smack as punk had been by speed and garage rock by bad acid washed down with cheap suds; a voice of the age that denied all possibility of connection between one human and another, while insisting on putting itself directly in the listener's face, grunge produced paragons like Alice in Chains, Pearl Jam, Soundgarden, and Nirvana, who reveled in self-contradiction as the true, if unknowing, sons of *duh duh duh. duh duh* that they were.

Grunge bands performed nothing as retro as "Louie Louie," and their smeary sound made no accommodation to stop-time rhythms. Nevertheless, grunge at its best reproduced exactly the spirit of "Let's give it to em, *right now!*'" In fact, it treated that declamation as a basic manifesto of human experience, perhaps even as a human right.

The termite spirit embedded so deeply in grunge's biggest hit, Nirvana's 1992 "Smells Like Teen Spirit," that disc jockeys referred to it as "the 'Louie Louie' of the nineties." The comparison made less musical than cosmic sense, but it did not lack a practical side. Like "Louie," only more so, "Teen Spirit" reveals its secrets only reluctantly and then often incoherently. It's a yowl of pain and bitter anguish, a leap (for what? not anything so simple as riches and stardom) that hates itself for bothering to care. "Teen Spirit" is as mournful as it is angry, and it is one of the most pissed-off records ever made. It's a song whose subject can only be suggested after the blunt trauma of hearing it: death, stardom, fandom, consumption, production, overkill, underattention, obscenity, and feeling fucked in the head all loom toward you, even though they float up from a sonic soup so dense with remorseful guitar and ballistic drum attack that you'd have to be the sonic equivalent of an experienced anthracrite miner to parse out the exact details of what's going on.

I'm not sure anybody really knows what the words are, not even Nirvana's Kurt Cobain, who wrote and sang them. Lord knows what rumors could be construed from the fragments— "Hello, hello, hello / How long" and "Here we are now, entertain us / I feel stupid and contagious"—that leap out of the overamped guitar murk. So far, no such folklore has surfaced, though it needn't since the gossip about Nirvana's chemically saturated personal lives has taken its place.

In fact, I spent some time attempting to decipher the lyrics of "Teen Spirit," listening to it over and over again to try to decipher just what the hell Cobain was saying. I reached some interesting conclusions, convincing myself that the opening line must be "Well, the lifestyle it was dangerous" and that the first verse ended, according to my notes, "with two thoroughly incomprehensible lines in which he could be hollering anything: 'It's an idol,' 'I'm in denial,' or 'revival,' or 'I'm on vinyl,' followed by 'I'm a Beatle,' though for that matter it could just as easily be 'beetle.' " Fortunately, CD players operate at just one speed.

Despairing of reaching any conclusion, I stumbled into what seemed a piece of luck: an invitation to have cocktails with Johnny Rotten at Coco Pazzo, a chic New York restaurant. Introduced to Rotten, I immediately grilled him: "I figure you're the only person left to ask. Do *you* know the lyrics to 'Smells Like Teen Spirit'?"

"Yes." He unveiled his ferociously toothsome grin. "But I know something more important." A long leering pause. "Never get involved with drugs. You *always* get caught." Well, even I knew that much.

There were no frat-house buddies to turn to, no school bus rides on which to speculate, and anyway, such is the failure of the contemporary imagination that "Smells Like Teen Spirit" had already been written into rock'n'roll history as incomprehensible. But I wanted—by now, I *needed*—to know what kind of barside shaggy dog story Kurt Cobain, true scion of Richard Berry that he'd proven to be, might have invented. Or at least, I wanted a version more trustworthy than the evidence of my own ears.

So I got into a taxi and traveled cross-town to a music store where, with a blush, I asked for a copy of "Smells Like Teen Spirit." It cost $3.79 plus tax.

Now, the sheet music of rock'n'roll songs is notoriously meaningless. Half the time, the notes and chords are so shredded and mangled that the transcribers can't make them out, the band certainly hasn't bothered to write down what it plays before it starts rolling tape, and anyhow, it's just another tiny part of the cash flow, less lucrative than T-shirt concessions, so most rock'n'roll songwriters probably never even bother to look at their own lead sheets. Why would they? *They* know what they're singing and playing. And why should they give it up, since part of the whole reason for making rock'n'roll is to do something that speaks directly to those who get it and remains utterly unfathomable to everybody else, even if they have gotten elected governor or appointed head of the secret police?

But I coughed up that $3.79 anyway and I took the flimsy document home and put "Teen Spirit" back on the box and let it blast, 'round midnight. I read along as the music played. All that stuff about revival, denial, and beetles turned out to be "A mulatto, an albino, a mosquito, my libido." What's worse, it scanned perfectly.

The point, if there is one, is that what I imagined was quite a bit better (at least, more gratifying) than what Nirvana actually sang. The story I constructed made sense out of both the restless noise the group created and their own rebellious, self-immolating posture in the face of fame. The fact that my version bore only the most fragmentary relationship to what the group said it sang (and what I now believed it to be singing) didn't extinguish the song. But I won't deny that it diminished it a bit. Worst of all, I'm not sure that I know more about "Smells Like Teen Spirit" now than before I plunked down for the official version of the facts.

Or maybe that should be "best of all." Knowing what's in the documents results in elephantine bloat. But a true termite knows the stories that reside in the heart and soul of the matter. If there is a rational reason why "Louie Louie" and our love for it persists, words will come no closer to its essence than that. Therefore . . .

Me gotta go.

Maximum "Louie Louie": A Discography

This Discography is by "Louie"cologists Doc Pelzel, Stretch Riedle, and Phil Dirt.

This listing of different versions of "Louie Louie" contains, for each entry:

Artist
Title of LP, EP, CD, 12-inch, 45, VHS
Label, Catalog Number   Format
Date Recorded and/or Released   Length
Musical Genre
Notes

The Date Recorded and/or Released, if not printed somewhere on the version itself, is listed with an estimated year as "circa." The Musical Genre is a loose categorization identifying in which section of a record store the version would most likely be found. The Notes contain additional information to identify or differentiate the version. If a version has a title other than "Louie Louie," that title is listed in Notes, except for 45s, in which case that title is in Title. If composer credits for the version are other than Richard Berry, those credits are given in Notes. To help minimize confusion for seekers of additional "Louie Louie" versions not listed here, some Notes list other releases on which the version being discussed has appeared, especially if that appearance was as an imitation "live" version or with a different real or erroneous Length. Also as a convenience for version seekers, this discography does not conform to the *Phonolog* convention of separate listings for "Louie Louie" and "Louie, Louie."

To be listed in the discography, a version must be a performance of "Louie Louie" distinctly different from any other recording listed. Edits, remixes, and overdubs of one performance do not count as different versions, but are listed when possible in the Notes section of the version of which they are alterations. Some artists, therefore, who have "Louie Louie"'s of different lengths on different albums, or who have studio and live "Louie Louie"'s on different albums, may only be listed in this discography once if those "different versions" are actually reprocessed from one recorded performance. Conversely, artists may have multiple listings for versions with the same length if those versions were recordings made at different times and/or with different personnel performing.

It would be gratifying but ludicrous to call this listing "The Complete 'Louie Louie' Discography," because only those versions that could be physically located and verified by the discographers have been included. Versions that "informed sources" said they "were sure" existed did not get included (even if, as Isaac Asimov said about life forms on other planets, it is mathematically certain they exist). Because this discography is the largest listing of renditions thus far, the title "Maximum 'Louie Louie' " still seems appropriate.

Additional versions of "Louie Louie" are still being sought and readers are encouraged to submit documentation of existing versions that are not listed. Submissions should include all available information and fulfill the criteria for being a different version outlined above. Submissions should be made to:

Maximum "Louie Louie"
% KFJC-FM
12345 El Monte Road
Los Altos Hills, CA 94022

Readers who submit information about versions not listed in "Maximum 'Louie Louie' " will receive an updated discography incorporating all additions to the master list given here.

Africa
Music From 'Lil Brown'
Ode Records, Z1244010   LP
Circa late 1960s   (5:40)
Rock/funk
NOTE: This version is part of a medley with "Ode to Billie Joe."

Andress, Tuck
Reckless Precision
Windham Hill, WD-0124   CD
1990   (3:41)
Acoustic folk/jazz

Angels, The
A Halo to You
Smash Records, MGS 27048   LP
Circa 1964   (2:29)
Pop female vocal

Los Apson
"Ya No Lo Hagas"   Import
Peerless Records, EDP1263   45
NOTE: Group is from *A*gua *P*rieta, *SON*ora, Mexico.

Arnold-Hedgecock Experience
Charade Records, CH-186434   45
1987   (2:41)
Rock
NOTE: Roger Hedgecock, former mayor of San Diego,
    was removed from office for accepting illegal
    campaign funds.

Australian Crawl
The Final Wave   Import
Freestyle Records, SFL1 0142   LP
1966   (5:06)
Rock
NOTE: Song entitled "The Last Louie Louie" credited to
    (Berry, Wheatley); live recording, Australian import.

Barner, George and the Original Trendsetters
Breadline Records, 3528597   45
Circa 1985   (2:58)
Rock with horns
NOTE: George Barner, at time of recording, was Thurston
     County Commissioner in the state of Washington.

Basement Wall
Texas Punk Volume 8 (compilation)
Cicadelic Records, CIC 978   LP
Song recorded 1967; album issued 1986   (1:22)
Garage rock

Beach Boys
Shut Down Volume 2
Capitol Records, T2027   LP
1964   (2:21)
Pop surf
NOTE: This version also on *Best of the Beach Boys*
     Volume 1, Capitol DT 2545; *For All Seasons*, Pair/
     Capitol PDL2-1068; Japanese Import CD *Shut Down*
     Volume 2, Capitol CP216005; American *Shut Down*
     Volume 2 later retitled "Fun Fun Fun."

Beau Brummels
Beau Brummels '66
Warner Brothers Records, WS1644   LP
1966   (2:12)
Rock

Beau Brummels
Volume 44
Vault Records, 121   LP
1967   (2:41)
Rock
NOTE: This version is a different performance from the
     version on *Beau Brummels '66*.

Bedient, Jack and the Chessmen
Live at Harvey's
Fantasy Records, 8365   LP
1965   (2:10)
Lounge jazz
NOTE: Song is entitled "Louis Louis" on LP.

Belushi, John
Animal House (soundtrack)
MCA Records, MCA 3046   LP
1978   (2:55)
Frat rock
NOTE: This version is also on the *Animal House* CD,
   MCA D31023 and on a single, MCA 40950.

Berry, Richard and the Pharaohs
Flip Records, Flip 45-321   45
1956   (2:10)
R&B
NOTE: The original 45 issue had "Louie Louie" as the B
   side to "You Are My Sunshine." A later 45 issued with
   the same Flip 45-321 catalog number had "Louie
   Louie" as the A side and "Rock Rock Rock" as the B
   side. If this discography were being compiled
   chronologically, the version listed here would be
   number one. This studio version is also on *12 Flip
   Hits*, Flip Records, Flip 1001, 1959; *Golden Era Series,
   Volume 3*, Era Records, ESVOL3, circa 1967; *Louie,
   Louie*, Earth Angel Records, JD901, 1986; *Born Bad
   Volume 4*, Australian import LP, Born Bad Records,
   BB004, 1989; *Hawk*, Condor Records, 100.

Berry, Richard
Casino Club Presents Richard Berry Combo Live Session is listed on
   LP front, and *Richard Berry and the Soul Searchers Live Session* is
   listed on the LP center label.
         , PR151-02   LP
Circa 1960s   (3:06)
R&B
NOTE: There is no name for the record company issuing
   this LP, neither on the center labels of the disc nor
   on the front, back, or spine of the jacket.

Berry, Richard
Great Rhythm and Blues Oldies Volume 12
Blues Spectrum Records, BS112   LP
1977   (2:13)
R&B
NOTE: This version produced by Johnnie Otis.

Berry, Richard
Best of Louie, Louie
Rhino Records, RNEP 605   LP
1983   (2:18)
R&B
NOTE: When Limax Music denied permission to Rhino
 Records to use the original 1956 Richard Berry
 "Louie, Louie" on their *Best Of* compilation, Rhino
 commissioned Richard to re-record the song in a style
 reminiscent of the original.

Black Flag
Poshboy Records, PBS 13   45
1981   (1:27)
Punk
NOTE: Credited to (Berry, Cadena). Despite different
 times being listed, this version also appeared on *Posh
 Hits Volume 1*, Poshboy PBS 8138, 1983; *Everything
 Went Black*, SST Records, SST 015, 1983; *The First
 Four Years*, SST Records, SST 021, 1983; *Wasted
 Again*, SST Records, SST 166, 1987 (colored vinyl);
 Duck and Cover, SST Records, SST 263, 1990. The
 single has been re-issued as SST 175 numerous times
 on different colored vinyl.

Black Flag
Who's Got the 10½
SST Records, SST CD060   CD
Live recording August 23, 1985, Portland, Oregon   (4:13)
Punk

Blondie
Wet Lips Shapely Hips   Bootleg
Old London Records, OL91011   Import
1979   LP
New wave   (4:20)
NOTE: Recorded live in London.

Bloodclots
Raw Deal   Import
Raw Records, RAWL 1   LP
1977   (2:14)
Live garage punk
NOTE: British import.

Broth
Broth
Mercury Records, SR 61298   LP
1967   (3:40)
1960s' inner-city peace and love pop rock
NOTE: Group consisted of one member of each major
    ethnic group, wearing bell bottoms and tie-dyes, posed
    around a VW van.

Burgett, Jim
Recorded Live at Lake Tahoe
Wolfgang Records, LP 4321   LP
Circa mid-1960s   (2:12)
Casino lounge music

Cannon, Ace
Sweet 'n' Tough
Hi Records, SHL 32030   LP
June 1966   (2:11)
Pop jazz

Cano, Eddie and His Quintet
Brought Back Live from P. J.'s
Dunhill Records, DS50018   LP
Circa late 1960s   (2:05)
Latin pop jazz
NOTE: Besides "Louie Louie," LP also contains "Slip
    Slip," "Wack Wack," and "Monday Monday."

Cats Under the Stars
Monkey Business Records, MBR 001   45
1982   (3:00)
Pop jazz/lounge vocal

Challengers
California Kicks
GNP Crescendo, GNP 2025   LP
1966   (3:15)
Pop surf instrumental

Chan-Dells
Arc Records, 8102   45
August 1963

Checkmates, Inc.
Too Much
Ikon Records, IER 121-4   LP
Circa 1960s
Casino lounge
NOTE: Recorded live at Harvey's Resort Hotel and
    Casino; Side 1 begins with "Louie Louie" and Side 4
    ends with "Louie Louie."

Clarke, Stanley and George Duke
Clarke/Duke Project
Epic Records, FE 36918   LP
1981   (5:06)
Fusion jazz

Cramer, Floyd
Here's What's Happening
RCA Records, LPM 3746   LP
1967   (2:30)
Easy listening
NOTE: Credited to (Barry [sic], Ortega, Decaro)

Crescent Street Stompers
Aquarius Records, AQ5041   45
Circa early 1970s   (2:45)
Pop psychedelic

Crest, Dick
Would You Believe the Dick Crest Orchestra
Mar-Tur Records, S1001   LP
Circa late 1960s   (2:32)
Big band

Cult, The
Lil' Devil   Import
Beggars Banquet Records, BEG 188TD   Double 12" 45
Recorded January, 1986   (3:30)
New wave
NOTE: "Louie Louie" is part of a live medley; British
    import.

Day, Otis and the Knights
Otis My Man   Video
MCA Home Video, 80392   VHS HiFi
1986
R&B

Don and the Goodtimes
The Hitmakers
Jerden, JRL 7005   LP
Circa mid-1960s   (5:12)
Rock
NOTE: Don Gallucci, former Kingsmen member.

Doucet, Michael
Cajun Brew
Rounder Records, 6017   LP
1988   (3:09)
Cajun

Dunn, Kevin
Tanzfeld   Import
Press Records, P4007   LP
1985   (3:40)
Industrial new wave
NOTE: British import.

Duplex
Battle of the Bands
Star Records, SRM101   LP
1964   (2:10)
Garage rock
NOTE: Hawaiian battle of the bands competition. This
    version re-issued on *Pebbles Volume 16*, AIP Records,
    AIP 10023, 1985.

Eddie and the Subtitles
Skeletons in the Closet
The record label is called "No Label"   LP
1980   (2:20)
Garage punk
NOTE: This version also issued on a 45 with no label, no
    catalog number. This version replaces Black Flag's
    version on the CD of Rhino's *Best of Louie, Louie*
    compilation.

Ely, Jack and the Courtmen
Bang Records, B-520   45
"Louie Louie '66"   (2:32)
1966
Rock
NOTE: "Ely" is misspelled as "Eely" on label.

Experience
Experience   Import
Vogue Records, SLVLX575   LP
Circa 1970s   (7:03)
Progressive
NOTE: French import.

Falcons, The
Phillips Records, 333-527JF   Import
Circa 1966   45
Garage punk   (2:38)
NOTE: This Dutch single was included on *The V-Lips
Greatest Hits* compilation album, Frizzbe Records,
Frizz 6, 1985, released in Holland.

Fat Boys
Coming Back Hard Again
Tin Pan Apple/Mercury Records, 835809-2   CD
1988   (5:42)
Mainstream rap
NOTE: This version also available as a 12″ single, Tin
Pan Apple/Mercury Records, 871011-1, with the
(5:42) version and a (3:50) edit. The (3:50) edit also
issued as a 7″ single, Tin Pan Apple/Mercury Records,
871010-7. Credits for rap lyrics to Jim "Jimbo"
Glenn.

Feelies
Jerden Records, 904   45
Circa mid-1960s   (2:59)
Rock
NOTE: This group is no relation to the 1980s' group with
the same name.

Flamin' Groovies, The
Still Shakin'
Buddah Records, BDS5683   LP
1976   (6:45)
Rock
NOTE: This studio version also on *Still Shakin'* CD, Big
Beat Records, W1K925.

Flamin' Groovies, The
Slow Death, Live
Lolita Records, 5004   LP
Recorded 1971; released circa 1983   (8:02)
Rock

NOTE: This version recorded at the Fillmore, San
Francisco, on June 30, 1971, which closed a week of
live quadraphonic broadcasts carried on KSAN-FM,
San Francisco (front two channels) and KOME-FM,
San Jose (rear two channels). The version on this LP is
from the KOME channels. A poor quality mono
recording of the KSAN channels appears on *Bucket
Full of Brains*, Voxx Records, VXS200.015, in 1983.
Also, a (7:20) length printed on album, but version
times at over 8 minutes.

Flamin' Groovies, The
Studio '70   Import
Eva Records, EVA12045   LP
Recorded in 1970; released in 1984   (6:14)
Rock
NOTE: This version recorded live at a rehearsal at the
Matrix club. This French import version is also on the
Groove In CD, limited edition of 1,000 copies printed
for Caroline, Revenge Records, EV300.

Flash Cadillac and the Continental Kids
American Graffiti (movie)
MCA Home Video, VHS 66010   VHS Hi-Fi
1973 movie; 1984 video release
Rock
NOTE: This version has Flash Cadillac and the
Continental Kids portraying "Herby and the
Heartbeats." Version released on video only and is not
on the soundtrack or any Flash Cadillac albums.

Flippers, The
Pebbles, Volume 28   LP
Archive International Productions, AIP10046
Recorded 1966; released 1986
Garage R&B
NOTE: This version was originally released in Sweden in
1966 as a 45 on Karusell Records, KFF634.

Fountain, Pete
I've Got You Under My Skin
Coral Records, CRL 757488   LP
Circa 1967   (2:08)
Easy listening

Friar Tuck
Friar Tuck and His Psychedelic Guitar
Mercury Records, SR61111   LP
1967   (4:56)
Parody
NOTE: Friar Tuck is Gary Paxton and cronies. Song title
is listed as "Louis Louis." This version lampoons
many of the then-current soft rock groups (The
Mamas & The Papas, Fifth Dimension, etc.).

Bobby Fuller Four
EVA Records, EVA12032   Import
Recorded 1964   LP
Pop rock   (2:33)
NOTE: This French import was also released in
Germany on Line Records, OLLP 5302, in 1983. The
version is part of a medley: "Louie Louie"/"Farmer
John"/"Jenny Lee."

Girl Trouble
Stomp and Shout and Work It on Out
Dionysus Records, ID 123318   LP
Recorded January 19, 1985; released 1990
Rock

Guru Josh
Infinity
Deconstruction Records, 2358-2-R   CD
1990   (4:09)
Dance

Half Japanese
Our Solar System
Iridescence Records, K6   LP
1981   (1:25)
New wave
NOTE: "Louie Louie" is about half of a studio medley.

Harper, Charlie
Stolen Property   Import
Flicknife Records, SHARP 100   LP
Recorded September, 1981   (2:42)
British pub rock
NOTE: Charlie Harper was a member of UK Subs.
"Louie Louie" is credited to the Kingsmen (but this
British import LP also has "Hey Joe" credited to
"Traditional").

Harrison, Wilbert
Let's Work Together
Sue Records, SSLP 8801   LP
1969   (5:11)
R&B
NOTE: Also on 45, Juggernaut Records, 70SUG405,
       (3:00)

H. B. and the Checkmates
Lavender Records, R1936-1   45
Circa 1966   (2:30)
Garage rock
NOTE: Reissued on Pebbles' *Highs in the Mid Sixties,
       Volume 7—The Northwest*, AIP Records, AIP 10012,
       1984. Song is entitled "Louise, Louise."

Heavy Cruiser
Heavy Cruiser
Family Production Records, FPS 2706   LP
1972   (3:26)
Rock
NOTE: Heavy Cruiser was a Neil Merryweather group.

Hermanos Carrion
Lagrimas de Cristal Que Manera de Perder   Import
Dimsa Records, DML 8672   LP
1971   (2:41)
Folk-rock
NOTE: Song is entitled "Alu, Aluai" and is credited to
       (Barry [sic], Ortega). Recording is a Mexican issue for
       South American distribution.

Honey, Ltd.
Lhi Records, 1216   45
Circa mid-1960s   (2:59)
Easy listening
NOTE: Produced by Lee Hazelwood, this 45 is identical
       on both sides, except for a short intro voiced by
       Hazelwood on one side only.

Die Hornissen
"Spin Radio Underground Program"   Broadcast
Promo Only, NC 007U2   LP
1986   (1:08)

New wave

NOTE: German group "The Hornets" do a live medley that includes "Louie Louie" for this segment of the "Spin Radio Underground Program" out of Los Angeles.

Iggy and the Stooges
Metallic K.O.
Skydog Records, IMP 1015
1976
Rock
NOTE: This version also issued as a French import CD *Metallic 2 × KO*, Skydog Records, 622322CD.

Import
LP
(3:24)

Impossibles, The
Best of Louie, Louie
Rhino Records, RNEP 605
1983
Choral parody

LP
(:37)

Invictas
A Go-Go
Eva Records, EVA 12016
Recorded circa mid-1960s; released circa early 1980s
Top 40 cover club
NOTE: French import.

Import
LP
(2:25)

I Trappers
"Lui, Lui Non Ha"
CGD Records, ND9606

Import
45
(2:26)

Jan and Dean
Command Performance
Liberty Records, LST 7403
1965
Pop surf
NOTE: This live version also on *Golden Hits Volume 3*, Liberty Records, LST 7460.

LP
(2:44)

Bobby Jay and the Hawks
The Watusi
Warner Brothers Records, WS 1562
Circa mid-1960s
Instructional pop dance

LP
(2:30)

Jones, J. J.
Misty
Wyncote Records, SW 9170   LP
Circa mid-1960s   (2:47)
Piano bar organ

Joske Harry's
Arsa Records, AR107.   Import
                                                            45

Junior Cadillac
Junior Cadillac Is Back
Great Northwest Records, GNWRC 000002   LP
Circa early 1970s   (3:45)
Bar band
NOTE: Junior Cadillac is Buck Ormsby's band.

Kingsmen Featuring Jack Ely
60's Dance Party
Era Records, PBU 5000   LP
Recorded 1976; released 1982   (2:42)
Rock
NOTE: This recording was made 13 years after the
    original and is definitely not a remix.

Kingsmen, The
Jerden Records, 712   45
1963   (2:42)
Rock
NOTE: This version is the original studio recording with
    Jack Ely vocals. It was also issued as "Louie Louie
    '64–'65–'66" with the same Jerden catalog number.
    This version was also issued as a 7" 45 on Wand
    Records, 143; Scepter Records, SWF 21011 (with the
    time incorrectly listed as 3:00); and Eric Records,
    4007.
        This version was overdubbed with concert audience
    noise to create a "live" version, which was issued on
    the *In Person* LP, Wand Records, WDM or WDS 657,
    1963. The original studio version was issued on the
    Kingsmen *Greatest Hits* LP, Wand Records, WDS 681,
    1966.
        This original version is probably the most
    commonly anthologized version. Although the times
    listed for it usually vary between (2:24) and (2:42), the
    song has been on more than 50 compilations,

including *Time-Life Presents '1964 The Beat Goes On,'*
Time-Life Classic Rock Series, 1988, SCLR09; *The
Northwest, Nuggets Volume 8*, Rhino Records, RNLP
70032; *Cruisin' 1963*, Increase Records, INCM 2008,
1972; *Quadrophenia*, original movie soundtrack,
Polydor Records, PD-2-6235, 1979; *Spud's
MacKenzie's Party Favors*, Capitol Records, C1-48993,
1988; *Music to Watch Cartoons By*, Phoenix Records,
8406; *Encyclopedia of 100 Rock and Roll Super Hits*,
TVP Records, TVP-1009, and (naturally) *Best of Louie,
Louie*, Rhino RNEP 605, 1983. The original studio
version is also the one most likely to be found on
syndicated radio program discs, tapes, and CDs, such
as "Continuous History of Rock and Roll, the Great
American Dream the Garage Bands," Rolling Stone
Magazine Show #8, broadcast November 28, 1981,
RSMP 81-8.

Kingsmen, The
10 Big Hits of the Rock and Roll Era
Audio Encores Records, AE1-1006   LP
1980   (2:42)
Rock
NOTE: This 1980 Nashville re-recording may or may not
have included appearances by original members of the
Kingsmen.

Kinks
Kinksize
Reprise Records, RS 6158   LP
1965   (2:57)
Rock
NOTE: This version also appears on *Kink Kingdom*,
Reprise Records, 6184. An edit (:51) of this version
appears on a promo-only LP, *Then, Now, and in
Between*, Reprise Records, PRO 328, as part of a
crudely spliced medley.

Last, The
Best of Louie, Louie
Rhino Records, RNEP 605   LP
1983   (3:21)
Rock
NOTE: This version also appears on a French import LP,
Painted Smiles on a Dead Man, Lolita Records, 5005.

Les Dance and His Orchestra
  Best of Louie, Louie
  Rhino Records, RNEP 605   LP
  1983   (2:40)
  Parody
  NOTE: This version contains a David Bowie sound-alike
    vocalist singing the words to "Louie Louie" over a
    "Let's Dance"-ish musical arrangement.

Little Bill with the Adventurers and Shalimars
  Topaz Records, T-1305   45
  Circa 1960s   (2:25)
  R&B

London, Julie
  Yummy Yummy Yummy
  Liberty Records, LST 7609   LP
  Circa 1968   (2:40)
  Pop vocal
  NOTE: The single of this version was Liberty Records
    56085.

Lyres, The
  Live at Cantone's
  Pryct Records, PR1003   LP
  Recorded late 1970s; released 1987   (5:10)
  Garage rock

Maddalena
  "Lui Lui"   Import
  RCA Italiana Records, PM45-3413   45
  NOTE: Italian import.   (2:45)

Magazine 60
  Barclay Records, 200191   Import
  Released 1981   12″ single
  Dance   (1:03)
  NOTE: This French import 12″ club single contains
    "Louie Louie" at the end of a long medley of 1960s
    covers.

McCallum, David
  Music—It's Happening Now!
  Capitol Records, ST 2651   LP
  Circa mid-1960s   (3:13)

Easy listening
NOTE: Yes, Illya Kuryakin from "The Man from
   U.N.C.L.E." No, he doesn't sing. It's an instrumental.

MC5
Kick Copenhagen   Bootleg
Lawn Mower Records, MOW 11   Import
November 1972   LP
Pre-punk   (6:40)

M.C.K. and the Surfettes
"Life's a Beach"
Music Force Records, 30694   12″ single
1988   (4:33)
Dance/rap
NOTE: There are four mixes: Radio version (4:33)
                           Instrumental version (5:30)
                           Summer Club Mix (5:30)
                           Spring Break Mix (6:01)

Mellodramatics
First American Records, FA 1209   12″ single
1981   (7:23)
Dance
NOTE: There are two mixes: Vocal (7:23), Instrumental
   (8:04)

Messengers, The
The Messengers
Rare Earth Records, RS 509   LP
1969   (3:11)
1960s pop rock

Mitchell, Willie
On Top
Hi Records, SHL 32048   LP
January 1969   (2:08)
Pop jazz instrumental
NOTE: Willie Mitchell was *Cashbox* magazine's
   Instrumentalist of the Year, 1968.

Morticians, The
Morticians Records, 102   45
Circa 1968   (3:10)
Texas garage rock

Motorhead
Bronze Records, BRO 60   Import
1978   45
Metal   (2:42)
NOTE: This British import version has also been on the
     LP *No Remorse*, Pro Records, 823303-1, 1984; and on
     Anthology, Raw Power Records, RAWLP011, 1985.

Nat and John
Charly Records, C92A   Import
                                                                    45
                                                                 (2:31)

Nelson, Sandy
Boss Beat
Imperial Records, LP 12298   LP
Circa 1966   (2:28)
Alternative easy listening

Our Brothers Keeper
King Records, 6399   45
Circa 1960s   (2:30)
Rock

Outcasts, The and The Sting Rays
Battle of the Bands Live, Round One
Cicadelic Records, CICLP 990   LP
Recorded 1967; released 1984   (3:25)
Garage rock

Outta Place
We're Outta Place
Midnight Records, MIR 102   LP
1984   (2:14)
Garage rock

Pink Chunk
Monster Wax Records, 79-120   45
Circa 1979   (4:57)
Self-abuse (Wild Man Fisher impaled on Portsmith
     Symphonia)

Pink Finks
Raven EP LP Volume 3   Import
Raven Records, RVLP20   LP
Recorded circa mid-1960s; released 1984   (3:12)
Garage rock
NOTE: Australian import.

Piranhas, The
Somethin' Fishy
Custom Fidelity Records, CF-1452   LP
Circa mid-1960s   (4:04)
Teen garage rock

Les Players
"Si C'Etait Elle"   Import
Polydor Records, PPN1879   45
NOTE: French import.   (2:25)

Plunkett, Steve
My Attitude
Quality Records, 15179   CD
(Circa ??)   (4:48)
Dance
NOTE: Also on CD single with Club Mix (4:48), Radio
    Mix (3:14)

Promenaders
Promenaders   Import
Y Records, Y31   LP
1982   (1:52)
Polka
NOTE: This British import version is part of a medley.

Psychotic Petunias
Mayhem Records, Mayhem 1   45
(Circa ??)   (3:58)
Dirge instrumental with chipmunk vocals

Purple Helmets
Ride Again   Import
New Rose Records, Rose 160   LP
1988   (3:13)
British pub rock
NOTE: The "Louie Louie" on this French import is live.
    The band consists of members of the Stranglers (J. J.
    Burnel, Dave Greenfield), Vibrators (John Ellis),
    and Interview (Manny Elias).

Pyramids, The
The Original Penetration
Best Records, BRS36501   LP
1964   (1:55)

Surf
NOTE: Re-issued as *Penetration*, What Records, W12-
2404, 1983.

Redding, Otis
Pain in My Heart
Atco Records, 33-161   LP
1965   (2:05)
Soul

Red Square
Best of Louie Louie Volume 2
Rhino Records, R1 70515   LP
1989   (3:01)
Russian rock

Renaud, Line
MGM Records, K14500   45
1973   (2:46)
Pop female vocal

Paul Revere and the Raiders
Sande Records, 101   45
1962   (2:41)
Rock
NOTE: This version was issued in June 1963 on
    Columbia Records, 4-42814, a 45 backed with "Night
    Train." It was first on LP in June 1967 on the *Greatest
    Hits* album, Columbia Records, CL2662 (mono) and
    CS9462 (stereo). (Later, KCL2662 and KCS9462,
    when list prices went up.) The stereo LP contains the
    original mono mix, which was "electronically re-
    recorded to simulate stereo" for the May 1972 *All-
    Time Greatest Hits* collection, KG31464. This version
    also appeared on the Rhino Records *Best of Louie
    Louie Volume 2* compilation, R1 70515, released in
    late 1989; and on Columbia's CD anthology, *The
    Legend of Paul Revere*, CZK 45311.

Paul Revere and the Raiders
Here They Come
Columbia Records, CL2307 (mono) and CS9107 (stereo)   LP
August 1965   (2:48)
Rock
NOTE: This was a real "live" version, not just an overdub
    of crowd noise onto the studio version.

Paul Revere and the Raiders
"Louie Go Home"
Columbia Records,   45
Circa late 1963
Rock
NOTE: This is the "answer" song to "Louie Louie." It
   was later used as the flip side to the Sande version on
   Columbia Hall of Fame 45 4-33082.

Paul Revere and the Raiders
Special edition
Raider/America Records, RA 682   LP
1982   (3:14)
Rock
NOTE: This live version, recorded at the Milwaukee
   Summer Festival, was available through the Paul
   Revere and the Raiders Fan Club.

Paul Revere and the Raiders
Paul Revere Rides Again
Hitbound Records, 51-3013   Cassette only
1983   (2:12)
Rock
NOTE: This cassette-only version was a 1983 studio
   recording custom-manufactured for Radio Shack.

Rice University Marching Owl Band
Rice University Marching Owl Band
MOB Records, MOB 121682   LP
1982   (1:09)
Marching band
NOTE: This version later issued on *Best of Louie Louie*,
   Rhino, RNEP 605.

Ripp Tides, The
Surf Wax Records, 1001   EP
1981
Horn-based surf band
NOTE: This version was on a 10″ EP.

Robbs, The
W'R IT Records, 1340   45
Circa mid-1960s   (2:45)
Rock

Roberts, Rockin Robin
Etiquette Records, ET 1   45
1961   (2:40)
Northwest R&B
NOTE: Roberts fronts The Wailers.

Sandpipers
Guantanamera
A&M Records, SP 4117   LP
1966   (2:45)
Spanish easy listening
NOTE: This version was credited to (Barry [sic], Ortega,
    and DeCaro). It was also issued on *Sandpipers Four
    Sider*, A&M Records, SP 3525; as a 45, A&M
    Records, 819; and on Rhino Records *Best of Louie
    Louie*, RNEP 605.

Santamaria, Mongo
Hey, Let's Party
Columbia Records, CS 9273   LP
1967   (2:16)
Pop Latin

Sentinals
Vegas Go-Go
Sutton Records, SSU338   LP
Circa mid-1960s   (3:15)
Top 40 cover band

Shaffer, Paul
Coast to Coast
Capitol Records, C1-48288   LP
1989   (3:31)
Pop

Shaggs, The
"Louis, Louis"
Concert Records, 1-78-65   45
1965
Garage rock
NOTE: This all-girl garage band from New Ulm,
    Minnesota, issued this variation on "Louie Louie"
    backed with "Summertime News," a variation on
    "Summertime Blues."

Shockwaves, The
Best of Louie Louie Volume 2
Rhino Records, R1 70515   LP
1988   (2:03)
Surf

Sisters of Mercy
"Possession," "Rough Diamonds," "Cryptic   Bootleg
Flowers," "Ghost Riderz"   Promo
Skeleton Songs Records, Skelet 03;   Import
Easy Flyte Records, Flight 140;   LP
Metropol Records, no catalog #;   (7:35)
Takrl Records, 1402;   (11:00)
3/28/83 at Paradiso, Amsterdam, Holland;   (6:35)
6/5/84 at Nijmegen Doornroosje, Holland;   (5:30)
11/84, Germany;
3/16/85 at Leeds University, England
NOTE: The above four versions are all portions of
    medleys in Sisters of Mercy live shows. Although they
    are distinctively different recordings and not remixes
    of one recording, their repeated performance as a
    regular song in their tour act classifies them closer to
    different takes or different mixes of the same session.

Slack
Deep Like Space
C/Z Records, CZ011   LP
February 1988

Smith, Patti
Teenage Perversity and Ships in the Night   Bootleg
ZE/Anonym Platten Spieler Records, ZAP 7854   LP
January, 1976   (1:10)
Punk/new wave
NOTE: As with Sisters of Mercy, many variations exist,
    all from live performance bootlegs on which "Louie
    Louie" segues out of "Pale Blue Eyes.

Sonics, The
Etiquette Records, ET-23   45
1966   (3:00)
Raw garage rock
NOTE: This version also appeared on The Sonics *Boom*
    LP, Etiquette Records, ETALB027, released in 1966.

Sonics, The
Sinderella
Bomp Records, BLP 4011   LP
Recorded 1967; released 1980   (4:02)
Garage rock

Sounds Orchestral
Janus Records, J124   45
Circa late 1960s   (3:46)
Easy listening

Springsteen, Bruce
Rockin Days   Bootleg
Amazing Pig Records, TAP 009   LP
1983   (2:11)
All-American rock'n'roll

Standells
In Person at P.J.'s
Liberty Records, LST 7384   LP
Circa 1967   (4:10)
Primordial punk
NOTE: This version also on Sunset Records, SUS 5136,
   Live and Out of Sight LP.

Stewart, Dave and Barbara Gaskin
Spin
Rykodisc, RCD 20213   CD
1991   (5:08)
Soft rock
NOTE: Version is part of a medley entitled "Cast Your
   Fate to the Wind/Louie Louie," credited to (V.
   Guaraldi, R. Berry). Stewart and Gaskin were
   members of Hatfield and the North, and National
   Health.

Stupid Set
"Soft Parade"   Import
MMMH Records, MMMH0001   12" Single
Recorded 1980; released 1981   (10:28)
Industrial
NOTE: This version credits (R. Berry, P. Bassani, G.
   Huber, G. LaVagna, F. Sabbioni).

Los Supersonics
Los Supersonics   Import
DCA Records, DIC1001   LP
NOTE: San Salvadoran import.

Surfaris
Hit City '64
Decca Records, DL-4487   LP
1964
Surf

Surfaris
Surfaris Live
Koinkidink Records, KWK 102   LP
Recorded September 18, 1981; released 1983   (2:32)
Surf

Surkamp, David
Butt Records, MGLS003   Import
1984   45
Rock
NOTE: David Surkamp is a member of Pavlov's Dog.

Swamp Rats
Disco Sucks
Keystone Records, K111541-39   LP
Recorded July 1966; released 1979   (3:13)
Garage rock
NOTE: This version was also on 45, St. Clair Records,
    MF69. The timing is listed as (2:35) on the disc but is
    really (3:13).

Swingin' Medallions
Double Shot
Smash Records, SRS67083   LP
1966   (2:44)
Rock

Tams
A Little More Soul
ABC Records, ABCS 627   LP
Circa late 1960s   (2:57)
R&B

Tek, Denniz
Denniz Tek   Import
Revenge Records, MIG 13   CD
Recorded 1974; released 1989   (3:38)
rock
NOTE: Denniz Tek is guitarist for Radio Birdman. This
    French import was recorded in Australia and mixed in
    Texas.

Tempos, The
The Tempos
Crypt Records, 010   LP
Recorded 1966; released 1987

39 Clocks
Subnarcotic   Import
Psychotic Promotion Records, PS1-B   LP
Circa 1980   (2:50)
New wave
NOTE: German import. This version was also on a British
    import in 1983 on Flicknife Records, catalog number
    Sharp109. This band contains former members of
    Clock DVA.

Thunders, Johnny
In Cold Blood   Import
New Rose Records, Rose 18   LP
Recorded August 1982; released 1983   (3:05)
Punk

Tiger Moon
Vision Records, VR 1205   12″ single
1988   (5:04)
Dance
NOTE: There are three mixes: Club mix (8:32), Doub-A-
    Louie Mix (7:43), Urban Radio Mix (5:04)

Toots and the Maytals
Funky Kingston
Mango Records, MLPS 9330   LP
1975   (4:25)
Reggae
NOTE: The timings listed on different printings of this
    LP and CD vary considerably from each other and
    reality. (One printing credits F. Hibbert with writing
    "Louie Louie" and R. Berry for writing "Funky
    Kingston.") The import CD on Trojan Records, TRLS
    201, at (5:45) real time is the longest version.

Topics, The
Living Evidence
Topic Records, LP1001   LP
Circa 1970s   (6:16)
Pop rock

Troggs
From Nowhere   Import
Page One Records, TL5355   LP
1966   (3:00)
Rock
NOTE: This British import version is also on *With a Girl
Like You*, DJM Records, DJML047, 1975, a German
import LP *Original Troggs*, DJM 0044202, and a
French import LP the *Very Best of the Troggs*, Vogue
P.I.P. Records, 404520, 1980.

Tucker, Maureen
Playing Possum
Trash Records, TLP 1001   LP
1982   (2:40)
Rock
NOTE: Maureen Tucker was drummer for the original
Velvet Underground.

Turner, Ike and Tina
Ike and Tina Turner's Greatest Hits, Volume 2
Saja Records, 91224-2   LP
Recorded circa 1968; released 1988   (2:45)
R&B
NOTE: This version is also available on *Best of Louie
Louie, Volume 2*, Rhino Records, R1 70515.

Tyme Code Featuring Steve Sparling
Macola Records, MRC0949   12″ single
1986   (3:33)
Dance
NOTE: There are two mixes: Short version (3:33)
                           Long version (5:10)
The short version is included on Rhino Records *Best of
Louie Louie, Volume 2* LP, R1 70515.

Underground All Stars
Extremely Heavy
Dot Records, DLP25964   LP
Circa late 1960s   (3:20)
Psychedelic rock
NOTE: A Kim Fowley production.

USC Trojan Marching Band
Let the Games Begin
(There is no record label or catalog number.)   LP
1984   (1:12)
Marching band

Ventures, The
A Go-Go
Dolton Records, BST 8037 LP
Circa 1965 (2:10)
Pop instrumental

Ventures, The
Play Guitar with the Ventures Guitar Phonics Volume 7 LP
Liberty Records, LST 17507
Circa mid-1960s
Surf-instructional

Viceroys, The
At Granny's Pad
Bolo Records, BLP 8000 LP
1963 (1:04)
1960s cover band

Wailers, The
The Wailers and Company LP
Etiquette Records (2:32)
Circa early 1960s
Northwest R&B
NOTE: Re-issued as Imperial Records, LP9262, *Tall Cool One.*

Wammack, Travis
Atlantic Records, 45-2322 45
1966 (2:03)
Fuzz guitar instrumental
NOTE: This version is on a British CD, *Scr-Scr-Scratchy,* Zuzazz Records, Z2010, 1989; and a French import LP, Formidable Rhythm N Blues, Atlantic 40254.

Whitcomb, Ian
Sock Me Some Rock
Tower Records, ST 5100 LP
Circa 1967 (4:44)
Pop jazz
NOTE: This version was shortened, overdubbed with crowd noise, and issued as a 45 by "Sir Arthur," Tower 216. This 45 edit was subsequently issued on Ian Whitcomb's *Instrumentals* LP, First American Records, FA 7751, in 1980.

White, Barry
Beware
Unlimited Gold Records, FZ 37176   LP
1981   (7:14)
Easy soul
NOTE: A shortened edit (3:35) was issued as a 7" 45, ZS5
    02425, and a 12" promo-only single was issued
    concurrently with the LP.

Wig, The
Live at the Jade Room
Texas Archive Records, TAR 3   LP
Recorded 1966; released 1983
Rock

Wilson, Ron and the Surfaris
Lost It in the Surf
Bennett House Records, BHR 116   Cassette
Recorded 1985; released 1986
Scottish surf
NOTE: Ron Wilson sang vocals and pounded on a
    Scottish ceremonial drum, accompanied by Sean
    Fulsom playing bagpipes.

Winter, Johnny and Friends
A Lone Star Kind of Day
Relix Records, RRCD 2042   CD
1990   (3:24)
Boogie rock

XL 5 Minus 1
"Booga Louie"
Cove Records, 101   45
Circa 1967

Young and Restless
Something to Get You Hyped
Pandisc Records, PD-8809   CD
1990   (5:07)
Rap
NOTE: "Louie Louie" credited to the group, with no
    mention of Richard Berry.

Young and Restless
Coupe de Ville (soundtrack)
Cypress Records, LP 71334   LP
1990   (several)

Rap

NOTE: The four mixes below also appear on the Cypress
    LP "Coupe de Ville," 74500.

The four mixes: "Louie Rap"	(3:38)
"Louie Vocal Attack"	(3:45)
"Louie Louie House Mix"	(3:38)
"Louie de Palma Mix"	(0:57)

Zappa, Frank

Uncle Meat

Bizarre/Reprise Records, 2MS2024   LP

1968   (2:28)

Orchestral aside

NOTE: The version is entitled "Louie Louie at the Royal
    Albert Hall in London." There are no composer
    credits on the LP, but Richard Berry is credited on the
    CD (Rykodisc 10064-65). An actual performance of
    "Louie Louie" is on the *Unmitigated Audacity* bootleg
    LP, GLC Records, D549, 1981.

Index

Abbot, Gary, 111
Abbott, Keith, 69
Adams, Dorothy, 37
"Ain't That Love," 173
Aladdin, 15
Alice in Chains, 204
"All Day and All of the Night," 143
Allemang, Ross, 93
Allen, Steve, 56
"AlleyOop," 56
AMC, 172
"American Bandstand," 90, 92
American Berry Music, 1, 196
"Angel of My Life," 30
"Angel of the Morning," 149
Angels, 144
Animal House, 145, 162, 163, 165, 171
Animals, 146, 152
Annabella, 167
"Annie," 28
"Annie Fannie," 88
Apple, 152
April-Blackwood, 149, 150
Apson, Los, 148
"Are You a Boy or Are You a Girl," 146
Arlen, Harold, 32
Armo Music, 27
Armstrong, Louis, 51
Artists Rights, 194, 196, 197, 198
Ashby, Irving, 33
Asheton, Ronald Frank, 159, 160
Asheton, Scott, 159
Astaire, Fred, 32
Atlantic Records, 25, 194
Australian Crawl, 147

"Baby, That Was Rock'n'Roll," 24
Baker, James, 28
Baker, LaVern, 28

Ballard, Hank, 27, 50, 90, 118
and the Midnighters, 50, 64
Bangs, Lester, 102–3, 145
Bank Records, 113
Barbarians, 146
Barnes, George, 169
Barnum, H. B., 173
Barretto, Ray, 31
Bay State Distributors, 107, 109
Beach Boys, 14, 52, 59, 109, 123, 144, 170, 171
Beatles, 52, 59, 64, 70, 74, 96, 101, 108, 124, 140, 144, 152, 177
"Beatnik Sticks," 91, 92
Beau Brummels, 147, 184
Beck, Jeff, 152
Behind the Hits, 150
Belushi, John, 45, 162, 163, 165, 166
Belvin, Jesse, 14, 17–19, 21, 168, 173, 198
"Be Mine," 16
"Be My Baby," 105
Bennett, Richard, 197
Bernal, Gil, 24
Berns, Bert, 113, 180
Berry, Chuck, 11, 26, 31, 32, 59, 61
Berry, Dorothy, 37, 148, 172
Berry, Richard, 10, 11, 12–14, 16–40, 42, 45–46, 54, 57, 61, 66, 68, 74, 76, 79, 94, 118, 119, 122, 130, 140, 141, 142, 143, 144, 148, 152, 158, 168, 169, 172–77, 180–2, 184, 192, 201, 202
and the Soul Serchers, 175
Best of 'Louie Louie', 41, 44, 186, 196
Best of the Kingsmen, 103

"Be True to Your School," 123
Beware, 168
"Beware," 168
Big Bopper, 59
"Big Boy Pete," 81, 101, 112, 178
"Big Break," 26
Big Chill, 7
Bihari, Joe, 18, 21, 25, 29, 33, 34, 37, 39, 44
Bihari, Jules, 18, 21, 33, 34, 37, 44
Bihari, Saul, 18, 21, 33, 34, 37, 44
Blackboard Jungle, 115
Black Flag, 166
Blackwell, Bumps, 50, 51
Blaine, Hal, 105
Bland, Bobby, 46
Blecha, Peter, 103, 110
Bloodclots, 165, 184
Bloom, Allan, 4
Blossoms, 194
"Blue Moon," 59
Blues Brothers, 164
Blues Magoos, 145
BMI, 29, 40, 42, 43, 196, 197
Bobby Fuller Four, 145
"Bodies," 166
Bold Soul, 172
Bolster, Ken, 99, 100
Booker T. and the MGs, 87, 196
"Book of Love," 178
Boone, Pat, 64, 148
Bottiger, Ted, 192
Bowl of Slugs, 184
Bow Wow Wow, 167
Boy George, 5, 167
"Boy Next Door," 109
Bradford, Alex, 16
Briggs, Willie, 175
"Brother Louie," 152–54
Brothers Four, 93
Brown, Charles, 16, 21
Brown, Errol, 152, 154

Brown, James, 61, 95
Brown, Michael, 153
Brown, Rabbit, 24
Brown, Roy, 16
Brunvand, Jan Harold, 115
BT Express, 58
Buckley, Tim, 157
Bumble, B. and the Stingers, 92
Butera, Sam, 26
"Bye Bye," 26

Cadets, 15, 21, 26, 29. *See also* Jacks
Cadillac, Junior, 192
California Cooler, 195, 196
Callender, Red, 33
Calloway, Cab, 51
"Calypso Blues," 33
Cannibal and the Head-hunters, 146
"Can't Get Enough of Your Love, Baby," 168
Capital Records, 108
Cash, 20
Cashbox, 68, 123
"Castles Made of Sand," 69, 151
"Casual Look, A," 30, 38
"Cathy's Clown," 56
Challengers, 147
Chambers Brothers, 184
Chandler, Gene, 81, 86, 101
Chantry, Art, 69
Chapman, Reid, 124–25, 126
Charles, Ray, 16, 37, 51, 52, 103, 142, 173, 174
"Charlie Brown," 25
Chase, Ken, 87–88, 96, 97, 98, 109, 111, 112, 131
Checker, Chubby, 64
Checkers, 59
Checkmates, Ltd., 147
Cheplowitz, Mel, 183
"Cherrie Pie," 23
Cherry, Don, 16
Chimes, 22
Christian, Charlie, 31
Christmas, 71
Christopher, Jordan, 149, 150
  and the Wild Ones, 149
Chudd, Lew, 30
Clark, Dee, 86, 101
Clark, Dick, 61, 64, 65, 70, 89
Clark, Doug, and the Hotnuts, 146
Clarke, Stanley, 170
Clash, 165, 166
Class, 15, 29
Clay, Andrew Dice, 5
Cleveland, James, 16

Cliques, 18
Clothes, Todd, 36
Clovers, 90
Coasters, 21, 25, 26, 194
Coates, Dorothy Love, 16
Cobain, Kurt, 205
Cocker, Joe, 163
"Cock in My Pocket," 159
Cohen, Stanley, 115
Colbert, Godoy, 30
Cole, Nat King, 16, 33
Collins, Billy, 175
Collins, Noel, 30
Columbia Records, 99, 108
"Come Softly to Me," 56
Comets, 90
Command Performance, 145
Commercial Recorders, 65
Como, Perry, 44
Connick, Harry, Jr., 4
Connick, Harry, Sr., 4
Contours, 74
Cooke, Sam, 18
"Cop Killer," 203
Coryell, Larry, 52, 59
Count Five, 146
Coupe de Ville, 7–10
Courtmen, 112
Cramer, Floyd, 147
Craven, Michael, 187
Crawford, Brother J. C., 158
Crayton, Pee Wee, 22
"Crazy Lover," 26
Criss, Cherry, 17
Criss, Dolphy, 17
Criss, Farmer, 17
Criss, Sonny, 17
Crowns, 27
Crystals, 194
Culture Club, 167
Curtis, Barry, 111, 179

"Da Doo Ron Ron," 59
Dale and Grace, 123
Dalley, Robert, 83
Daltrey, Roger, 144
Dance Halls, Teen Fairs and Armories, 65
Dangel, Rich, 66, 68, 70, 72, 97
Darin, Bobby, 50
"David's Mood," 51
Davies, Ray, 143
Davis, Helen, 192
Davis, Jimmie, 34
Davis, Maxwell, 14, 21, 22, 29, 36
Davis, Sammy, Jr., 174
Dawson, Jim, 17, 19
Day, Doris, 100
"Death of an Angel," 24, 30, 46, 113, 178
Debbie and the Panty Lines, 184

DeBella, John, 186–90
Debonairs, 20
Dejarnatt, Arlie, 192
Delp, Brad, 155
Deltas, 162
Dennon, Jerry, 98, 99, 107–9, 131, 135, 193
Dick James Music, 150
Diddley, Bo, 65
Dirt, Phil, 183
"Dirty Robber," 65
"Dirty Water," 146
Disco Twits, 184
Dixon, Floyd, 21
Dixon, Luther, 108
"Does Your Chewing Gum Lose Its Flavor on the Bedpost Overnight?," 107
"Do It ('Til You're Satis-fied)," 58
Dolphin, John, 18, 20–21, 22
Dolphin/Dolton, 64, 66
Dolphy, Eric, 16
"Dominique," 123, 124
Domino, Fats, 15, 26, 30, 64, 119
Don and Dewey, 15
Don and the Goodtimes, 179
Donegan, Lonnie, 107
Donna/Del-Fi Records, 56
Donovan, 152
"Don't Believe in Christ-mas," 71
Dootone, 15
"Double Shot," 145
Downbeats, 91
"Down Here on the Ground," 175
"Do You Love Me," 59
Dreamers, 26
Drifters, 194
Duke, George, 170
"Duke of Earl," 59
Dunlap, Jim, and the Horsemen, 87
Durr, Dorothy, 175
Dylan, Bob, 71, 141
Dynamics, 59

"Earth Angel," 18, 23, 30
Easton, Lynn, 81–88, 94, 97, 98, 100, 103, 105, 111, 117, 122, 137, 140, 141, 179
Eddy, Duane, 88
"Ed Sullivan Show," 85
El-Chords, 118
Elektra Records, 179
"El Loco Cha Cha," 13, 31, 33, 147
"El Watusi," 31

Ely, Jack, 81–88, 95, 97, 98, 100, 102, 104, 110, 111, 112, 122, 130, 136, 180, 184, 193, 198, 201
Ely, Ken, 85
Emerson, Lake, and Palmerisms, 92
"Emma," 152
Empire, 29
Engelhart, Little Bill, and the Bluenotes, 47–50, 51, 53–55, 56, 57, 58, 61, 64, 66
Entertainment Machine, 75
Entwistle, John, 144
Epic Records, 155
Era, 177
Ermines, 26
Etiquette Records, 66, 70, 71
"Every 1's a Winner," 152
"Express," 58

Fabulous Wailers Live at the Castle, 70, 74
Faggen, Gil, 124–25
Farmer, Art, 16
"Farmer John," 145, 146
Fat Boys, 170–71
Feirtag, Max, 15, 30, 33, 35, 37, 42, 44, 45, 98, 117, 122, 126, 131, 137, 148, 168, 173, 193, 195
Fellers, Rocky, 109
"Fever," 50
Finley, Larry, 25
Finn, 133
First Thing Coming, 69
5 Hearts, 22
5 Royales, 23
Flairs, 14, 15, 16, 21–26, 30, 37, 54
Flaming Caucasians, 188
Flamingos, 20, 23
Fleetwoods, 56, 64
Flippers, 147
Flip Records, 15, 30, 33, 34, 42, 68, 98, 137, 172, 177, 178
"Fog Cutter," 57
Foos, Richard, 42
Foreigner, 188
Forrest, Jimmy, 95
Fountain, Pete, 147
Four Seasons, 59
Fowley, Kim, 92
Fox, Pete, 20, 26, 30
Foxx, Redd, 146
"Framed," 25
Francia, Johnny, 57
Frantics, 57, 58, 61, 66, 71, 74
Frazier, Thurston, 19
Freberg, Stan, 56

Fred, John, and His Playboy Band, 146
Freed, Alan, 15, 43, 59
Freeman, Ernie, 33, 42
Fright Night 2, 197
"F--- Tha Police," 203
Fulson, Lowell, 50
Funhouse, 158
Funky Kingston, 148
"Funny," 18

Gallucci, Don, 81, 86–87, 92, 98, 103, 179
Gants, 146
"Garageland," 166
Gardena Records, 92
Gene & Eunice, 44
Gentrys, 146
Gibbs, Georgia, 27, 43
Gillet, Charlie, 102
"Gimme Some Lovin'," 196
Ginsberg, Allen, 24
Ginsburg, Arnie, 106–7, 110, 183
"Girl of My Dreams," 18
"Girl Who Stopped the Duke of Earl," 173
"Give Her All the Love I've Got," 175
"Give Peace a Chance," 152
Glass, Phillip, 5
Glenn, Jim "Jimbo," 170
"Gloria," 27, 146, 151
GNP, 15
"Go Away Little Girl," 110
Golden Crest, 64, 65
"Golden Teardrops," 23
Goldman, Albert, 4
Goldmark, Goldie, 31
Goldmine, 65, 83, 95
"Goodnight My Love," 18
"Good Rockin Daddy," 16, 28
Gordon, Dexter, 16
Gordon, Rosco, 21
Gordy, Berry, 59, 74
Gore, Tipper, 4
Grace, Robert J., 131, 135, 138
Graham, Bill, 70
Gramm, Lou, 188
Granahan, Gerry, 149
Grant, Amy, 122
Greek, John, 62, 65
Greenberg, Florence, 108, 136
"Green Onions," 59, 87, 196
Grendysa, Peter, 119
"Guantanamera," 147
Gubow, Lawrence, 134
Guess Who, 18, 109
Gunter, Cornelius, 20

Gunter, Cornell, 26
Guss, John, 91, 92, 95

Hackett, Buddy, 184
Hagar, Sammy, 202
Haley, Bill, 31, 90, 115
Hamilton, Chico, 17
Hancock, Hunter, 15, 35–38, 198
Hansen, Randy, 184
Haris, Gail, 61, 62
Harris, Robert, 30
Harris, Wynonie, 15–16
Harrison, George, 124
Harrison, Wilbert, 147
Hart, Roger, 89, 93, 94, 96, 98, 99, 110, 174
Hasil, 172
Hatfield and the North, 169
"Haunted Castle," 98
"Havana Moon," 32, 33
"Have Love, Will Travel," 70, 39, 142, 174
"Have You Seen Your Mother, Baby, Standing in the Shadows," 146
Hawkins, Jennell, 27, 30, 172
Hawkins, Screamin' Jay, 31
"Heat Wave," 59
Hedgecock, Roger, 169
Henderson, Stanley, 30
Hendrix, Jimi, 47, 53, 59, 69, 151–52
"Henry," 28
Hensen, Gary, 175
Here Are the Sonics, 142
Hermans's Hermits, 152
"He's a Rebel," 194
"He's So Fine," 59
"Hey, Henry," 16, 28
"Hey Joe," 183
Hibberts, Toots, 148
"Hi-Heel Sneakers," 146
Hirt, Al, 52
"Hit the Road, Jack," 59
Hodge, Alex, 20
Hodge, Gaynel, 19, 20
Holden, Dave, 55
Holden, Oscar, 50, 51, 55
Holden, Ron, 51, 55–61, 66, 80, 122
and the Playboys, 55, 57
Holly, Buddy, 48, 59, 61, 81
Hollywood Blue Jays, 20
Hollywood Flames, 19
Hollywood Recorders, 33
"Honeydripper," 17
"Honey Love," 50
Hooker, John Lee, 21
Hopkins, Lightnin', 21
Horne, Lena, 32
Hot Chocolate, 152
"Hound Dog," 24, 25

Houston, Whitney, 170
Hover, H. D., 174
Howlers, 22
Howlin' Wolf, 15
"Huggy Boy," 15, 20
Hynde, Chrissie, and the
    Pretenders, 166

Ian, Janis, 153
"I Can't Explain," 144
Ice Cube, 25, 202, 203
Ice-T, 25, 202, 203
"I Had a Love," 21, 22
"I Love an Angel," 56, 57,
    61
"I'm a Man," 146
"I'm Gonna Love You Just a
    Little More, Baby," 168
"I'm Leaving It Up to You,"
    123
Imperial Chief, 15
Imperial Records, 30
"I'm Ready," 26
"I'm Still in Love with You,"
    22, 26
"I'm Wild About That
    Thing," 119
"I Need You," 144
"In My Room," 109
"In the Midnight Hour,"
    146
"I Put a Spell on You," 31
"I Saw Her Standing
    There," 96
Island Records, 148
Isley Brothers, 142
"It's Ecstasy When You Lay
    Down Next to Me," 168
"It Will Stand," 45
Ivy, Percy, 22n
"I Wanna Be Your Dog,"
    159
"I Wanna Testify," 146
"I Want to Hold Your
    Hand," 124, 140
"I Want You Back," 96

Jack, Wolfman, 15
Jacks, 23, 26. See also
    Cadets
Jackson, Chuck, 108, 175
Jackson, Jesse, 5
Jackson 5, 96
Jacquet, Illinois, 51
"Jailhouse Rap," 170
"Jailhouse Rock," 25
"J.A.J.," 51
"James Alley Blues," 24
James, Elmore, 21
James, Etta, 14, 16, 21, 27,
    43–44
Jan and Dean, 145
Javna, John, 150

Jazz on a Summer's Day,
    143
Jefferson Airplane, 148
Jefferson, Joe, 20
Jefferson, John, 20
"Jenny Lee," 145
Jerden, 98, 100, 107, 108
Jessie, Obie "Young," 20, 22
John, Little Willie, 50, 53
Johnson, Ron, 150
"Jolly Green Giant," 112,
    113, 178
Jones, Gloria, 30, 33
Jones, Quincy, 51, 52, 53
Jones, Ricky Lee, 15
Jordan, Louis, 31, 33, 51
"Judy in Disguise," 146
"Juke Box Jury," 25

Kalvert, Scott, 171
Kama Sutra Records, 153
K&G, 172
Kansas, 154
"Kansas City," 59, 147
Kapralik, David, 100
Keen, Bob, 56
"Keep On Dancing," 146
Kelton, Frank, 27
Kennedy, John, 140
Kenny G., 51, 53
Kerner, Kenny, 153
"Killer Joe," 109
King, B. B., 21, 49, 50
King, Carole, 153
"King Creole," 25
Kingsmen on Campus, 141
Kingsmen in Person, Featur-
    ing "Louie Louie," 111
Kingsmen Trio, 10, 11, 31,
    35, 68, 74, 76, 78, 79,
    81–89, 93, 94, 97,
    98, 99, 100, 101, 107,
    108, 109, 110, 113, 117,
    119, 120, 122,123, 124,
    126, 127, 128, 131, 136,
    137, 141, 142, 144,
    148, 149, 153, 162, 165,
    166, 177–180, 184,
    193, 196, 198
Kinkdom, 144
Kinks, 143, 144
Kink-Size, 144
"Ko Ko Mo," 44

"La Bamba," 145
Laboe, Art, 61
La Juive, 31
Lamarr, Hedy, 140
Lancaster-Barker, Lisa, 65,
    72
Landis, John, 162
"Land of 1,000 Dances,"
    146
"Last Kiss," 56

"Last 'Louie Louie'," 148
Latin Rascals, 170
Lawrence, Steve, 110
Led Zeppelin, 155
Left Banke, 153
Leiber, Jerry, 15, 21, 24–25,
    26, 33, 67
Lemmings, 163
Lennon, John, 101, 124,
    152, 202
Letterman, David, 141, 169
Levin, Drake, 174
Levinson, Bob, 106–7, 109
Levy, Morris, 194
Lewis, Dave, 51, 53
    and the Dynamics, 52
Lewis, Jerry Lee, 15, 59, 90
Liberty Records, 56, 68, 71
Liggins, Joe, 16, 17
"Like, Long Hair," 92
Limax Music, 1, 39, 44,
    117, 126, 129, 137, 195,
    196
Lindall, Bob, 95, 97
Lindsay, Mark, 89, 91, 110,
    122, 174
Lipstick Traces, 79
Little Esther, 15
"Little Green Thing," 51
"Little Latin Lupe Lu," 146
Little Richard, 14, 15, 26,
    52, 59, 65, 67, 81, 118,
    196
    and the Upsetters, 50
Lloyd, Ian, 153, 154
"Loco-Motions," 59
Lois Music, 27
London, Julie, 147, 149
Look at the Fool, 157
"Louie, Go Home," 113,
    142, 174
"Louie Louie '66," 113
Louie Report, 115
"Louis Quatorze," 167
Love, Darlene, 194
"Love Me Girl," 26
"Love You So," 51, 55, 56,
    57, 61
"Lucille," 65
Luft, Frank, 183
Lulu, 152
Lymon, Frankie, and the
    Teenagers, 194
Lynn, Loretta, 49, 52

Mabon, Willie, 24
"Mad About You," 26
Madonna, 5
Magnum, 36
Manson, Charles, 100
Marcus, Greil, 78, 79, 143
Margolis, Chuck, 55
Marsalis, Wynton, 4
Martindale, Wink, 92

Martinez, Ray, 33
Marvin and Johnny, 21, 23
Marx, Richard, 14
"Mary Lou," 22, 26
Master Recorders, 21
"Mau Mau," 57, 61, 65
"Maximum 'Louie Louie'," 183
May, Joe, 16
"Maybelline," 26
Maye, Arthur Lee, 27, 30
Mayfield, Percy, 16
MC5, 132, 133, 158, 165
McCallum, David, 147, 184
McCartney, Paul, 96, 101, 124
McKuen, Rod, 149
McLaren, Malcolm, 167
McNeely, Jay, 17
McPhatter, Clyde, 50
Melcher, Terry, 100
"Memories of El Monte," 37
Mercer, Johnny, 32
Merilee, 61
Mermaids, 124
Messengers, 147
Metallic KO, 159, 165, 179
Meyer, Augie, 140
Milburn, Amos, 16
"Milk Cow Blues Boogie," 96
Milton, Roy, 16
"Mind Disaster," 71
Mineo, Art, 65
Mingus, Charles, 16
"Miss Molly," 118
Mitchell, Mike, 81, 86, 97, 108, 137, 178, 179
Mitchell, Willie, 147
Modern Records, 14, 15, 18, 21, 25, 28, 37, 43
"Moments," 30
"Moments to Remember," 172
Monarch Records, 37
"Money," 74, 88, 112
Monotones, 178
"Mony Mony," 141
Moon, Keith, 104, 105, 144
Moore, Johnny, 16, 21
Morales, Mark, 170
"More Than a Feeling," 155
Morrill, Kent, 65, 66, 70, 72, 82
Morrison, Van, 151
Morris, William, 111, 112
Most, Mickie, 152
Mothers of Invention, 78
Motola, George, 29
Moussorgsky, 5
"Mr. Blue," 56
Muddy Waters, 24, 26, 49
Music Machine, 145

"Mustang Sally," 146
"My Boyfriend's Back," 144–45
"My Generation," 144, 152
Mystery Train, 78

Naked Gun, 197
Nashville Teens, 146
National Lampoon, 163
Negativland, 31
Nelson, Larry, 55
Nelson, Mary, 55
Nelson, Sandy, 147
Never Mind the Bollocks, Here's the Sex Pistols, 166
"Never Never Gonna Give You Up," 168
New, Leroy K., 127
Newman, Randy, 14
New Musical Express (N.M.E.), 142
New York Dolls, 165, 169
"Next Time," 26
"Night Train," 95, 100
"19th Nervous Breakdown," 146
"96 Tears," 146
Nirvana, 71, 103, 204–7
Nite Owl, 55
"No Kissin' and Huggin'," 34
"No Matter What Shape Your Stomach's In," 178
Nordby, Bob, 81, 86, 88
Norman, Gene, 15, 22
"No Room," 38
Northwest Recorders, 95, 97
Nunn, Bobby, 24, 26
"Nut Rocker," 92
N.W.A., 25, 202, 203

Okeh, 31
Oliver, Carson, 175
Olympics, 81, 112, 178
"One for My Baby," 32
"One Little Prayer," 22
"Only the Lonely," 59
Orbison, Roy, 72
Original Gospel Harmonettes, 16
Original Trendsetters, 169
Ormsby, Buck, 47–50, 53–55, 58, 61, 62, 63, 65, 66, 68, 70, 71, 80, 84, 122, 140, 146, 191, 192
Otis, Johnny, 15, 16, 27, 37
"Out of My Tree," 71
Owens, Buck, 52

Pain in My Heart, 145
Palmer, Earl, 15

Palmer, Robert, 24
PAM Records, 172, 175
Parker, Junior, 46, 50
Parliament, 146
"Party Lights," 59
Patty Smith Group, 165, 184
"Paul Revere's Ride," 92
Pavlov's Dog, 169
Paxley, 172
Peaches, 27
Pearl Jam, 204
Peel, David, 184
Pelzell, "Doc," 75, 182–86
Penguins, 18, 20, 23
"Peppermint Stick," 118
Perez, Ralph, 12
"Peter Gunn Rock," 88
Peterson, Dick, 111, 177, 179
Pharoahs, 30, 33, 35, 42, 66, 146, 177
Phillips, Sam, 15
Pickett, Wilson, 146
"Pipeline," 183
Platters, 20
Playing Possum, 169
Pop, Iggy, 158
  and the Stooges, 158, 159, 165, 179
"Popsicles and Icicles," 124
Potlatch, 79–80
Potter, Peter, 25
Predoehl, Eric, 115, 162
Premiers, 146
Presley, Elvis, 15, 25, 56, 59, 84, 85, 96, 105, 148
Presley, Reg, 150
Pretenders II, 166
Price, Lloyd, 15
Prima, Louis, 26
Priority Records, 203
"Problem," 158
"Problems," 166
Propes, Steve, 16, 20, 21, 22, 27, 29, 39, 46, 55, 173
"Psychotic Reaction," 146
"Purple Haze," 151, 152, 201

Quadrophenia, 143
"Quarter to Three," 59
Quatro, Suzi, 152
? and the Mysterians, 146

Raelette, 37
"Raindrops," 101
Rainey, Ma, 119
RAK Records, 152
Ramones, 165
Rams, 22
Rare Earth, 147
Ravens, 23
Raw Power, 158

Ray, Robert B., 77
Reagan, Ronald, 5
"Real Frank Zappa Book,"
    4
"Reconsider, Baby," 50
Recorded in Hollywood, 18,
    20, 22
Record Mirror, 142
Redding, Otis, 145
Reisdorff, Bob, 66
Remains, 146
"Remote Control," 166
Rene, Leon, 15, 29
Revere, Paul, 89, 98, 99
    and the Raiders, 89–101,
    108, 109, 110, 113, 117,
    138, 142, 174, 179
Rhino Records, 41, 42, 44,
    103
Rhythm and Blues, 21, 36
Rhythm Rockers, 31, 32
Richard, Keith, 11
"Rich Bitch," 159
Richman, Jonathon, 184
Ricky and Jennell, 27
Riddle, Nelson, 32
"Ride Ride Baby," 113
Riedle, Jeff, 182–86
Righteous Brothers, 94, 146
Rillera, Barry, 12–14, 32,
    57, 140, 146
Rillera, Bobby, 12–14, 32,
    57, 140, 146
Rillera, Ricky, and the
    Rhythm Rockers, 11
"Riot in Cell Block #9," 14,
    24, 25, 26, 202
"Roadrunner," 65, 146
Roberts, Rockin' Robin, 14,
    24–26, 48, 54–55, 61,
    62, 66–70, 67, 68,
    70, 72, 73, 74, 79, 80,
    82, 84, 94, 122, 131,
    140, 149, 152, 154, 167,
    192, 198, 201
Robinson, Damon "Kool
    Rock-ski," 170
Robyn, Abe "Bunny," 15, 21
"Rock, Rock, Rock," 177
Rock Action, 159, 160
"Rock Around the Clock,"
    115
Rocket, 69
Rocking Kings, 59
"Rockin' Man," 26
Rock of Ages, 76
Roddam, Frank, 143
Rogers, Dan, 65
Rolling Stone Illustrated
    History of Rock & Roll,
    103, 154
Rolling Stones, 31–34, 140,
    146
Rollins, Henry, 166

"Roll with Me, Henry," 27
Rolontz, Bob, 21, 22
Roman Wheels, 62
Roth, Joe, 7, 10
Rotten, Johnny, 205
Roulette Records, 194
RPM, 18, 15, 21, 24
Rubin, Chuck, 194, 197
Ruffin, Jimmy, 175
Ruhlmann, William, 89, 93,
    95, 110
"Run Joe," 33
Rupe, Art, 18, 37
Rush, Merrilee, 149
Ryder, Mitch,
    and the Detroit Wheels,
    146

Sahm, Doug, 140
Sam and Dave, 194
Sam the Sham and the
    Pharoahs, 146
Sande, 95, 98, 99
Sandpipers, 147, 149
Santamaria, Mongo, 147
"Satisfaction," 11, 183
"Saturday Night Live," 166
Scepter/Wand Records,
    108–9, 125, 126, 132.
    See also Wand Records
Schlachter, Marv, 108–9,
    126, 133
Scholz, Tom, 154–55
"Scotch on the Rocks," 65
"Search and Destroy," 159
Secrets, 109
Seeger, Pete, 130
"See See Rider," 119
"Set 'Em Up, Joe," 32
"17," 166
Severinson, Doc, 169
Sex Pistols, 165, 166, 167
Shadows of Knights, 146
Shaffer, Paul, 169
"Shaking All Over," 109
"Shanghaied," 71
Shannon, Bob, 150
"ShBoom," 5
"She Loves You," 140
"She's About a Mover," 146
"She Wants to Rock," 16,
    21, 22
Shields, 18
Shindig, 136, 140, 141, 146
Shirelles, 108
Shirley and Lee, 27
"Shout," 59, 142
Showmen, 45
Sill, Lester, 24
"Since I Lost My Baby," 7
"Sincerely," 43
Singing Nun, 123
Sir Douglas Quintet, 140,
    146

Sir Mixalot, 53
Six Teens, 30, 38
Sky's the Limit, 32
Smash, 172
"Smells Like Teen Spirit,"
    71, 204–7
Smith, Bessie, 119
Smith, Mike "Smitty," 92,
    96
Smith, O. C., 17
"Smokey Joe's Cafe," 25
"Society's Child," 153
"Sock It to Me," 146
"So Fine," 18
"Somewhere There's a
    Rainbow," 33
Sonics, 39, 53, 70, 71, 147,
    165
Soul Stirrers, 16
"Soul Train," 168, 169
Soundgarden, 53, 204
"Spanish Castle Magic," 69,
    151
Spark Records, 24
Specialty Records, 15, 16,
    18, 37, 50
Spector, Phil, 25, 105, 194
Spector, Ronnie, 105
Spencer Davis Group, 196
"Splish Splash," 50
"Spread Your Love," 175
Springsteen, Bruce, 39, 169
"Stagger Lee," 59
Stallone, Sylvester, 5
Standells, 146
Starr, Ringo, 124
"Stay," 59
Stengel, Casey, 59
Stierman, Vern, 126
Stokes, Geoffry, 76–77, 79
Stoller, Mike, 15, 21, 24–25,
    26, 33, 67
Stompers, 62
Stooges, 158, 159, 165
Stories, 153–54
"Straight Flush," 57
Straight Outta Compton,
    203
"Stranded in the Jungle,"
    26
Stranglers, 170
Strong, Barrett, 112
"Strychnine," 71
"Stuck on You," 56
"Submission," 166
"Sugar Sugar," 141
Sundholm, Norm, 111, 179
Sun Records, 15
"Surfing Bird," 124
"Surfin' U.S.A.," 59
Swaggart, Jimmy, 105
Swallows, 23
"Sweet Sugar You," 33
Swingin', 36

Swingin' Medallions, 145, 146

"Take the Key," 34
"Talk Back Trembling Lips," 109
"Talk Talk," 145
"Tall Cool One," 57, 61, 63, 65
Talmy, Shel, 143, 144
T.A.M.I. Show, 145
Tams, 147
Taylor, Billy, 51, 52
Taylor, Chip, 149, 150
T-Bones, 178
Teen Queens, 21
"Tell Me You Love Me," 21, 22
Temptations, 7
"That's What the Good Book Says," 24
"There, I've Said It Again," 124
Thomas, Rufus, 118, 123
Thompson, Beverly, 20
Thornton, Big Mama, 24, 26
Three Blazers, 21
"Three O'Clock Blues," 50
Thunderbirds, 55
Thunders, Johnny, 169
Thurston, Scott, 159, 160
Tillman, Julia, 175
Tillotson, Johnny, 109
Til, Sonny, and the Orioles, 23
Tiny Tony and the Statics, 61
"Tobacco Road," 146
Toles, Billy, 51
Toll, Robert C., 75
Tolson, Clyde, 134
Toots and the Maytals, 148
Toussaint, Allen, 147
Touzet, Rene, 13, 31, 122, 136, 143
Townshend, Peter, 143, 144, 154
Tracy, Ben, 94
Trammell, Charles, 20, 22
Trashman, 124
Trash Records, 169
Travelers, Pilgrim, 16
Triad, 154
Troggs, 149, 150
"Truly," 16
Tucker, Maureen, 169
Tucker, Tommy, 146
Turks, 20
Turnabouts, 61, 149
Turner, Ike, 15, 21, 145
Turner, Tina, 145
"Tutti Frutti," 196

"Tweedle Dee," 28
"25 Players! 1 guitar!," 166
"Twist," 64, 170, 171
"Twist and Shout," 113
2 Live Crew, 122, 141
Tympani Five, 33

U2, 31

Valens, Ritchie, 59, 61
Valjo Music, 27
Vance, Kenny, 165
Vee, Bobby, 68, 109
Velvet Underground, 169
Ventures, 53, 57
Vinson, Fred M., Jr., 135
Vinton, Bobby, 124
Visible Language, 77
Vulgar Boatmen, 77

Wailers, 53, 56, 57, 58, 61, 62, 63, 64, 65, 66, 68, 69, 70, 71, 72, 73, 74, 81, 89, 94, 143, 144, 151, 165
"Walk Away, Renee," 153
"Walk Don't Run," 57
Walker, Dick, 93
Walker, T-Bone, 16, 31
"Walking the Dog," 123
"Wallflower," 14, 16, 27, 28, 31, 43
Wall Street Journal, 75, 185
Wammack, Travis, 147
"Wanda Lu," 157
"Wanderer," 59
Wand Records, 108, 109, 110, 122, 126, 127, 128, 129, 131, 132, 133, 135, 136, 178, 193. *See also* Scepter/Wand Records
Waple, Ben F., 128
Ward, Carlos, 57
Warhol, Andrew, 5
Warners, 56
Warrant, 14
Warren, Rusty, 146
Warwick, Dionne, 108
Waters, Muddy, 14
Watson, Johnny "Guitar," 21
"We Ain't Got Nothin' Yet," 145
"We Gotta Get Out of This Place," 146
Weiner, Russell, 154
Wells, Ed, 38
Welsh, Matthew K., 124–25, 126, 128
"Werewolf," 57

West, Steve, 93
"What'd I Say," 59, 103, 142
"Where the Action Is," 89, 179
White, Barry, 168, 169, 170, 176
Who, 94, 104, 143, 144, 155
"Whole Lot-ta Shakin' Goin' On," 90
"Why Do Fools Fall in Love?," 194
"Why Don't You Write Me," 23, 26
"Wild Berry," 175
Wild Berry! Live From H. D. Hover's Century . . ., 175
"Wild Thing," 104, 149, 150, 151, 196
Willard, Maxine, 175
Williams, Al, 191
Williams, Curtiss, 20
Williamson, James, 159, 160
Wilson, J. Frank, 56
Wilson, Jackie, 140
Wilson, Phillips, 14
Wilson, Tony, 152
Wimbley, Damon, 170
"Wipe Out," 59
Wise, Richie, 153
Witherspoon, Jimmy, 21
Wonder, Stevie, 154
Woods, Donald, 24, 30, 113, 178
"Wooly Bully," 5, 146
"Work with Me, Annie," 27, 50, 118

"Yakety Yak," 25
"Yama Yama Pretty Mama," 26, 30
Yardbirds, 146
Yes, 154
"Yesterday," 183
"Yesterday and You," 109
"You Are My Sunshine," 33, 34, 37
"You Can't Catch Me," 32
"You Cheated," 18
"Young Blood," 25
Young Jessie, 26
"You Really Got Me," 143
"You're the First, the Last, My Everything," 168
"You Sexy Thing," 152

Zappa, Frank, 4, 37, 142, 154, 201
Zeiger, Hal, 37
Zucker, Irwin, 92

dehmett